CERTIFIED COURSE IN

EARN YOUR CERTIFICATE THROUGH
SELF-PACED INSTRUCTION

David Himmel

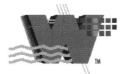

WAITE GROUP PRESS ™
Corte Madera, CA

Publisher • Mitchell Waite
Editor-in-Chief • Scott Calamar
Editorial Director • Joel Fugazzotto
Managing Editor • Kurt Stephan
Content Editor • Harry Henderson
Technical Reviewer • David Calhoun
Production Director • Julianne Ososke
Cover Design • Cecile Kaufman
Design • Kristin Peterson
Production • Wald Design
Illustrations • Pat Rogondino

Himmel, David
      Certified course in C / by David Himmel.
      p.   cm.
      Includes index.
      ISBN 1-878739-92-1 : $39.95
      1. C (Computer program language) I. Title.
   QA76. 73.C15H53 1995
   005.13'3--dc20   94-45130
                                                                              CIP

DEDICATION

I dedicate this book to my mother,
who so ably wrote my first chapter.

ABOUT THE AUTHOR

Dave Himmel, author of *Workout C* from Waite Group Press, develops graphics and multimedia applications for Boeing Computer Services in Seattle, Washington. He also provides software consulting services for businesses and has taught college courses in C. He holds a BS degree in Physics from the University of Illinois, an MS in Electrical Engineering from Washington University, and an MBA from Southern Methodist University. Dave has 30 years of experience with a variety of programming languages, including Assembly, Basic, C, C++, FORTRAN, and Pascal.

ACKNOWLEDGMENTS

This book is the result of important contributions from many talented people. Mitch Waite and Scott Calamar collaborated to develop the concept for *Certified Course in C*. Kurt Stephan successfully guided the project through the publishing maze. Harry Henderson provided insightful reviews and made many excellent content suggestions. David Calhoun provided valuable technical corrections. My wife, Marilyn, kept me honest with the English language. Mike Seiden and Greg Temple of the University of Phoenix devised and implemented the book's unique certification procedure, and Joanne Miller of the Waite Group was an invaluable liaison as the process was being developed. Borland International supplied the Turbo C++ Lite compiler included with the book, and Nan Borreson of Borland provided ongoing support, as well as material included in the book. And the entire staff of Waite Group Press deserves credit for making *Certified Course in C* possible. Thank you all.

TABLE OF CONTENTS

CONTENTS

CHAPTER 8

CHAPTER 9

FOREWORD

The University of Phoenix is excited to work with Waite Group Press and David Himmel in presenting *Certified Course in C*—an innovative approach to learning the C language. This approach makes it possible for you, upon completion of certain requirements, to be rewarded with college-level credit. While self-paced tutorial approaches are not new, the combination of two tiers of certification and the awarding of a certificate with credit is new. (Appendix D, "Certification and Course Credit," explains how the two-tier testing procedure works.)

Approximately three years ago, the University of Phoenix began offering a Masters-level degree in Information Systems at its Denver campus. Since that time, the degree program has been expanded to include a Bachelor of Science in Business with a major in Information Systems. The degrees are offered at a number of campuses throughout the western U.S. The program started with an enrollment of 70 in 1991, and is up to nearly 1,000 students now.

One of the most important factors that drives the various University of Phoenix Information Systems degree programs is the recognition of "Open Systems" and its effect on computerization and information networks. More and more companies in the corporate marketplace desire to become independent from specific brands of hardware and software. The C language is a cornerstone within the Open Systems world, and consequently demands the attention of programmers and managers alike. This is a major reason why the University of Phoenix is pleased to be the certifying organization for *Certified Course in C*.

In the near future, our Technology Programs department expects to work with the University of Phoenix On-Line division to begin offering Information Systems degrees within an electronic environment. The On-Line division is unique, as students use PCs or terminals to connect to the host computer in San Francisco. From there, they interact with instructors and classmates from around the world.

As you complete the chapters of *Certified Course in C*, you will have the opportunity to explore the topics presented through the completion of the numerous laboratory exercises included in each chapter. As instructors, we encourage you to work each of the exercises and think about the results of your investigations into the C language. As with most learning, the time you invest will be repaid many times over in your understanding of the material. A language such as C demands time to learn its powerful capabilities. We encourage you to take the time necessary.

After you have completed and submitted the enclosed final exam and received a passing score (as explained in Appendix D), we hope you will submit a request for Level II certification. The exam for this level of certification provides you with an opportunity to apply your knowledge of the C language by creating program code in response to questions. Upon achievement of Level II certification, you will be awarded three credits in the University of Phoenix's undergraduate C programming language course.

We hope to receive requests from you for both levels of certification. We look forward to returning a certificate to you for each level.

Gregory Temple
Michael Seiden
The University of Phoenix

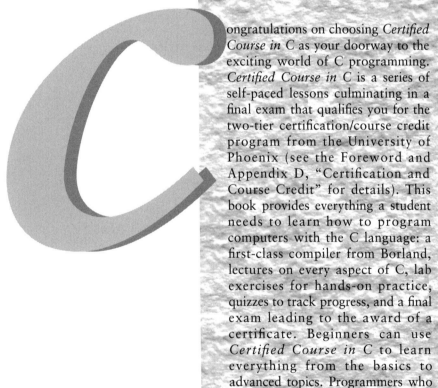

1

GETTING STARTED

ongratulations on choosing *Certified Course in C* as your doorway to the exciting world of C programming. *Certified Course in C* is a series of self-paced lessons culminating in a final exam that qualifies you for the two-tier certification/course credit program from the University of Phoenix (see the Foreword and Appendix D, "Certification and Course Credit" for details). This book provides everything a student needs to learn how to program computers with the C language: a first-class compiler from Borland, lectures on every aspect of C, lab exercises for hands-on practice, quizzes to track progress, and a final exam leading to the award of a certificate. Beginners can use *Certified Course in C* to learn everything from the basics to advanced topics. Programmers who already know C can expand their knowledge or test their programming abilities.

Because each chapter is organized into lecture, lab, and quiz sections, *Certified Course in C* is also an excellent textbook for a basic or intermediate class in C. The 12 lectures furnish prepared material for classroom presentations, the lab exercises come complete with supplied solutions, and the on-line quizzes provide a ready mechanism for monitoring student progress.

Certified Course in C concentrates on the most important ingredient for learning programming: hands-on practice. The book was written specifically to provide lab exercises and quizzes that let you learn by doing. The labs are full of practical examples of C programs for accomplishing real-world tasks such as organizing addresses and telephone numbers or evaluating a home loan. The lessons cover all aspects of the C language; chapter-by-chapter they increase your skills, developing your ability to write more complex programs. Chapter 1 tells you how to install the Borland Turbo C++ compiler, familiarizes you with the Integrated Development Environment (IDE), then leads you through the steps of writing and running your first C program. Chapter 2 gives an overview of the C language and its history. Then each of Chapters 3 through 14 contains a lecture section that explains a major topic of C, followed by a lab section with practice exercises and a quiz to check your progress. Chapter 15, "Putting It All Together," guides you through the steps of developing a major C program (the same program that you use for taking the quizzes).

Using This Book

Each chapter in *Certified Course in C* covers one major topic of the C language. If you have no previous experience with C, you should proceed through the book from beginning to end; however, it is possible to study each chapter independently. This method can be useful if you have some prior programming experience and want to extend your knowledge or brush up on a particular aspect of C. The total time to complete the course is approximately four weeks (160 hours). The introduction to each chapter estimates the time you will need to spend on that topic. However, these times are only approximate averages. You should take as little or as much time as needed to feel comfortable with each topic—after all this is *your* self-paced course. The quizzes will serve as your guide to how fast to proceed. At the end of each chapter, an interactive quiz on the computer tests your knowledge of the chapter material.

Reading the Lectures

The first step in learning each topic is to read the lecture. The lecture guides you through the chapter material in manageable subtopics. You should read through it once without worrying too much about absorbing all the detail. After a first reading, proceed to the lab exercises, referring back to the lecture as needed. Then take the quiz, and for any wrong answers, review the lecture material.

Working the Lab Exercises

The best way to learn C is to write programs. The labs give you this opportunity, so you should diligently work out all the exercises. You will spend about two-thirds of your time in this course on the exercises. Most of the exercises are practical problems, designed to have you thinking like a "real-world" C programmer. The solutions will often not be obvious; this is intentional, but don't worry—the material will lead you through the process of finding the answers. Solutions to all the exercises are supplied on the companion disks. You can refer to them, but you should do so only to compare your own solutions or when you need some hints to work out an answer. C programming is a process of thinking logically and using the language to implement solutions, and the labs are your best opportunity to develop these skills. When you get to the lab section of each chapter, roll up your sleeves, get a cup of coffee, and go to work.

The lab exercises are structured as shown below, with five headings in bold type:

EXERCISE #:   Topic of the exercise.

✳ **STARTER FILE:** Name of a file containing some C code that is part of the problem statement

```
The starter file contents are listed here.
```

✳ **DO:** Here are instructions for working the exercise.

✳ **SOLUTION FILE:** Name of a file that contains a solution.

✳ **RESULT:**

```
The output of the provided solution program will appear here.
```

✳ **DISCUSSION:** This is a discussion of some important details of the problem and an explanation of the solution.

For example, here are the first two exercises from Chapter 3.

EXERCISE 1A: Determine sizes of fundamental data types.

✳ **STARTER FILE:** EX03-1A.C

```
#include <stdio.h>
void main()
{
    printf( "Size of char = %d\n", sizeof( char ) );
}
```

✳ **DO:** Type in the above program and run it.

✳ **RESULT:**

```
Size of char = 1
```

✳ **DISCUSSION:** This program displays the size of data type *char*. The *printf* statement sends data to the screen, guided by the formatting characters located between the double quotes (" "). The characters %d constitute the decimal conversion specifier for the data that follows the comma. The '\n' character specifies the newline escape sequence that causes the cursor to move to the next line.

EXERCISE 1B: Add other data types.

✳ **DO:** Add *printf* statements to display the sizes of data types *short, int, long, float, double,* and *long double*.

✳ **SOLUTION FILE:** EX03-1B.C

✳ **RESULT:**

```
Size of char = 1
Size of short = 2
Size of int = 2
Size of long = 4
Size of float = 4
Size of double = 8
Size of long double = 10
```

✳ **DISCUSSION:** Notice that Turbo C++ assigns the same size to *short* and *int*, and different sizes to all three types of floating-point numbers.

Not all exercises will have a starter file; some will have both starter and solution files. Solutions are always provided, but you should work out your own solution before comparing it with the supplied program. An exercise will often have a follow-up (like 1B above) that asks you to modify the program and run it to see the effect.

Notice the numbering system for the solution files in the above examples. File EX03-1B.C contains the program that solves the second exercise (1B) for the Chapter 3 lab (EX03). We suggest that you use the same numbering system for the solutions that you develop, but substitute your initials for EX—for instance the author, David Himmel, would develop the solution for this exercise in file DH03-1B.C.

You will develop many complete, and very practical, programs in the chapter lab sections, including a calculator program, a program to balance your checkbook, a program to evaluate home-loan refinancing, a linked-list program for holding names and addresses, and a program to look at data in any disk file. You may find these programs useful after finishing the course, and you may wish to customize them for your own purposes.

Chapter 15, "Putting It All Together," guides you through the development of a program for presenting on-line exams. This is an exercise that gives you the experience of designing and developing a major C program.

Taking the Quizzes

Each chapter has a quiz that will assess your knowledge of the topics presented and serve as a guide to whether you should review the lecture material. You can take any of the chapter quizzes by running the supplied exam program. Figure 1-1 shows the main selection screen for the exam program, and Figure 1-2 shows a quiz question.

Just select the desired quiz and answer the multiple-choice questions (using cursor keys and (ENTER)); the program will display your score upon completion of the quiz (when you press (END)). Figure 1-3 shows the quiz results screen.

The results screen displays your score, a list of any questions with wrong answers, and a recommendation as to whether you should review the chapter or progress to the next chapter. From the results screen, you can press (ENTER) to print a graded copy of the quiz; you can also press (SPACEBAR) to return to the quiz and change any of your answers. If you press (ESC), you can select another quiz from the main menu. The best approach is to work back and

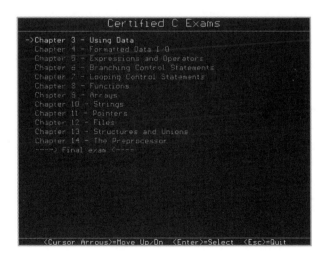

FIGURE 1-1 Exam
selection screen

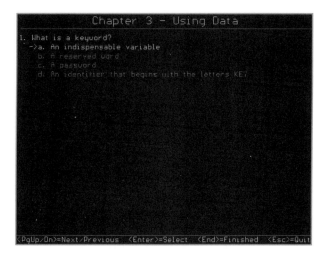

FIGURE 1-2   Quiz
question

forth between the quiz and lecture in each chapter until you achieve a good result. Treat the quiz as an open-book test. After successfully completing all the chapter quizzes, you can take the final exam (listed at the bottom of the exam selection screen). You may want to retake the quizzes just before attempting the final exam.

The exam program won't show your score for the final exam—to apply for certification, you must send your answers to the University of Phoenix for grading. When you've answered all the questions to your satisfaction, the program will prompt you to press (END), causing it to save the exam to a hard disk file (C:FINAL.XAM). You can then copy this file to a 3.5 inch floppy disk and mail it to the University of Phoenix, following the specific instructions given in Appendix D. Upon achieving a score of 75 percent or better on the final exam, you will be awarded a certificate similar to that shown in Figure 1-4.

Installing Turbo C++

The Turbo C++ system comes compressed in file TCLITE.EXE on the installation disk; you can easily extract and install the system by following the simple instructions below. You can also review installation instructions by running the README.COM program on the disk as follows:

`A:\> README`

To install and run Turbo C++ Lite, you will need a PC system consisting of an 80386 or better processor (math coprocessor not necessary) with at least 2 Megabytes (MB) of memory, a VGA display, a mouse, 20MB of free hard disk

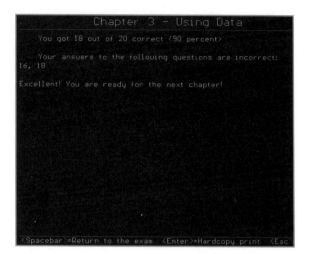

FIGURE 1-3   Quiz results screen

FIGURE 1-4   Sample certificate from University of Phoenix

space, a 3.5 inch disk drive, and DOS 3.0 or higher. You need to be familiar with DOS commands for formatting disks (FORMAT), creating directories (MD), changing directories (CD), listing directory contents (DIR), and copying files (COPY).

Installation Procedure

To install Turbo C++ Lite, insert the disk, then change to the drive with the disk and run the batch file, INSTALL.BAT. You must first decide in which drive you want the system to reside, but you can change this. Assuming you insert the disk in drive A and want to install to the default directory on drive C, you should type the following commands (commands are listed in bold type):

    C:\> **A:**

    A:\> **INSTALL C:**

If you want to install to drive D instead, then the last command should be:

    A:\> **INSTALL D:**

The installation program will then create directories, uncompress files, and copy them to your disk.

Please note: should you choose to reinstall TCLITE, the installation will overwrite any files with the same names.

ALTERNATE INSTALLATION PROCEDURE

The Turbo C++ installation program (INSTALL.BAT) defines some new DOS environment variables; if your system already uses many environment variables, the installation can fail, indicating "OUT OF ENVIRONMENT SPACE." If this happens, you can use the following procedure to install Turbo C++:

With the installation disk in drive A and your default directory set to A:, type:

    A:\> **TCLITE C:**

The self-extracting program will create the C:\TCLITE directory and display the name of each file as it expands and copies it to the directory. You can choose to install on drive D with the command:

    A:\> **TCLITE D:**

After you've installed Turbo C++, you might try the DOS RENAME command to rename the directory.

After the files are installed, you should add the subdirectory C:\TCLITE\BIN to the PATH setting in your AUTOEXEC.BAT file (located in the C:\ boot directory). For example, if you used the default installation directory, you need to have the following line in your AUTOEXEC.BAT file:

```
PATH C:\TCLITE\BIN
```

If you already have a line with some PATH items, just add a semicolon (;) followed by the new path (C:\TCLITE\BIN) at the end. You can then start Turbo C++ from any directory (after saving the AUTOEXEC.BAT file and restarting) by typing TC, and your screen will look like Figure 1-5:

```
C:\> TC
```

Features of Turbo C++

Turbo C++ Lite is a simplified version of the professional Turbo C++ product; it is a teaching version intended for learning C and C++. The Turbo C++ Lite Integrated Development Environment (IDE) will be the "laboratory" that you will use to develop your programs throughout this book, so let's overview its features and operation.

The IDE combines all the necessary elements of programming in a unified graphical user interface. In the menu bar at the top of Figure 1-5 you can see the programming menus. Perhaps the most important of these is the *Help* menu on the far right—by clicking there and selecting *Contents*, then *Menu* commands, you can browse through explanations of all other menus. There are so many useful functions in the IDE that it is impossible to discuss them all here, so make frequent use of the *Help* facility until you become familiar with the system.

The *File* menu provides for opening, closing, and saving disk files; you will use this to access C source files. After you *Open* a file or ask for a *New* source file, you can type program statements in the window area below the menu bar (look up the *Editor* under *Help* for more information). The *Edit* menu contains operations such as cut, copy, and paste for altering text lines. The *Search* menu allows you to find particular words or phrases in source files. You will use the *Run, Compile*, and *Debug* menus to run an executable program, process a source file to create an executable program, and track down problems that might occur. The *Project* menu is a facility for handling larger programs that often consist of several different files. The *Options* menu lets you designate directories for your programs and certain other environmental parameters, and the *Window* menu allows you to have several windows operational at one time and to switch between them at any time.

IMPORTANT: As a final step in the installation of the IDE, select the *Options* item, then *Directories...* and make sure the path names of the include and library directories for Turbo C++ are as shown in Figure 1-6 (provided you installed to C:\TCLITE).

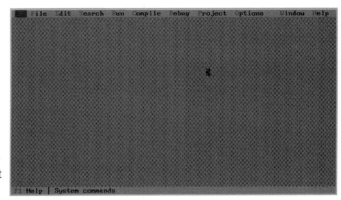

FIGURE 1-5 Turbo C++
Lite Integrated Development
Environment (IDE)

Installing Lab Files

To complete the software installation, you will need to copy files from the companion disk and set up the exam program for taking quizzes. Insert the companion disk in drive A (or B if necessary). Create a directory for your source files—the name CCC (for *Certified Course in* C) would be a good choice for a name.

```
C:\> MD C:\CCC
```

Then set your prompt to the CCC directory, copy files, and load the IDE with the following commands

```
C:\> CD CCC
```

```
C:\> COPY A:\*.*
```

```
C:\> TC
```

This will put all the source code files (starter files and solution files) in the CCC directory along with a few project (.PRJ), header (.H), and data files.

Now compile, link, and run the exam program. Click on the *Project* menu item and select *Open project...*, then double click on file EXAM.PRJ. Project files like this one contain references to all source code files necessary for a complex program. Select the *Run* menu item and click again on the *Run* item that appears. The IDE will compile all source files associated with the exam program, link them, and run the program. You should see the screen shown in Figure 1-1. You're not yet ready to take an exam, so press (ESC) to quit.

When you're ready to take the quiz at the end of each chapter, you will use the *Project* and *Run* menus as above to run the exam program; however, the IDE won't have to repeat the compile and link steps each time.

Now you are ready to develop your first program!

ALTERNATE DOS VERSION OF EXAM.EXE

You cannot run the exam program that was compiled in the IDE directly from a DOS prompt because the Borland IDE linker does not permit it. If you prefer to run the exam program from the DOS prompt, you can copy the file EXAM.EXE from the companion disk. We compiled and linked this standalone version of the exam program with the Borland C++ compiler, Version 3.0 (not supplied with the book). To copy and run this version of EXAM.EXE, exit from the IDE, insert the companion disk in drive A, and type the following lines:

```
C:\> COPY A:\EXAM.EXE
C:\> EXAM
```

The operation of this program is identical to the IDE version.

Developing C Programs

Figure 1-7 shows the process for developing programs.

The figure includes two generic cycles that apply to all computer software: the development cycle and the maintenance cycle. The code development cycle iterates through the edit, compile, link, and run steps. The maintenance cycle begins after initial development is complete and the program becomes fully operational for the first time. Maintenance occurs whenever you introduce new or different features into a program, or whenever you discover an operating deficiency or bug. The following paragraphs explain how to use the Turbo C++ IDE system to accomplish program development and maintenance.

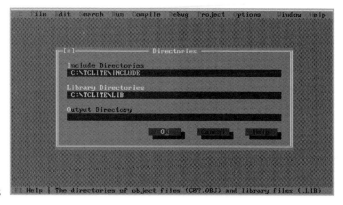

FIGURE 1-6 Setting Turbo C++ Lite directories

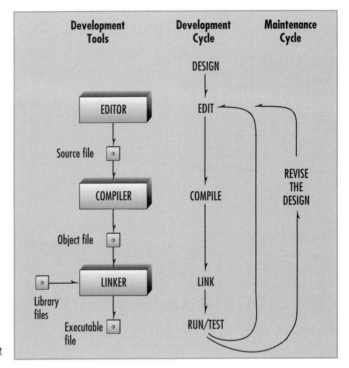

FIGURE 1-7   C
programming development

Design

In the design phase, you collect information about what a program is required to do and you make an outline of how the program will operate. For a small program, you may simply develop ideas in your head. A larger program may require you to sketch out a flow diagram and make some notes about things like data structures. Very large programs require formal documentation to spell out details of files, data relationships, program sequencing, and other parameters. You should take as much time as necessary to complete the design thoroughly. A good design translates into much saved time and effort during the development phase, and it results in a quality program that performs as required.

Edit

The second step in developing a program is to create the source code. You create a source file of C statements with an editor like the one included with the IDE. Here is how you can create a little program that is famous among C programmers as the "hello world" program because it displays that phrase on the screen (see Chapter 2 for the history of C).

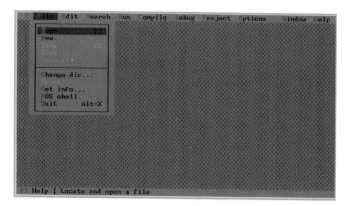

FIGURE 1-8(a) File
operations

Set your prompt to the new directory (CCC) that you created during installation
and start up the IDE system:

```
c:\> CD CCC

c:\> TC
```

Open a new file and start the editor by selecting (clicking on) *File*, then *New*, as
shown in Figure 1-8(a).

Now type in the following lines using lowercase letters exactly as shown:

```
#include <stdio.h>
main()
{
    printf("hello, world\n");
}
```

Notice that the two characters in column one directly under the *m* in *main* are
curly braces and not parentheses. Save this program to a file by selecting the *Save*
option on the *File* menu as shown in Figure 1-8(a) and typing the name HELLO.C
as shown in Figure 1-8(b).

Compile

The third development step is to compile the source code and create an object file.
The object file is a translation of the source file that is meaningless to humans, but
suitable for the computer to process. You could compile the hello program with
the IDE *Compile* menu, but we prefer to use the *Run* menu to combine the
compile, link, and run steps (which you can do in a minute).

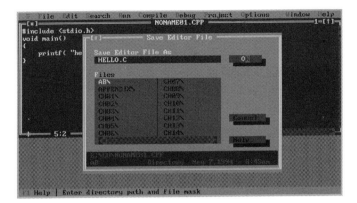

FIGURE 1-8(b) File
operations

Link

The link step combines object files (from compiled source code files and from system libraries) into a single, executable file. You could link the hello program by selecting the *Link* option from the *Compile* menu, but again, we prefer to use the *Run* menu.

Run and Debug

The final development step is to run the program and test its operation. You can run the hello program by selecting *Run* on the main menu bar then clicking on *Run* from the list, as shown in Figure 1-9.

To see the output, "hello, world," you must select *Output* under the *Window* menu item (see Figure 1-10).

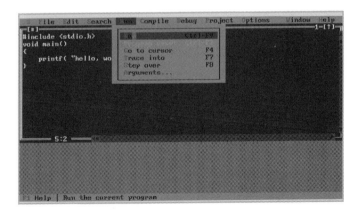

FIGURE 1-9 Run
operation

FIGURE 1-10 Window
selection

If a program does not perform as desired, you can use a debugger to examine program flow and data items to understand what is wrong. Then you can correct errors by modifying source code and performing another complete development cycle of edit-compile-link-run. Refer to the *Help* menu item for instructions on the IDE debugger.

SUMMARY

At this point you've installed the software, learned about the tools and procedures for writing C programs, and written and executed your first program. Chapter 2 introduces the C language; then you'll be ready to move on through the lessons of *Certified Course in C*.

2

ABOUT C

efore you become immersed in the details of C, let's take a little time to discuss some interesting aspects of the language. In this chapter, you will learn a bit of the history of C and the people and organizations responsible for the language. You will see the relationship of C to the newer language C++, which is part of the name of the compiler that comes with this book (Turbo C++). You will also learn the advantages of C over other programming languages, tour the basic ingredients of a C program, and get some tips on writing good C programs.

Who Invented C?

C was developed in 1972 by Dennis Ritchie at the Bell Laboratories of AT&T. He collaborated with Ken Thompson, who also worked at AT&T, on designing this new language for the UNIX operating system. They carried over some features from a language called B that Ken Thompson had written in 1970 for the first UNIX system, and so they extended the name to C. B was heavily influenced by a language called BCPL, developed by Martin Richards. Thus, C was designed by and for experienced programmers who needed an efficient language for implementing an operating system.

One of the central themes of UNIX was portability, and during the 1970s, C and UNIX evolved together on many different computer platforms. By the early 1980s, C had become a mature and powerful language for minicomputers and workstations. However, several implementations existed, each differing in certain details, and the only governing specification was a book titled *The C Programming Language* (Brian W. Kernighan, Dennis M. Ritchie, Prentice Hall, 1988.) Versions of C based on this book are known as *Common C* or *K&R C*. Many programmers got their first taste of C by coding the famous "hello, world" program described in the first few pages of the Kernighan and Ritchie book (and in Chapter 1 of this book). The second edition of *The C Programming Language* includes ANSI C definitions.

What Is ANSI C?

In 1983, the American National Standards Institute (ANSI) established a committee to consolidate the definition of C to a single version. In 1988, the ANSI committee completed its work and adopted the standard known as ANSI C; this standard is now accepted worldwide as the true definition of C. ANSI C includes most features of Common C so as not to make older programs obsolete.

What Is C++?

Perhaps you are wondering, "If this is a book on C, why is the compiler called Turbo C++?" C++ is a newer language that encompasses C as a subset; that is, a C++ compiler will also compile ANSI C programs. The Borland Turbo C++ system included with *Certified Course in C* is an excellent ANSI C compiler as well as a C++ compiler. C++ shares some of the constructs of C, so by learning C you will also be taking a step toward learning C++.

C++ was designed at AT&T as a language for object-oriented programming. C programming follows the traditional procedural approach to software that separately defines data elements, then sequentially executes statements to process the data. Object-oriented programming combines the processing functions and data into a single entity called an object. This approach reduces the complexity of large programs and encourages the development of reusable software. The ideas behind C++ take time to master; learning standard C is still a good way to get started writing moderately complex programs using proven techniques.

Why Learn C?

For at least a decade, C has been growing in momentum. It is now the language of choice for professional programmers using personal computers (PCs) and workstations. The vast majority of commercial software products for these computers are written in C—word processors, spreadsheets, engineering software, games, compilers, and more. C is also widely used to develop business software for mainframes, a domain long dominated by the COBOL language. The following characteristics explain why C is so popular.

C Is Portable

Portability means that you need to make very few changes to a program in order to move it to another computer system. Because it was intended for the UNIX operating system, C was designed from inception to be portable. The ANSI C standard reduced differences between compiler implementations to make portability a solid reality. Also, as part of the design strategy for making C portable, the authors placed the input and output (I/O) operations outside the central definition of the language. Most programming languages make I/O commands an integral part of the language, but C places them in function libraries outside the core language. This removes a major computer-platform dependency from the language. Libraries also make it possible to deal with other hardware-dependent issues such as graphics.

C Is Efficient

C programs run fast. There are several features in the language that programmers can use to make programs efficient.

- A rich set of data types allows a programmer to access information as required by the application.
- Pointers in C allow direct access to data in computer memory.
- Many C operators match similar operations found in computer hardware.

C Is Concise

There are only 32 reserved key words in C, and source code statements are small. You can accomplish several tasks at once by combining commands within statements, and some operators actually perform two functions simultaneously. This is attributed to the designers of C, who provided well chosen commands that can do maximum work with minimum overhead.

C Hits Both High and Low

High-level languages allow you to think about the application. They provide statements that correspond to relevant tasks instead of computer operations. On the other hand, assembly languages give you access to the technical details within a computer. C gives you both: it provides high-level control statements for structured program flow, and it supplies low-level access to powerful computer operations.

What Are the Disadvantages of C?

Over the last 20 years, a large audience of users has expressed satisfaction with C, but a few disadvantages have also surfaced.

Some find the syntax of C to be strange or difficult to learn; however, this objection recedes quickly as the user gains experience with the language.

A few of the symbols in C have more than one meaning. For example, the asterisk (*) is the multiplication operator and the indirection operator. The meaning of this, and other symbols, is resolved by context. Confusion about operators can lead to programming errors.

The power of C gives programmers unrestricted access to data and computer internals; it is possible to abuse this power and write programs that are unstable or contain dangerous mistakes.

What Is in a C Program?

Most C programs are similar in layout, especially those that adhere to good programming practice. The basic building block for C programs is the function; even the main program is a function, as you will soon see. A C program comprises a collection of functions that call one another in a sequence that you specify by placing call references in the program. Figure 2-1 shows the ingredients of a function.

The source code statements make up what is called the *function definition*. The first line contains three items: the function type, the function name, and a list of parameters. You can return a data value to the calling function, and the type declares what kind of data you wish to return—in this case type *void* declares that there is no return value. You use the name *(display)* to refer to the function when calling it. Within the parentheses, you declare both the types and names of parameters (or data) that you want to pass into the function when you call it; here, a single message parameter is declared that is a pointer to a character string (you'll learn about pointers in Chapter 11). Below the first line, braces mark the

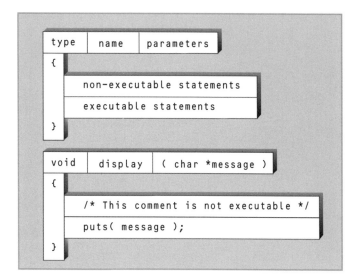

FIGURE 2-1 Function definition

beginning and end of the function body. Between the braces a function contains statements; this is where a function does its work. Executable statements are those that actually perform tasks when the program runs; the *puts* statement in this function displays a line of text. Nonexecutable statements are used only by the compiler to set up the executable program. Figure 2-2 shows two functions integrated into a C program.

This program has five major parts: an information header, a *#include directive*, a function *prototype*, and two functions. The information header contains comments explaining the purpose of the program, who wrote it, and other pertinent information. *#include* directives copy the contents of header files (STDIO.H in this case) into the program during compilation. Header files primarily contain nonexecutable statements that the compiler needs. You normally group *#include* directives together at the top of a program file. Function prototypes usually also occur at the top of a program; they give the compiler information about functions so that it can check for the correctness of each call statement. The first function is the central part of the main program. The word *main* identifies where the program begins executing. All this particular *main* function does is call the display function with an argument that is a message to be displayed. The bottom function is the same one you just saw in Figure 2-1, which uses the *puts* statement to display a message.

INFORMATION HEADER

```
/****************************************
        File: HELLO.C
    Purpose: Display a message on the screen
    Programmed: D. Himmel, April 24, 1994
    Functions: main
                display
 ****************************************
```

INCLUDES

```
#include <stdio.h>
```

PROTOTYPES

```
int display( char *message );
```

MAIN FUNCTION

```
void main()
{
    display( "hello, world\n" );
}
```

FUNCTION

```
void display( char *message );
{
    /* This comment is not exectuable */
    puts( message );
}
```

FIGURE 2-2   Layout of a C program

How Do You Write Good C Programs?

This section provides a few guidelines for writing good C programs. Keep these suggestions in mind as you write programs in the lab sections of upcoming chapters. Appendix B contains additional guidelines for producing quality C programs—you should study these guidelines after completing the chapters.

Use Plenty of Comments

In general, about 80 percent of the total cost of software occurs after a program is put into operation. Comments are important because they clarify what is intended and how a program works, making maintenance much easier. As a rule of thumb, about 25 percent of the lines in a program should be comments. Figure 2-3 contains examples of each of three kinds of recommended comments: information headers, variable comments, and code comments.

An information header precedes each function; it describes the function, its arguments, its return type, and the author. A variable comment is attached to the definition of each variable; it explains how the variable will be used. Code

INFORMATION HEADER

```
/**********************************************************
    Function: depreciate

    Purpose: Calculate depreciation.

Call example: ret = depreciate( schedule )

            char *schedule; Pointer to schedule name.
            int ret; Return code
                0 = successful
                1 = failed

  Programmed: D. Himmel, April 20, 1994
***********************************************************/
#define NUM_ITEMS 100      /* Number of inventory items */

int depreciate( char *schedule )
{
    int fullDep;            /* Number of items fully depreciated */
    float totalCost;        /* Accumulated cost of machinery */
    float Cost[NUM_ITEMS];  /* Array of costs for purchased items */

/*-------------------- Initialize ----------------------*/

/* Clear accumulators */

    fullDep = 0;
    totalCost = 0.0;

/* Open files */

    file1 = fopen( 'INV", "r" ); /* Inventory file */
    file2 = fopen( "PUR", "r" ); /* Cost file */

/*---------------- Calculate depreciation -------------*/

}
```

VARIABLE COMMENTS

MINOR CODE COMMENTS

MAJOR CODE COMMENTS

LOCAL COMMENTS

FIGURE 2-3   Comments

comments can be of three types: major code comments separate larger, significant program sections; minor comments clarify blocks of code within major sections; and local comments explain details of individual statements.

Here are two *don'ts* that will help you do a good job with comments:

1 Don't put off the task of commenting—the easiest approach is to add comments while the code is fresh in your mind

2 Don't just repeat what the code says:

```
void myFunction()
{
    while ( notDone )            /* 1st level indent (function block) */
    {
        ++numFinished;          /* 2nd level indent (while block) */
                                /* Blank line for clarity */
        for ( i=0; i<TOTAL; ++i )
        {
            if ( value > 0 )    /* 3rd level indent (for block) */
            {
                sum += value;   /* 4th level indent (if statements) */
            }
        else
        {
            break;
        }
    }
    }
}
```

FIGURE 2-4   Indentation example

```
gallons = quarts / 4; /* Divide by 4 */
```

Instead, add information to the statement:

```
gallons = quarts / 4; /* Convert quarts to gallons */
```

Indent

The ANSI standard does not dictate how to place C statements on a line; it allows you to place them anywhere and even to split statements between lines. However, you generally should use only one statement per line, and you should indent statements to show their relationship to one another. Figure 2-4 shows how to indent all statements within a function and how to indent statements controlled by looping or branching statements (*for, while, if*).

Follow a Consistent Layout

C allows much flexibility in the placement of program elements, but you will find it beneficial to adopt an ordering and stick with it, especially on software projects involving several other programmers. Figure 2-5 gives a suggested ordering for the major elements of a C program.

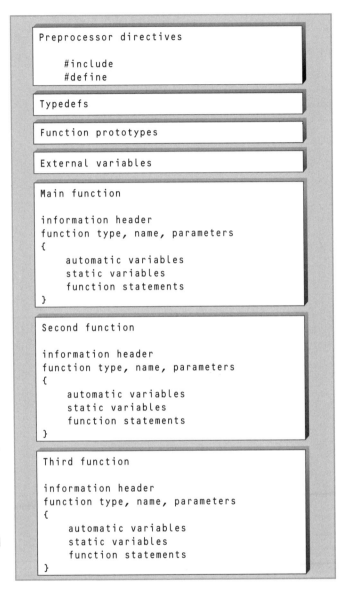

FIGURE 2-5 Suggested ordering of C program elements

Often it is best to put the second three elements (defines, *typedefs*, and prototypes) in a header file and use an *#include* directive to insert them in the program.

SUMMARY

In Chapter 1, you installed Turbo C++ and learned how to use it to edit, compile, link, and run programs. In this chapter, you reviewed a brief history of C and the basic structure and elements of a C program. Now it's time to move ahead and start learning C in depth.

*Average time to
complete this chapter
(including lab and
quiz) is 4 hours.*

USING DATA

has a rich set of data types suitable
for any computing requirement.
One of your most important jobs as
a programmer is to choose data
types that are appropriate to a task.
Your choices will affect not just
whether a program works, but how
much memory it consumes and how
fast it runs.

This chapter gives you a solid
understanding of the different data
types and their characteristics. You
will learn how to use *identifiers* for
constants and variables, and how to
control access to variables among
different sections of a program.

LECTURE

Basics of Computer Data

Data is everywhere in your computer, as shown in Figure 3-1. It's stored on your disks (hard disk, floppy disk, or CD-ROM disk) and in the random access memory (RAM); it passes down the wires to your printer and display; and it travels to and from remote locations via your modem. Computer data represents text and numbers and it also constitutes executable programs. The computer operating system (DOS or Windows) is data in the form of a program always running in RAM. When you run a program by typing a command or clicking on an icon, the operating system responds by loading the program file from disk to RAM, where it begins executing. This program can then read and write other disk data files or communicate data with other destinations.

Figure 3-2 illustrates the smallest elements of computer data: *bits*, *bytes*, and *words*. A bit (which stands for *binary digit*) can have a value of either 0 or 1. A byte is made of 8 bits and can hold 256 different numeric values. Words comprise 2 or more bytes depending on the computer model—PCs based on the Intel 286, 386, or 486 central processor have 2-byte words, whereas machines like the Sun SPARCstation have a 4-byte word. There is also an element called the *nibble*, which is 4 bits or one-half of a byte. The nibble is referred to much less often than bits, bytes, or words, but it is sometimes useful because it corresponds to one digit of a hexadecimal number.

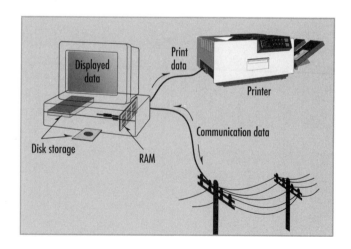

FIGURE 3-1   Data in
and around your computer

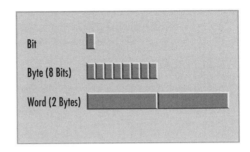

FIGURE 3-2 Bits, bytes, and words

Types of Data

Before you can use data in a program, you must allocate storage for it. You do this by *defining* the data type with key words like *int, char,* and *float.* The type determines the amount of memory required, the range of values that can be stored, and how the program processes the data. You can use other qualifying key words (*long, short, unsigned*) to alter the definition of data. Table 3-1 lists the basic data types of C, along with storage sizes and intended values.

Key Word	Usage	ANSI C Size	TURBO C++ Size
char	Text or integers	1 byte	1 byte
short int	Integers	Minimum of 2 bytes and less than or equal to *int*	2 bytes
int	Integers	Less than or equal to *long*	2 bytes
long int	Integers	Minimum of 4 bytes	4 bytes
float	Real numbers	Less than or equal to double	4 bytes
double	Real numbers	Less than or equal long double	8 bytes
long double	Real numbers		10 bytes
void	Type only	Has no size	1/N

Table 3-1	C data types

Notice that C does not explicitly specify the size of some of the data types; different compilers are free to set most data sizes within the constraining limits.

You can discover the size (in bytes) of any data type with the *sizeof* operator. For example, you can obtain the size of *int* with:

```
sizeof( int )
```

The parentheses are optional, so you can also write:

```
sizeof int
```

But in the context of a program, the connection to the operator is more obvious with the parentheses included. You can also feed the name of a variable to *sizeof* and it will return the number of bytes required for that variable. Here is how you would define and find the size of a floating-point variable named *distance*:

```
int size;
float distance;
size = sizeof( distance )
```

The value of variable *size* would be 4. In the lab section you will write programs to display the sizes of various data types.

Character Data Type

The *char* key word declares the character data type. This data type always occupies 1 byte of storage (on any modern computer system). Because the number of values that a byte can hold is 256, a character can represent up to 256 different letters—more than enough for the uppercase and lowercase English alphabet, plus many special symbols.

Text Data in Characters

The character data type normally holds one letter of text information in the form of a character code. Appendix A lists the numeric codes corresponding to the American Standard Code for Information Interchange (ASCII) alphabet. If you look in that appendix you will see that the code for 'A' is 65 and the ASCII code for the space character (' ') is 32. PCs use ASCII codes for characters but other computer systems use different codes; IBM mainframe computers use Extended Binary Coded Decimal Interchange Codes (EBCDIC).

Here's how you can define a character variable named *oh*:

```
char oh;
```

Here's how you can define it and store the code for the letter 'O' at the same time:

```
char oh = 'O';
```

Numeric Data in Characters

C is different from some other programming languages in that it allows you to use the character data type to work with integer numbers. This means you can save space in programs that use a lot of small integers (values less than 256) because you can define 1-byte character data types instead of 2-byte integers. C does not specify whether the *char* data type is signed or unsigned; thus, compilers default to different choices. If you use characters for numeric calculations, you should be aware of the compiler's choice of signed or unsigned—the lab section shows how you can test for this. Turbo C++ defaults to *signed char*. You can override the compiler default by declaring either *signed char* or *unsigned char*. Table 3-2 shows the allowed range of numeric values for these two data types.

	Minimum Value	Maximum Value
unsigned char	0	255
signed char	−128	+127

Table 3-2	Limits for character value

Integer Data Types

Integers are whole numbers, like 1776 or -50, without a fractional part. C provides key words for three types of integers: *short, long*, and *int*, each of which can be further declared to be *signed* or *unsigned*, for a total of six integer types. Integers default to the signed type.

You can define a 2-byte signed integer named *smallNumber* as follows:

```
int smallNumber;
```

Or you can do it this way (but the *signed* keyword is redundant):

```
signed int smallNumber;
```

Some compilers make *short* integers different from type *int* (allowed by the rules in Table 3-1), but Turbo C++ makes them the same, so the following five statements are equivalent:

```
int smallNumber;

short smallNumber;

short int smallNumber;

signed short smallNumber;

signed short int smallNumber;
```

Notice that *short* and *short int* are synonymous—you can leave out the key word *int*. You can define a 4-byte signed integer named *bigNumber* with the key word *long*:

```
long bigNumber;
```

Here are some equivalent statements:

```
signed long bigNumber;
```

```
long int bigNumber;
```

```
signed long int bigNumber;
```

How do you choose the type of integer to use? Select the smallest data type that will contain the largest number expected by your program. This way the program will properly compute integers and it will consume the least amount of memory. Table 3-3 gives the limits for each type of integer.

Data Type	Minimum Value	Maximum Value
signed char	-128	+127
signed int	-32768	+32767
signed long	-2147483648	+2147483647
unsigned char	0	255
unsigned int	0	65535
unsigned long	0	4294967295

Table 3-3   Limits for integer values

If you have correctly identified the maximum and minimum values that will occur, then your program will not experience problems. If you can't be sure of the range of values, it would be a good idea to add statements to your program to check for invalid values. But what if a program does try to insert a number that is out of range for an integer? This is called *underflow* if the number is smaller than the minimum allowed and *overflow* if it is larger than the maximum allowed. The computer will not indicate an error for underflow or overflow even though something is wrong. Figure 3-3 illustrates the continuous, circular nature of integer values. Just as a clock rolls over to 1 o'clock when it reaches the limit of 12, a 2-byte, unsigned integer *(unsigned int)* overflows from 65535 to 0 at the limit. Therefore if you attempt to assign 65536 to an unsigned integer variable, the actual value will be 0, and 65537 will yield 1. Figure 3-4 shows the allowed range of values for a 2-byte signed integer *(int)*. In this case, a value of +32768 will overflow to -32768 and -32769 will underflow to 32767.

Floating-Point Data Types

Floating-point numbers are real numbers, such as 3.1416 and 1.50, that have both an integer part and a fractional part. C stores a floating-point number as a fraction and an exponent. For instance, C would store the average temperature of the human body, 98.6, as the fraction .986 with an exponent of 2, which says to move the decimal point two places to the right.

There are three kinds of floating-point numbers: type *float*, type *double*, and type *long double*. They differ only in the precision (number of significant digits) of the fraction and in the range of the exponent. Table 3-4 shows the sizes of these data types, along with the precision and allowed range of values.

Data Type	Precision	Minimum Value	Maximum Value
float	7 digits	1.e-37	1.e38
double	16 digits	1.e-307	1.e308

(Minimums and maximums are positive or negative)

Table 3-4   **Limits for floating-point values**

Floating-point variables usually take more memory than integers and they require far more time to process, so you should choose integers over floating-point data types if possible. However, floating-point numbers are essential when a program uses fractions or encounters values larger than integers will accommodate.

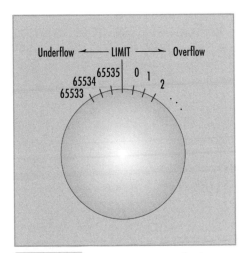

FIGURE 3-3 Continuous range of values for *unsigned int*

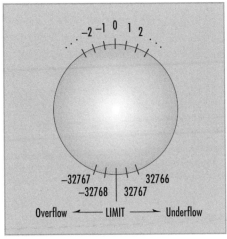

FIGURE 3-4 Continous range of values for *signed int*

Even though floating-point numbers permit an extremely wide range of values, they still will overflow and underflow at the range limits. A floating-point overflow will result in an unpredictable value, and an underflow will result in a zero value. Integers live in a circular world where they can keep going back around to the same values over and over. However, floating-point numbers live in a flat world where they drop off into uncharted regions at the limits. Figure 3-5 illustrates the linear nature of floating-point values. Notice the peculiar "island" where zero is separated from other values by the underflow regions; however, there is a bridge that allows underflows to reach zero. The only way you can be absolutely sure that a variable is zero is to assign the value of zero explicitly. Don't trust a calculated floating-point result to be exact, and never attempt to compare it with 0.0 or any exact real constant. When you perform calculations with floating-point numbers, the result could be off by one in the last digit of precision and be 0.000001 instead of 0.000000, or 0.999999 instead of 1.000000.

The *void* Data Type

C defines a unique data type called *void*. This is a generic type that has no specific size and no range of allowed values. There is no sense in defining a variable of type *void* because you cannot assign a value of any kind to it. "Then what good is it?" you might justifiably ask. C has two principal purposes for type *void*: One is to declare that a function will not have a return value (discussed in Chapter 8), and the other is to provide for a pointer that can hold the address of any type of data (discussed in Chapter 11).

The *typedef* Statement

You can declare your own data types with the *typedef* statement. This statement consists of the key word *typedef*, followed by a data type, and then the name of the new type, ending with a semicolon. For example, programmers often use the name *BYTE* as a convenient way to represent an *unsigned char* data type.

```
typedef unsigned char BYTE;
BYTE someBits;
BYTE moreBits;
```

This is the equivalent of:

```
unsigned char someBits;
unsigned char moreBits;
```

There are two benefits of *typedef*: it makes programs simpler and more readable, and it can make them more portable. Suppose a 16-bit integer is type *int* on one computer and type *short* on another. For the first machine you can declare

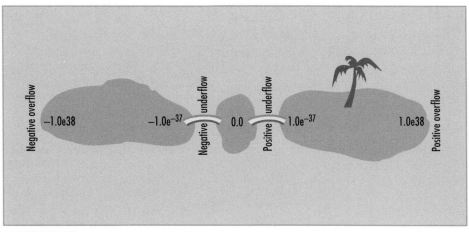

FIGURE 3-5   The flat world of floating-point numbers

```
typedef int INT16;
```

and define all 16-bit variables using the synonym, INT16. Then when you want to port the program to the second computer, all you need to do is change the declaration to

```
typedef short INT16;
```

and all variables that were defined with type INT16 will automatically convert to *short* when the program is compiled.

There are two categories of data types in C: *fundamental* data types represented by key words such as *int*, *char*, and *float*, and *derived* data types, which are assemblages declared by you, such as arrays, functions, and structures. The *typedef* statement is particularly powerful when used with derived data types, as you will see in Chapter 13.

To conclude this discussion of data types, imagine that you have to write a program to process registration data for a group of students. How will you choose data types for variables such as name, age, social security number, and tuition? Because names are made up of characters, type *char* would be the choice for names. You won't be performing arithmetic with social security numbers, so type *char* is a good choice for this data. The age would best be represented as an integer of type *int* (or possibly *char* to save space—all ages will certainly be less than 255). Because tuition is a dollar value with a decimal point, a natural choice for data type would be *float;* however, you could eliminate the decimal point by storing tuition as an integer value in cents instead of dollars (this is probably overkill because the amount of saved space would not be significant).

Constants

Constants are values that cannot be changed. You will use constants for many things in your programs: to initialize variables, to set the size of arrays, to limit the number of times a processing loop repeats, and more. Each basic data type, character, integer, and floating point, is associated with a different constant.

Character Constants

Character constants correspond to the data type *char;* they are used with variables of type *char* and sometimes with integer types. Character constants are letters, digits, or symbols enclosed by single quotes; here are some examples:

```
'A', 'z', '@', '\n'
```

Notice that the last constant contains two symbols, a backslash (\) and the letter *n.* Any constant prefixed with a backslash (\) is called an *escape sequence.* Escape sequences translate to numeric ASCII codes for controlling operations such as a printer line feed ('\n'), carriage return ('\r'), or form feed ('\f'). Table 3-5 lists some common character constants that are escape sequences.

Escape Sequence	ASCII Code	Meaning
\a	7	Alert or bell
\b	8	Backspace
\f	12	Formfeed
\n	10	Newline
\r	13	Carriage return
\t	9	Horizontal tab
\v	11	Vertical tab
\\	92	Backslash
\?	63	Question mark
\'	39	Single quote
\"	34	Double quote
\<octal digits>		Octal number
\x<hex digits>		Hexadecimal number

<octal digits> and <hex digits> represent a sequence of digits

Table 3-5   **Escape sequences**

Integer Constants

Integer constants are numbers that don't change. Most frequently they are decimal (base 10) integers, like 1776, 99, and -1, but C also allows you to write *hexadecimal* (base 16) and *octal* (base 8) constants. In C, hexadecimal (hex) constants are preceded by 0x (such as 0xFF), and octal constants are preceded by zero (such as 07). A *long* constant is any constant that is too big for an *int,* or that ends with the letter *l* or *L*. Table 3-6 lists a sequence of integer constants written in decimal, hex, and octal notation.

Decimal (base 10)	Octal (base 8)	Hexadecimal (base 16)
0	00	0x0
1	01	0x1
2	02	0x2
3	03	0x3
4	04	0x4
5	05	0x5
6	06	0x6
7	07	0x7
8	010	0x8
9	011	0x9
10	012	0xA
11	013	0xB
12	014	0xC
13	015	0xD
14	016	0xE
15	017	0xF
16	020	0x10
64	0100	0x40
100	0144	0x64
128	0200	0x80
256	0400	0x100

Table 3-6   **Counting up with decimal, octal, and hex integers**

Floating-Point Constants

Floating-point constants are decimal numbers that contain either a decimal point (.) or an exponent (e or E). By default they are of type *double*; you can force a constant to be type *float* by appending the letter *f* or *F*, or to be type *long double* by appending the letter *l* or *L*. Here are some floating-point constants:

```
98.6                     /* type double */
-100.f                   /* type float */
1.5e2                    /* type double */
3.1415926535897896L      /* type long double */
```

Symbolic Constants

Symbolic constants are synonyms for other constants; you create them with the *#define* preprocessor directive. Here is how you would make the symbolic constant *DISTRICTS* correspond to the actual number of districts, 22:

```
#define DISTRICTS 22
```

Preprocessor directives are commands that the compiler performs before it begins the real task of compiling. The *#define* directive instructs the compiler to replace every occurrence of the symbol (*DISTRICTS* in this case) with the associated value (22). Chapter 14 gives a more complete explanation of preprocessor directives, including the use of *#define* to produce more complex substitutions called *macros*.

Symbolic constants have two very important purposes: they make programs much more readable—you should always define symbolic constants in place of numbers, and they make program maintenance much easier—to change the number of districts in this example you would change only the *#define* statement instead of every occurrence of the value 22 in a program.

You can use any C identifier for the name of a symbolic constant, but it is good practice to use uppercase letters because this differentiates symbolic constants from variables.

Variables

A variable is a memory location that can be altered. You create a variable by defining it in a statement containing a data type key word followed by an identifier. You can also use a synonym from a *typedef* statement to establish the data type. Here are some examples of variable definitions:

```
unsigned long largeNumber; /* unsigned long int definition */
char monogram;             /* character definition */
double price = 1.50;       /* optional initialization */
BYTE smallNumber;          /* uses typedef synonym */
signed INT16 twoBytes;     /* key word plus typedef synonym */
```

Definition statements always begin with the data type, then they name an identifier, and they end with a semicolon. You can optionally include an initialization, as for *price* above, but this is not a necessary part of the definition. The fourth definition uses the synonym, *BYTE*, declared as

```
typedef unsigned char BYTE;
```

The last definition combines the key word *signed* with *INT16* from the following *typedef* statement to declare the data type of *signed int* for *twoBytes*:

```
typedef int INT16;
```

The definition of a variable accomplishes three things: it establishes the type of data, it allocates storage space, and it assigns a name, or *identifier,* to the variable.

Define vs Declare

There is an important distinction in C between the terms *define* and *declare.* When you declare a data type, a function prototype, or a structure tag, you specify characteristics of the item (such as how big it will be and what kind of data will be associated with it). However, an item does not actually exist in a program until you *define* it. The definition of an item (a variable, a function, or a structure) not only registers characteristics, but it causes memory to be allocated to hold the item. We will defer discussions of functions and structures to later chapters, but here are examples that show the difference between declaring a data type and defining a variable:

```
typedef unsigned long ULONG;   /* A declaration */
ULONG bigNumber;               /* A definition */
unsigned long bigNumber; /* Combined declaration and definition,
                            usually just called a definition */
```

Identifiers

Identifiers are names that programs use to refer to data items. Identifiers in C can be almost any sequence of letters and digits, but you must observe some simple rules. An identifier must begin with a letter (A through Z, uppercase or lowercase) or underscore (_), and it must contain only letters, digits (0 through 9), or underscores. Identifiers are case sensitive; that is, if you change any letter from uppercase to lowercase, or vice versa, it becomes a different identifier. Table 3-7 shows both some legal and illegal identifiers.

These identifiers are OK:

```
num_allowed
first1
theOnlyWayToGo
SnowWhiteAndThe7Dwarfs
Route_66
ACAPITALPLAN      /* Caps recommended only for symbolic constants */
i                 /* Nondescriptive recommended only for indexes */
szFileName        /* Hungarian notation--sz stands for zero-terminated
                        string */
```

These identifiers are OK by the rules, but not recommended:

```
xxxx              /* Not descriptive */
_amount           /* Leading underscores are sometimes used
                        by the compiler and operating system */
owed_             /* ... and so are trailing underscores */
```

These identifiers are NOT OK:

```
9Pins             /* Illegal--can't begin with a number */
good@Golf         /* Illegal--can't use the at sign (@) */
Window Pane       /* Illegal--spaces not allowed */
Bullet-proof      /* Illegal--can't use hyphen (-) */
```

Table 3-7	Legal and illegal identifiers

There are many different conventions for identifiers: one scheme prefers only lowercase letters and separates words with underscores (example: *num_allowed*); another recommends beginning each word with uppercase and adding a prefix to denote the type of data (Hungarian notation). For this book, we have adopted a scheme that has gained widespread acceptance—it uses all lowercase letters for identifiers except for capitalizing the first letter of each word after the first word (example: *theOnlyWayToGo*).

Key Word *const*

You can make the value of a variable into a constant by adding the key word *const* to its definition.

```
const int bodyTemp = 98.6;
```

Thereafter *bodyTemp* is the same as the constant, 98.6, and you cannot change the value of *bodyTemp*. You can initialize a *const* item when you define it, but after that you cannot assign a value to it.

You can use *const* declarations for the same purpose as symbolic constants—to make a program more readable and more portable. A *const* declaration has the added advantage that the compiler recognizes it as a specific data type—Chapter 11 shows how this is important for declaring pointer constants.

Enumerated Data Type

There is a specialized data type in C called *enum* that you can use to declare a collection of constants having sequential integer values. This comes in handy when you need symbolic constants for related items like colors or days of the week. You can also use *enum* to define a variable, in which case the variable is restricted to the values that you previously declared for the *enum* type.

The general syntax for *enum* is:

```
enum TAG { enumeration list } variable name;
```

All the items in this syntax are optional except for key word *enum* and the semicolon. We recommend that you use *enum* in two parts: first declare an enumeration *template*, then define any needed *enum* variables. Here's an example of a template:

```
enum DAYS { SUNDAY, MONDAY, TUESDAY, WEDNESDAY,
            THURSDAY, FRIDAY, SATURDAY };
```

DAYS is the identifier for the template (called a tag); you can insert any C identifier, and we recommend using uppercase letters for tags. The enumeration list is the symbolic constants SUNDAY through SATURDAY enclosed by braces that, by default, take on values of 0 through 6. The above statement establishes an *enum DAYS* data type that can have the values SUNDAY through SATURDAY (or 0 through 6). Notice that the variable name is missing from the above statement.

Now you can define variables with the new data type that will be restricted to the enumerated values. For example:

```
enum DAYS anyDay;
```

Variable *anyDay* is type *int*, which can take any value from the enumeration list.

When you declare the enumeration list, the compiler assigns integer values to the symbolic constants in sequence starting with 0 and counting upwards. You can change the sequence by assigning values within the list. For example, you can renumber TUESDAY and FRIDAY like this:

```
enum DAYS { SUNDAY, MONDAY, TUESDAY=10, WEDNESDAY,
            THURSDAY, FRIDAY=-8, SATURDAY };
```

The items following TUESDAY and FRIDAY will also change, so that the whole sequence of constants becomes:

```
SUNDAY     0 /* Compiler starts with a default of 0 */
MONDAY     1 /* Count upward */
TUESDAY   10 /* Explicit renumber to 10 */
WEDNESDAY 11 /* Count upward */
THURSDAY  12 /* Count upward */
FRIDAY    -8 /* Explicit renumber to -8 */
SATURDAY  -7 /* Count upward */
```

Enumerated types provide two advantages: enumeration is an easy way to define a group of symbolic constants that make your program more readable, and enumeration can allow automatic compiler checking of values assigned to variables. Some compilers will generate an error if you try to assign a value that is not in the enumeration list, but C makes this an optional feature; many compilers do not perform this check. Turbo C++ issues a warning if you try to assign anything but one of the symbolic constants from the enumeration list.

Here is an easy way that you can check enumerated values even if your compiler doesn't. Add an extra symbol to the end of the enumerated list that will be the number of items in the list. For example:

```
enum COLOR { BLACK, RED, BLUE, GREEN, WHITE, NUM_COLORS };
```

Because the compiler starts numbering with 0, the last constant, NUM_COLORS, will be a number equal to the number of preceding items (five in this case). Now you can readily use NUM_COLORS to see if any variable has one of the color values (even if the variable was not defined with *enum*).

```
int paint;
if ( ( paint < 0 ) || ( paint >= NUM_COLORS ) )
{
    printf( "paint is not a valid COLOR" );
}
```

You don't get a full explanation of *if* statements for branching until Chapter 6, but the above statement makes the *printf()* execute if variable *paint* is less than 0 or greater than or equal to NUM_COLORS. If you add more colors to the list, the compiler will automatically adjust the upper bound, NUM_COLORS, accordingly.

Storage Classes

As you just learned, a variable has a type attribute that determines how much memory it requires and what kind of data it can hold. Variables have a second attribute, called *storage class,* which determines the lifetime of the variable (or how long the data will be retained by the program). There are two kinds of storage classes, *automatic* and *static.*

Automatic Storage Class

A program creates and destroys an automatic variable when it enters and leaves the *block* in which the variable is defined. A block consists of the group of statements between two braces ({ }). For instance, the braces of a function constitute a block within which you can define automatic variables.

```
void myFunction()
{                   /* beginning of block */
    int a;          /* a is automatic */
}                   /* end of block */
```

The name *automatic storage class* stems from the fact that a program automatically creates these variables upon entering a block and it automatically destroys them upon leaving. You can also define automatic variables with the key words *auto* and *register*. Here are several ways to define automatic variables:

```
void myFunction()
{
    int a;          /* automatic by default */
    auto int b;     /* key word auto is redundant here */
    register int c; /* automatic assigned to hardware register */
}
```

With the *register* key word, you can request that the compiler store a variable in a hardware register, which will process values faster than memory storage. However, a computer has a limited number of hardware registers, and the compiler will not be able to honor the request if none are available, or if the data type is not an integer compatible with registers. In that case, the compiler will just assign the variable to memory.

RESTRICTIONS ON THE REGISTER QUALIFIER

Beware; you cannot use the address operator (&) on a variable assigned to a *register* because hardware registers don't have memory addresses! (You will learn more about the address operator in Chapter 11.) In fact, most optimizing compilers assign variables to registers when appropriate anyway, so there is little need to use the *register* key word.

Static Storage Class

A program creates static variables before it begins executing and it destroys them when it quits. The word static means stationary, so this name is appropriate for variables that remain in place the entire time a program executes. You make a variable static by defining it outside all functions in a file or by attaching the key word *static*. Here are three ways of defining static variables:

```
int x;              /* static by default */
static int y;       /* key word static is redundant here */

void myFunction()
{
    static int z;   /* static inside a function */
}
```

Scope, Lifetime, and Initialization

When you define a variable, the compiler has to make three decisions about the variable:

1 It must decide which regions of the program know about the variable and have access to it—this is called *scope*.

2 It must decide when to create storage for the variable and when to destroy it—this is called *lifetime* or *storage class*.

3 It must decide whether or not to insert an initial value.

The scope, lifetime, and initialization of a variable are determined by a combination of the placement of the definition in the program and the key word qualifiers used. Table 3-8 shows the different ways you can define variables.

DEFINITION		PROPERTIES		
Location	Key word	Scope	Storage class	Initialization
Inside a function	none	Function	Automatic	None*
Inside a function	*auto*	Function	Automatic	None*
Inside a function	*register*	Function	Automatic	None*
Inside a function	*static*	Function	Static	To zero
Outside functions	none	File	Static	To zero
Outside functions	*static*	File	Static	To zero
Outside functions	*extern*	Program	Static	To zero

* Except for partially initialized arrays

Table 3-8 **Variable definition**

If you define a variable inside a function, the scope is limited to that function. Further, if an inner block of braces exists in a function, the scope of variables defined there is confined to the inner block.

```
void myFunction()
{
    int a;          /* scope of a is myFunction */
    {               /* beginning of inner block */
        int b;      /* scope of b is the inner block */
    }               /* end of inner block */
                    /* b does not exist here */
}
```

If you define a variable outside all functions in a file, the scope of the variable is the entire file—it is accessible to all functions in the file. However, it is not accessible to functions in other files. For large programs, it is often desirable to place functions in several different files. You can make a variable accessible across files (program scope) in the following way: define a variable outside all functions in one file, then in another file; declare a variable of the same name; and add the key word *extern*. As a consequence, the variable will be accessible to all functions in both files. Figure 3-6 illustrates this technique.

Notice that variable *width* is *defined* in file one and *declared* in the other files—*extern* is a declaration that does not allocate memory.

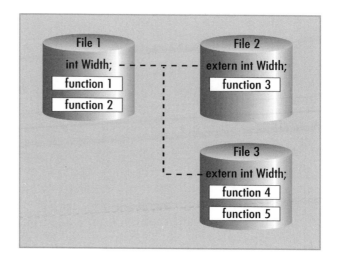

FIGURE 3-6 A static variable having a program scope

PORTABILITY OF IDENTIFIERS FOR *STATIC* ITEMS

Be forewarned about the following potential trap in connection with the static storage class. The C specification guarantees only that the first six characters of the names of static variables will be recognized, and it does not guarantee that compilers will recognize the difference between uppercase and lowercase characters for such names. This was done for compatibility with certain computer systems (IBM mainframes) that cannot process names with more than six characters. Most compilers will recognize at least 31 characters for static variables, but if you are concerned about a high degree of portability, you need to be aware of these restrictions.

Here is another way to affect the scope of a variable: if you include the key word *static* in a variable definition that is outside all functions in a file, you limit the scope to that file and prohibit access from functions in any other file.

The compiler does not initialize automatic variables. When a program creates an automatic variable, it takes whatever value happens to be in the memory location that is allocated. You should be aware of this and always explicitly set the values of automatic variables before using them. On the other hand, a program initializes all static variables to zero values before it begins executing.

LAB

EXERCISE 1A: Display sizes of fundamental data types.

✳ **STARTER FILE:** EX03-1A.C

```
#include <stdio.h>
void main()
{
    printf( "Size of char = %d\n", sizeof( char ) );
}
```

✳ **DO:** Type in the above program and run it.

✳ **RESULT:**

```
Size of char = 1
```

✳ **DISCUSSION:** This program displays the size of data type *char*. The *printf* statement sends data to the screen, guided by the formatting characters located between the double quotes (" "). The characters %d constitute the decimal conversion specifier for the data that follows the comma. The '\n' characters specify the newline escape sequence that causes the cursor to move to the next line.

EXERCISE 1B: Add other data types.

✳ **DO:** Add *printf* statements to display the sizes of data types *short*, *int*, *long*, *float*, *double*, and *long double*.

✳ **SOLUTION FILE:** EX03-1B.C

✳ **RESULT:**

```
Size of char = 1
Size of short = 2
Size of int = 2
Size of long = 4
Size of float = 4
Size of double = 8
Size of long double = 10
```

✳ **DISCUSSION:** Notice that Turbo C++ assigns the same size to *short* and *int*, and different sizes to all three types of floating-point numbers.

EXERCISE 2A: Display signed or unsigned default for type *char*.

✳ **STARTER FILE:** EX03-2A.C

```c
#include <stdio.h>
void main()
{
    char oneByte = 0;
    printf( "Value of oneByte = %d\n", oneByte );
}
```

✳ **DO:** Type in the above program and run it.

✳ **RESULT:**

```
Value of oneByte = 0
```

✳ **DISCUSSION:** This program displays the value of a variable defined as type *char*. The statement *char oneByte = 0;* does two things: it defines a variable and it initializes it to zero.

EXERCISE 2B: Discover the Turbo C++ default.

✳ **DO:** Change the value of the constant that initializes variable *oneByte* to the maximum possible for an 8-bit unsigned integer, 255.

✳ **SOLUTION FILE:** EX03-2B.C

✳ **RESULT:**

```
Value of oneByte = -1
```

✳ **DISCUSSION:** If *char* is unsigned, the program will display 255; if *char* is signed it will underflow to -1. Therefore, Turbo C++ defaults to signed *char*.

EXERCISE 2C: Declare an unsigned character.

✳ **DO:** Change the definition of *oneByte* to be *unsigned*.

✳ **SOLUTION FILE:** EX03-2C.C

✳ **RESULT:**

```
Value of oneByte = 255
```

✳ **DISCUSSION:** This result verifies that the *signed/unsigned* type determines the displayed value of *oneByte*.

EXERCISE 3A: Display the limits of integer data types.

✳ **STARTER FILE:** EX03-3A.C

```
#include <stdio.h>
void main()
{
    char aChar = 127;
    int anInt  = 32767;
    long aLong = 2147483647;

    printf( "Value of aChar = %d\n", aChar );
    printf( "Value of anInt = %d\n", anInt );
    printf( "Value of aLong = %ld\n", aLong );
}
```

✳ *DO:* Type in the above program and run it.

✳ RESULT:

```
Value of aChar = 127
Value of anInt = 32767
Value of aLong = 2147483647
```

✳ DISCUSSION: This program displays the maximum values for signed integers of type *char*, *int*, and *long*. Notice the %*ld* format specifier to display the long integer—without the *l*, the program will display the wrong value.

EXERCISE 3B: Induce overflow.

✳ DO: Add one to each initialization value; e.g., initialize *aChar* to 128 instead of 127.

✳ SOLUTION FILE: EX03-3B.C

✳ RESULT:

```
Value of aChar = -128
Value of anInt = -32768
Value of aLong = -2147483648
```

✳ DISCUSSION: Each signed integer has overflowed from the maximum positive value to the minimum negative value.

EXERCISE 4A: Test the precision of floating-point variables.

✳ STARTER FILE: EX03-4A.C

```
#include <stdio.h>
void main()
{
    float aFloat = 123456789876543210.;
    double aDouble  = 123456789876543210.;

    printf( "Value of aFloat = %25.20e\n", aFloat );
    printf( "Value of aDouble = %25.20e\n", aDouble );
}
```

✳ DO: Type in the above program and run it.

✳ RESULT:

```
Value of aFloat = 1.23456790519987104000e17
Value of aDouble = 1.23456789876543216000e17
```

✳ **DISCUSSION:** In order to test the precision of floating-point numbers, this program initializes the variables with an 18-digit number. The *printf* statement has a conversion specifier of *%25.20e*, which tells the compiler to display up to 25 digits in an exponential format and use 20 of the digits for the fractional part. Thus, you can know the precision by counting the number of correct digits in the displayed result. The value of *aFloat* (type *float*) is correct to 7 digits (7-digit precision) and the value of *aDouble* (type *double*) is correct through the 17th digit (17-digit precision). You should not expect the digits beyond the precision limit in your result to match those under RESULT above.

EXERCISE 4B: Find maximum limits for floating-point numbers.

✳ **DO:** Change the initialization values to 1.e40.

✳ **SOLUTION FILE:** EX03-4B.C

✳ **RESULT:**

```
Value of aFloat = +INF
Value of aDouble = 1.0000000000000000300e40
```

✳ **DISCUSSION:** This number is beyond the maximum limit for type *float*, causing an overflow error to occur (+*INF* indicates an infinite value). However it is within the range of numbers for type *double*—but notice that the answer is wrong beyond the 17th digit precision limit. You can experiment further to find the lower and upper limits by trying other initialization values.

EXERCISE 5:   Examine the *typedef* declaration.

✳ **DO:** Modify your program from Exercise 2C. Use a *typedef* statement to declare a new unsigned *char* data type, UCHAR, and use UCHAR to define the variable, *oneByte*.

✳ **SOLUTION FILE:** EX03-5.C

✳ **RESULT:**

```
Value of oneByte = 255
```

✳ **DISCUSSION:** The displayed result is the same as in Exercise 2C. If you have any difficulty with this modification, refer to program EX03-5.C on disk.

EXERCISE 6:   Try to define data type *void*.

✳ STARTER FILE: EX03-6.C

```
#include <stdio.h>
void main()
{
    void v;
}
```

✳ DO: Type and compile the above program.

✳ RESULT: A compile error occurs on line 4 stating that the size of variable *v* is unknown.

✳ DISCUSSION: This exercise proves that you cannot define a variable of type *void*. You will discover how to use *void* later in the book (Chapters 8 and 11).

EXERCISE 7A: Declare symbolic constants.

✳ DO: Modify your program from Exercise 2A. Use a *#define* statement to declare a new symbolic constant, MINBYTE, having a value of -128, and then initialize variable *oneByte* with MINBYTE.

✳ SOLUTION FILE: EX03-7A.C

✳ RESULT:

```
Value of oneByte = -128
```

✳ DISCUSSION: The best location for the *#define* statement is outside the main function just below *#include;* however, it will work as long as it appears anywhere before the synonym is used.

EXERCISE 7B: Declare character symbolic constants.

✳ DO: Add another *#define* statement to declare a new symbolic constant, LASTLETTER, having a value of 'Z', and then initialize variable *oneByte* with LASTLETTER.

✳ SOLUTION FILE: EX03-7B.C

✳ RESULT:

```
Value of oneByte = 90
```

✳ **DISCUSSION:** The *printf* statement displays the value of *oneByte* as a decimal number; the ASCII code for 'Z' is decimal 90 (refer to Appendix A). The preprocessor performs a literal substitution of the value for every occurrence of the symbolic constant, so you can declare symbolic constants to have values of any type of constant, integer, character, or floating point.

EXERCISE 7C: Use the key word *const*.

✳ **DO:** Replace the *#define* directive for LASTLETTER with a statement that defines it to be type *const char*.

✳ **SOLUTION FILE:** EX03-7C.C

✳ **RESULT:** Same as Exercise 7B.

✳ **DISCUSSION:** You can use *const* to declare symbolic constants as well as *#define*.

EXERCISE 7D: Attempt assignment to a *const* variable.

✳ **DO:** Add a statement that assigns a new value to LASTLETTER.

✳ **SOLUTION FILE:** EX03-7D.C

✳ **RESULT:** A compile error stating that an *lvalue* is required to accept an assigned value.

✳ **DISCUSSION:** You cannot change the value of a variable declared to be *const*.

EXERCISE 8A: Try different identifiers.

✳ **STARTER FILE:** EX03-8A.C

```
#include <stdio.h>
void main()
{
    int identifier = 0;
    int IDENTIFIER = 1;
    int Identifier = 2;
    int _id = 3;      /* Underscore is allowed */
    int id1 = 4;      /* Digits are allowed */
    int 1id = 5;      /* Illegal--must begin with letter */
    int @id = 6;      /* Illegal--not a letter or digit */
    int int = 7;      /* Illegal--cannot use key word */
    int id X = 8;     /* Illegal--cannot include spaces */
    int id-X = 9;     /* Illegal--not letter or digit */
}
```

✳ **DO:** Type and compile the above program (comments are not necessary).

✳ **RESULT:** Compile errors caused by lines 9 through 13.

✳ **DISCUSSION:** The compiler will not allow identifiers that violate the C rules. You can see the reason for each error in the comments above. Notice that the compiler displays different messages for the illegal identifiers—sometimes compiler errors will not tell you exactly how to fix the problem, as in lines 12 and 13 of the result, but they will usually be very close.

EXERCISE 8B: Test the scope of variables.

✳ **DO:** Modify your program from Exercise 8A. Delete lines 9 through 13 to get rid of illegal identifiers, and add a *printf* statement to display the values of all five defined variables.

✳ **SOLUTION FILE:** EX03-8B.C

✳ **RESULT:**

```
0 1 2 3 4
```

✳ **DISCUSSION:** The scope of all five variables is within the braces of the main function.

EXERCISE 8C: Test limited scope.

✳ **DO:** Change the scope of variable *id1* by placing its definition inside a separate block (insert an opening brace, {, before the defining statement and a closing brace, }, after).

✳ **SOLUTION FILE:** EX03-8C.C

✳ **RESULT:** A compile error on line 13 indicates that *id1* is not defined. Notice that a warning on line 10 also states that *id1* is not used.

✳ **DISCUSSION:** The *printf* statement attempts to access a variable that is out of scope—the program destroys *id1* when it encounters the inner closing brace.

EXERCISE 8D: Correctly use limited scope.

✳ **DO:** Delete *id1* from the existing *printf* and add a second *printf* statement for *id1* inside the inner block of braces.

✳ **SOLUTION FILE:** EX03-8D.C

✳ **RESULT:**

```
4
0 1 2 3
```

✳ **DISCUSSION:** Variable *id1* is accessible only within the inner block.

SUMMARY

There were quite a few topics in this chapter: data types, constants, variables, identifiers, *typedef, const, enum,* and storage classes. Some of them are specialized (*typedef, const, enum*). After you write enough C programs, these items will become quite familiar, but until then you may need to come back to Chapter 3 from time to time and review a particular topic. The most important things that you need to understand from this chapter are:

■ The fundamental data types, their sizes, and their ranges of values

■ How to express constants of different types

■ How to choose, define, and initialize variables

■ How to use storage class to control when and where variables are accessible

Now you are ready for Chapter 4, where you will format data from the keyboard for display on the screen.

*Average time to
complete this chapter
(including lab and
quiz) is 6 hours*

FORMATTED DATA INPUT AND OUTPUT

n important skill in programming is the ability to present information in a form that is meaningful to the user. This not only makes programs easier to use and more efficient, but it minimizes errors. "Garbage in, garbage out" is how an adage refers to computer data; properly formatted data eliminates a lot of the garbage.

In this chapter you will learn how to bring data into a program from the keyboard and display the program's results on the screen. You will use the specialized functions *getchar()*, *putchar()*, *gets()*, and *puts()* to transfer text characters and strings between programs and the outside world. Then you will use the functions *scanf()* and *printf()* to create custom-formatted data from characters, integers, and floating-point numbers. You will become familiar with using format strings, conversion specifiers, and conversion modifiers to instruct programs how to format data during input and output.

LECTURE

The process of moving data to your program from the keyboard, disk, or any other source is called *input,* and the process of moving it from your program to any destination is called *output.* Collectively, this transfer of data is called I/O (for input/output). As Figure 4-1 shows, a program always communicates with the outside world through the operating system (DOS in this case). In this chapter, we will limit the discussions to input from the keyboard and output to the screen; file I/O is covered in Chapter 12.

The data flow, called a *stream,* usually passes through a *buffer* (a reserved section of memory) that collects a certain amount of data before passing it on. Buffers smooth the flow of data, helping to regulate transfers and make them more efficient. You can verify the presence of your keyboard buffer by holding down a key until a warning beep begins to sound—this signals that you have completely filled the keyboard buffer and it cannot accept any more data. For most purposes you won't need to be concerned about these buffers because the operating system takes care of them. However, it's important to be aware of them because some of the I/O functions in C are affected by buffers, as you will soon see.

Data, both inside and outside your program, can be in any of several forms that correspond to the data types that we examined in Chapter 3: it can be ASCII character codes, integers, floating-point numbers, or other kinds of binary information. *Formatting* refers to the operations in the C program that convert different forms of data during input and output (I/O) transfer.

C performs I/O through function calls. The ANSI C specification includes a set of standard functions for keyboard, screen, file, and printer I/O, and most compilers add some non-ANSI functions of their own. An object library of these

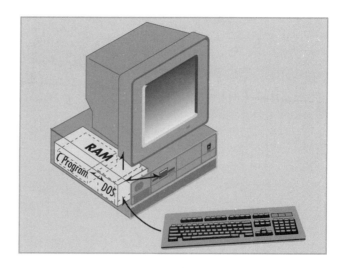

FIGURE 4-1   Data I/O

functions is supplied with your Turbo C++ installation in directory TCLITE/LIB. The following sections will familiarize you with these I/O functions.

Text I/O

Text I/O refers to the process of transferring character data, that is, bytes containing ASCII codes. C has functions limited to transferring single characters, plus other functions that are capable of transferring groups of characters.

Single-Character I/O

ANSI C specifies two functions, *getchar()* and *putchar()*, that are dedicated to single-character I/O. You can read a character from the keyboard with the following statement:

```
key = getchar();
```

The *getchar()* function waits until you press the (ENTER) key, then returns the ASCII code for the first key pressed before (ENTER). The above statement assigns that code to the integer variable *key*. You can use either type *char* or type *int* for the variable *key*. Because the ASCII code is 1 byte, if *key* is *int*, it goes in the first byte of the integer. Figure 4-2 illustrates the action of *getchar()*; each time you press (ENTER) the keyboard buffer empties out, feeding characters to the input function. (ENTER) acts as a control that opens the exit gate from the keyboard buffer. If you press several keys before (ENTER), *getchar()* will take only the first one, ignoring the others.

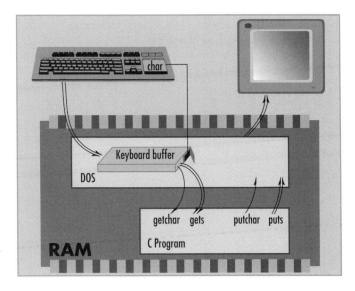

FIGURE 4-2 Character and string I/O

You can send a character to the screen with the following statement:

```
putchar( key );
```

The *putchar()* function transfers any of the 256 character codes to the screen, but only *displayable* characters will be visible. For example, the ASCII codes that correspond to the (ENTER) key are carriage return ('\r' or decimal 13) and newline ('\n' or decimal 10). These codes cause the cursor to move to the first column of a new line on the screen. Some other codes are nondisplayable too, such as bell ('\a' or 7), backspace ('\b' or 8), tab ('\t' or 9), and formfeed ('\f'or 12) (see Table 3-5).

String I/O

In C, character *strings* are sequences of characters (displayable or not) ending with a *null* character ('\0' or decimal zero). To store a string in RAM, you must define an *array* of variables. Chapters 9 and 10 give a more complete explanation of arrays and strings. The following statement defines a character array of 10 bytes:

```
char cityName[10];
```

You can read a string into *cityName* from the keyboard with this statement:

```
gets( cityName );
```

Figure 4-3 shows the string "New York" in the array *cityName*—note that we don't know (or care) what is in the last byte in the array. As Figure 4-2 illustrates, function *gets()* waits until you press the (ENTER) key, then it transfers characters from the keyboard buffer into the array. You can display the string on the screen with a similar statement:

```
puts( cityName );
```

Function *puts()* transfers the string characters to the screen, up to, but not including the ending null character.

FIGURE 4-3   Character array with string

Customized Text I/O

You can control conversions during I/O operations with functions *scanf()* and *printf()*. Here is the syntax of these functions:

```
scanf( format string, variable list );
printf( format string, variable list );
```

The *format string* allows you to customize the conversion of data from the *variable list* during input or output. The format string is usually a string constant enclosed by double quotes, but it can also be a variable (a character array containing a string). The variable list is a series of variable names separated by commas; for *scanf()*, it must be a list of addresses of (or pointers to) variables that you previously defined.

Formatted Character I/O

If *key* is a variable defined as type *char*, you can read a single character from the keyboard with this statement:

```
scanf( "%c", &key );
```

The format string is enclosed in double quotes; in this case it contains the *conversion specifier*, %*c*, which specifies that one character is to be transferred from the keyboard to variable *key*. Notice that *key* is preceded by an ampersand (&); this is the *address operator*, which tells *scanf()* where to place the data. In this case it specifies that the program store the data starting at the memory location of the variable *key*. You will learn more about the address operator in Chapter 11. You can also use the %*c* conversion specifier to display a single character on the screen with a *printf()* statement:

```
printf( "%c", key )
```

You don't need the address operator here because *printf()* takes the value of the variable.

The net effect of the *scanf()* and *printf()* statements above is the same as the previous *getchar()* and *putchar()* statements. The *getchar()* and *putchar()* functions are specialized for single-character or string I/O and are smaller and faster. However, *scanf()* and *printf()* are much more flexible because format strings can accommodate many types of conversion specifiers (see Table 4-1), and variable lists can specify any number of variables.

Formatted String I/O

Figure 4-4 shows formatted I/O for a string. In this example, the statement

```
scanf( "%s", cityName );
```

waits for the (ENTER) key, and then processes characters from the keyboard buffer according to the rules for conversion specifier *%s*. Under these rules, *scanf()* transfers characters until it encounters a *whitespace* character and then it adds a null character to the string variable. C defines a whitespace character as a space, tab, or newline character ('\n'). Therefore, strings entered through *scanf()* cannot contain spaces as they can with *gets()*—notice in Figure 4-4 how *scanf()* stops at the space between *New* and *York* so that the resulting input string is just *New*. On output, the following statement displays all the characters in the string except for the ending null character:

```
printf( "%s", cityName );
```

This *printf()* statement performs just like *puts(cityName);* with one difference—*puts()* automatically inserts a newline character ('\n') at the end of the output stream to move the cursor to a new line and *printf()* does not. However, you can do this by adding a newline to the *printf()* format string:

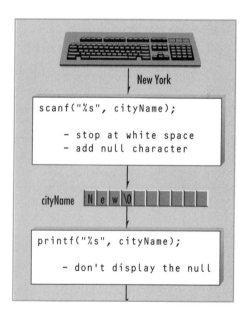

FIGURE 4-4 Formatted string I/O

```
printf( "%s\n", cityName );
```

You can also put some additional text in the format string:

```
printf( "The city name is %s\n", cityName );
```

This will display the phrase:

```
The city name is New
```

Sometimes you may want to sound the alert while displaying a message (like when displaying an error message). You can do this by inserting the alert escape sequence ('\a'):

```
printf( "\aThe city name %s is too long\n", cityName );
```

If you insert a lot of text in the format string, it can become too long to fit on one line conveniently. There are two ways to split a string into multiple lines; one way is to place a backslash (\) at the end of each line—this is called *line splicing*. Here is an example:

```
printf( "Now is the time for all good men \
to come to the aid of %s\n", cityName );
```

You can use line splicing to continue any statement on the next line. The other way to split a statement is to break the format string into phrases on separate lines and surround each phrase with double quotes:

```
printf( "Now is the time for all good men"
        " to come to the aid of %s\n", cityName );
```

The compiler will concatenate adjacent string constants into a single string constant. Note that this approach to continuation works only with string constants.

You might now wonder how to display a double quote, a backslash, or a percent character, since these are used as part of the syntax of the format string, escape sequence, and conversion specifier respectively. The answer is: you use an escape sequence (\") to display a double quote, a double backslash escape sequence (\\) to display a backslash, and two percents (%%) to display a percent. The following statements display each of these three characters:

```
printf( "Here is a double quote: \"\n" );
printf( "Here is a backslash: \\\n" );
printf( "Here is a percent: %%\n" );
```

The displayed result would be:

```
Here is a double quote: "
Here is a backslash: \
Here is a percent: %
```

Don't be confused by the newline ('\n') escape sequence at the end of each of these format strings—it just moves the cursor to the beginning of the next line after each display.

Formatted Integer I/O

Table 4-1 lists conversion specifiers for different types of data.

Conversion Specifier	Data Type	Example Output
%c	Single character	A
%d or %i	Signed decimal integer	123
%e or %E or %f	Floating-point number	.986e2 or 98.6
%g or %G	Floating-point number	.986e2 or 98.6
%o	Octal number	77
%p	Pointer	01F2
%s	Character string	Oregon
%u	Unsigned decimal integer	123
%x or %X	Hexadecimal integer	D8

Table 4-1   Format conversion specifiers

There are quite a few conversion specifiers that apply to integers (*%d, %i, %o, %u, %x, %X*). You can use any of these to reformat numeric ASCII characters from the keyboard into integer values, or reformat integer values to displayable ASCII characters. The *%d, %i,* and *%u* specifiers convert to and from decimal character representations; *%u* is for *unsigned* integers. The *%o* specifier converts to and from octal characters, and *%x* and *%X* convert hexadecimal representations. For output with *printf()*, uppercase X displays uppercase hex digits (A through F) and lowercase x displays lowercase hex digits (a through f). For input with *scanf()*, you can type either uppercase or lowercase letters for *%x* or *%X*. Table 4-2 shows the result if you use each of these conversion specifiers in a *printf()* statement to display the decimal number -1 (which is an integer with all bits on).

```
int allBitsSet = -1;
printf( "%d", allBitsSet );
```

Conversion Specifier	Displayed Value
%d or %i	-1
%u	65535
%o	177777
%x	ffff
%X	FFFF

Table 4-2 **Integer conversion specifiers for** *printf()*

You can also use these conversion specifiers in a *scanf()* statement to convert numeric keyboard characters to an integer. For example, the following statement will convert *ffff* typed from the keyboard and turn all 16 bits on in variable *allBitsOn*:

```
scanf( "%x", &allBitsOn );
```

Function *scanf()* converts integers according to the following rules:

1. Skip leading whitespace characters.
2. Accept one prefixed plus or minus sign character.
3. Accept any number of numeric digits ('0' through '9', or 'a' through 'f' for hex).
4. End at any nonnumeric character.

Figure 4-5 illustrates the application of these rules when the characters < >< ><3><9><y><r> (with several leading spaces) are typed on the keyboard. The *scanf()* statement skips the spaces, converts the digits 3 and 9 to an integer stored in *myAge*, and ends at the first nonnumeric character ('y'). The *printf()* integer conversion rules are much simpler—the value is converted to displayable ASCII characters. For a data type of *long*, you must add the *conversion modifier l* to a conversion specifier. This is especially important in *scanf()* statements. For example, if you want to input hexadecimal digits to long integer *bigNumber*, you should write:

```
scanf( "%lx", &bigNumber );
```

Formatted Floating-Point I/O

Conversion specifiers %e, %E, %f, %g, and %G apply to floating-point numbers. For input with *scanf()*, these specifiers are all equivalent; they will accept any sequence of characters that constitute a floating-point number in either fixed-decimal or exponential format. Here are two fixed-decimal values that you could type: -1.234 and 99.12; here are two exponential values: 1.23e45 and .9E-30. The rules for conversion of floating-point input are similar to those for integers except

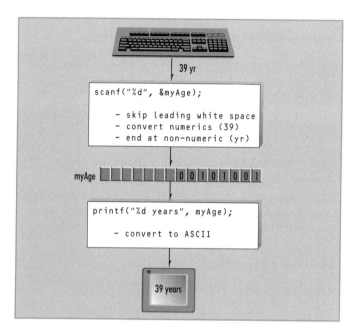

FIGURE 4-5   Formatted integer I/O

for allowing one decimal point ('.') and exponent ('e' or 'E') in the input stream. The rules are:

1. Skip leading whitespace characters.
2. Accept one plus or minus character prefix.
3. Accept any number of numeric digits ('0' through '9') and one decimal point.
4. Accept an exponent ('e' or 'E') followed by one plus or minus sign and one or two numeric digits.
5. End at any nonnumeric character.

If you are reading into a variable of type *double*, it is important to precede the conversion specifier with the letter *l*:

```
double aHugeNumber;
scanf( "%lf", &aHugeNumber );
```

For output with *printf()*, the %*f* conversion specifier displays a fixed-decimal format with seven significant digits and six fractional digits (-1.234567). Conversion specifier %*e* displays output in the fixed-decimal format with an exponent attached (9.876543e-21). Specifier %*E* displays an uppercase exponent (9.876543E-21). The %*g* and %*G* conversion specifiers are the same as %*e* and %*E* unless the number is small enough to fit in the %*f* format. For type *double*, you can add the *l* modifier to any of the specifiers, but this is not necessary.

Conversion Modifiers

You can assert additional control over I/O formatting by inserting *conversion modifiers* into the conversion specifiers. Table 4-3 lists conversion modifiers for input with *scanf()*.

Modifier	Effect
*	Suppression—skip the field
Integer	Specifies the maximum field width
h	Specifies a short integer
l	Specifies a long integer or double floating point
L	Specifies a long double floating point

Table 4-3   *scanf()* **conversion modifiers**

You have already seen the *l* used to specify input to a variable of type *long;* this modifier is important because *scanf()* will not yield the correct value without it. Likewise, an uppercase *L* specifies input to a *long double*, and an *h* specifies a *short* integer. Below are examples of each of these modifiers in a *scanf()* statement.

```
short aShortNumber;
scanf( "%hd", &aShortNumber );

long aLongNumber;
scanf( "%ld", &aLongNumber );

long double aLongDoubleNumber;
scanf( "%Lf", &aLongDoubleNumber );
```

You can limit the number of digits that *scanf()* will read by placing an integer modifier in the conversion specification. For example, the following statement will convert the first two digits you type to an integer and ignore any others between there and (ENTER):

```
scanf( "%2d", &anInteger );
```

You can make *scanf()* ignore a typed number altogether by inserting the asterisk (*) modifier.

```
scanf( "%*d %d", &anInteger );
```

In this case, if you type two integers separated by a whitespace character (65 87), *scanf()* will skip the first and convert the second (87).

Table 4-4 lists conversion modifiers for output through *printf()*.

Flag Modifier	Effect

Conversion modifiers have five optional fields that you can combine in the following order:

`<Flag><Width><.><Precision><Length>`

-	Left justify the item.
+	Show the sign of a number (+ or -).
space	Show the sign of a number (- if negative), show space if the number is positive.
0	Pad numbers with leading zeros.
#	Use an alternate form of numeric output. Add prefix 0 for octal (%o), add prefix 0x for hexadecimal (%x), and force a decimal point for floating-point numbers (%e, %f, %g), even if there is no fractional part.

Width Modifier	Effect
Integer	Specifies the minimum field width.
*	Width is given by next listed variable.

Precision Modifier	Effect
Integer	Specifies the number of digits after the decimal point for floating-point numbers (%e, %f, %g), the minimum number of digits to display for an integer (%d), or the maximum number of characters to display for a string (%s).
*	Precision is given by next listed variable.

Length Modifier	Effect
h	Specifies a short integer.
l	Specifies a long integer or double floating-point number.
L	Specifies a long double floating point.

Table 4-4   *printf() conversion modifiers*

You use these modifiers in the following syntax:

```
<Flag><Width><.><Precision><Length>
```

All of the syntax elements are optional—you can use some and omit others, but you must maintain the order. The *printf()* modifiers affect different data types differently. The following program (from lab exercise EX04-6.C) illustrates the effects of some of these modifiers:

```
#include <stdio.h>
main()
{
    int   i  = 123;
    char  s[] = "abcdef";
    float f  = -45.6;

    printf("\n\nMinimum width:/%10s/%10d/%10f/",      s, i, f);
    printf("\n\n    Precision:/%10.5s/%10.5d/%10.5f/", s, i, f);
    printf("\n\n Left justify:/%-10s/%-10d/%-10f/",    s, i, f);

    printf("\n\n Space prefix:/% 10d/% 10.5f/", i, f);
    printf("\n\n  Zero prefix:/%010d/%010.5f/", i, f);
    printf("\n\n  Sign prefix:/%+d/%+e/%+f/", i, f, f);

    f = i;
    printf("\n\n   Alternates:/%#o/%#x/%#f/", i, i, f);
}
```

Result:

```
Minimum width:/    abcdef/       123/-45.599998/

    Precision:/     abcde/     00123/ -45.60000/

 Left justify:/abcdef    /123       /-45.599998/

 Space prefix:/       123/ -45.60000/

  Zero prefix:/0000000123/-045.60000/

  Sign prefix:/+123/-45.599998/

   Alternates:/0173/0x7b/123.000000/
```

Each line of output from this program shows the effect of a particular modifier on several data types. The slash character (/) marks the beginning and end of each output field so that you can see the effect of the modifier. The first *printf()* statement specifies a minimum width of ten. The width modifiers cause both the string and integer to be padded on the left with spaces to fill out the ten characters specified. The floating-point number displays as a negative sign and decimal point plus eight significant digits. Eight digits is one more than type *float* will support, so the display appears not to be exactly -45.6 unless you mentally round it off to seven digits. The second *printf()* shows the effect of adding a precision modifier of 5. It displays only the first five characters of the string, it pads the integer out to five digits with zeros, and it displays the floating-point number with five digits to the right of the decimal point. Notice that the number is exact (-45.6) now that the number of significant digits is seven. The third *printf()* shows the affect of left justification; it moves all fields to the extreme left and pads with spaces on the right. The next three *printf()* statements show the use of flag modifiers to affix different prefixes to numeric displays: spaces, zeros, and a sign. The last *printf()* shows how the alternate flag (#) prefixes octal integers with zero and hexadecimal integers with 0x. The program assigns an integer with no fractional part to variable *f* so that the last *printf()* can illustrate how this flag forces the display of a decimal point.

Any character that appears before, after, or between conversion specifiers in the format string of a *scanf()* statement requires you to use that character as a separator in the typed input stream. For example, the following statement forces you to enter the dollar sign in front of *amount* or it won't read the correct value:

```
scanf( "$%f", &amount );
```

The next statement forces you to enter the lowercase x between *height* and *width* values:

```
scanf( "%dx%d", &height, &width );
```

Formatted I/O to and from a Buffer

The designers of C must have asked themselves, "Why limit all this conversion power to the keyboard and screen?" And so with a simple redirection of the I/O streams, they provided two very useful cousins of *scanf()* and *printf()* for converting between a character array and any other type of variable. Here is the syntax of the two functions:

```
sscanf( buffer, format string, variable list );
sprintf( buffer, format string, variable list );
```

These functions use the same conversion specifiers as their relatives, and they operate in the same way except for the character buffer array (the first item in the parameter list). Input for *sscanf()* comes from the specified memory buffer instead of the keyboard, and output from *sprintf()* goes to the buffer instead of to the screen. You will find *sprintf()* particularly useful in converting values from numeric variables to character strings for display. For example, the following code fragment converts integer variables *day*, *month*, and *year* to a date string in mm-dd-19yy format:

```
int day, month, year;
char date[11];

sprintf( date, "%2d-%02d-19%2d", month, day, year );
```

Notice that the array *date* is defined to hold 11 characters and there are only 10 in the date format—*sprintf()* always adds a null character to the end of the string and the extra character in *date* catches this terminating null. Notice also the conversion modifier 0 that pads any single-digit days with a leading zero. If variables *day, month,* and *year* had values of 3, 10, and 94 respectively, the output would be:

10-03-1994

LAB

EXERCISE 1A: Accomplish single-character I/O.

✳ **STARTER FILE:** EX04-1A.C

```
#include <stdio.h>
void main()
{
    char key;

    key = getchar();
    putchar( key );
}
```

✳ **DO:** Type in the above program, then run it three times. Each time you run it, type a different sequence of keystrokes: A (ENTER), then 123 (ENTER), then (ENTER) only. Watch carefully what the program displays after each step.

✳ **RESULT:**

```
A
A123
1
_    <- now the cursor is here on the second line below the 1
```

✳ **DISCUSSION:** Run 1 - The *getchar()* statement takes one character from the keyboard, and the *putchar()* statement displays it on the screen.

Run 2 - Notice how the cursor remains on the line with the last output—there is nothing in the program to move it after *putchar()* finishes. The input function *getchar()* takes the first character pressed on the keyboard (which is 1); therefore the remaining buffer contents are discarded when you press (ENTER).

Run 3 - The (ENTER) key issues a newline character ('\n') when you press it, and this time that was the first character from the keyboard, so *getchar()* accepts the ('\n') and *putchar()* displays it. When you pressed (ENTER), the newline moved the cursor to the line below the 1, and *putchar()* moved it one more line below that.

EXERCISE 1B: Display ASCII codes.

✳ **DO:** After the *putchar()* statement, add a *printf()* statement to display the ASCII character code in decimal form (remember, you can treat type *char* as an integer). Then run the program and type the same input as Exercise 1 above.

✳ **SOLUTION FILE:** EX04-1B.C

✳ **RESULT:**
```
A
A65
123
149

10
_       <- the cursor is here
```

✳ **DISCUSSION:** Now you can see the ASCII code just to the right of each character that *putchar()* displays—65 for the letter A, 49 for the numeral 1. Especially notice the value of 10 for newline. Also notice that the explicit newline in the *printf()* statement moves the cursor one extra line.

EXERCISE 1C: Accomplish single-character I/O with *scanf()* and *printf()*.

✳ **DO:** Replace *getchar()* with a *scanf()* statement and *putchar()* with a *printf()* statement, then run the program and type the same input as before.

✳ **SOLUTION FILE:** EX04-1C.C

✳ **RESULT:** Same as Exercise 1B.

✳ **DISCUSSION:** The result is the same, so *scanf()* and *printf()* can also perform character I/O.

EXERCISE 1D: Use two variables in one *printf()*.

✳ **DO:**   Combine the two *printf()* statements in Exercise 1C into one, then run the program and type the same input as before.

✳ **SOLUTION FILE:** EX04-1D.C

✳ **RESULT:** Same as Exercise 1C.

✳ **DISCUSSION:** If you correctly combined the two statements, the result will be unchanged.

EXERCISE 1E: Affect two-character I/O.

✳ **DO:**   Remove display of the integer ASCII codes from the *printf()* statement, then define another character variable and add to the *scanf()* and *printf()* statements so that they accept two characters from the keyboard and display them. Run the program three times and type ABC (ENTER), then (SPACE) A (ENTER), then A (ENTER).

✳ **SOLUTION FILE:** EX04-1E.C

✳ **RESULT:**

```
ABC
AB
A
A
A
A

_     <- the cursor is here
```

✳ **DISCUSSION:** The two %c conversion specifiers accept the first two keys pressed, so the C is discarded from the first input sequence. The second input sequence proves that (SPACE) is a valid input character. The third sequence shows that the newline generated by (ENTER) is also a valid input character because the second variable in *printf()* causes the cursor to move down one line.

EXERCISE 2A: Achieve string I/O with *gets()* and *puts()*.

✳ **STARTER FILE:** EX04-2A.C

```
#include <stdio.h>
void main()
{
```

continued on next page

continued from previous page

```
    char cityName[10];

    gets( cityName );
    puts( cityName );
}
```

✳ **DO:** Type in the above program, run it, and type "New York" (without the quotes).

✳ **RESULT:**

```
New York
New York
```

✳ **DISCUSSION:** The *gets()* statement reads the entire string into *cityName* and *puts()* displays it.

EXERCISE 2B: Achieve string I/O with *scanf()* and *printf()*.

✳ **DO:** Replace *gets()* with a *scanf()* statement and replace *puts()* with *printf()*, run the program, and then type "New York".

✳ **SOLUTION FILE:** EX04-2B.C

✳ **RESULT:**

```
New York
New
```

✳ **DISCUSSION:** The *scanf()* statement operates differently than *gets()*; it reads until it encounters a whitespace character (the space between *New* and *York*); therefore the array *cityName* contains just *New* and *printf()* displays that.

EXERCISE 2C: Examine I/O of two strings.

✳ **DO:** Define a second array, then modify *scanf()* to read a second string and modify *printf()* to display both strings. Run the program and type "New York".

✳ **SOLUTION FILE:** EX04-2C.C

✳ **RESULT:**

```
New York
New York
```

✳ **DISCUSSION:** The second input statement captures characters following the space character in the keyboard buffer (*York* in this case).

EXERCISE 3A: Use escape sequences.

✳ STARTER FILE: EX04-3A.C

✳ DO: Copy the starter file from the companion disk, run the program, and examine the output.

✳ RESULT:

```
\n causes
a line feed to occur
\" causes a double quote (") to be printed
\a causes the BELL, or beep, to sound_
\t can be used to align some numbers to tab columns
   1         2         3
   4         5         6

You use two % characters together to display the percent sign
```

✳ DISCUSSION: This program illustrates the effect of several escape sequences and shows how to display the double quote, backslash, and percent.

EXERCISE 3B: Display some escape sequences.

✳ DO: Add one *printf()* statement to display totals for the three columns of numbers as shown below in the RESULT.

✳ SOLUTION FILE: EX04-3B.C

✳ RESULT:

```
\n causes
a line feed to occur
\" causes a double quote (") to be printed
\a causes the BELL, or beep, to sound_
\t can be used to align some numbers to tab columns
           1       2     3
           4       5     6
         ------  ------ ------
"Total"    5       7     9
You use two % characters together to display the percent sign
```

✳ DISCUSSION: This output statement uses the following escape sequences: newline, tab, and double quote.

EXERCISE 4A: Examine integer I/O.

✳ **STARTER FILE:** EX04-4A.C

```
#include <stdio.h>
void main()
{
    int anyNumber;

    printf( "\nEnter something: " );
    scanf( "%d", &anyNumber );
    printf( "Here's what I see: %d", anyNumber );
}
```

✳ **DO:** Type in the above program, then run it four times. Type one of the following each time, and notice the resulting output: (SPACE)(SPACE)123 (ENTER), -123-4 (ENTER), (ENTER)+123.4 (ENTER), 1234567890 (ENTER).

✳ **RESULT:**

```
Enter something:    123
Here's what I see: 123

Enter something: -123-4
Here's what I see: -123

Enter something:
+123.4
Here's what I see: 123
Enter something: 1234567890
Here's what I see: 722
```

✳ **DISCUSSION:** Run 1 - The first rule of formatted integer input is "skip leading whitespaces."

Run 2 - The second rule is "accept one leading sign"; rule three is "end on a nonnumeric."

Run 3 - The first three rules are operating here.

Run 4 - The number is too big for type *int*—your last output may be different from that above.

EXERCISE 4B: Try incorrect *long* input.

✳ **DO:** Change the definition of the integer to type *long*, then run the program and type 1234567890.

✳ **SOLUTION FILE:** EX04-4B.C

✳ **RESULT:**

```
Enter something: 1234567890
Here's what I see: -31072
```

✳ **DISCUSSION:** Your output may be different from that above, but something is still wrong here—go to the next exercise to correct it.

EXERCISE 4C: Accomplish long integer I/O.

✳ **DO:** Add conversion modifier *l* to the *scanf()* conversion specifier.

✳ **SOLUTION FILE:** EX04-4C.C

✳ **RESULT:**

```
Enter something: 1234567890
Here's what I see: 1234567890
```

✳ **DISCUSSION:** The modifier is important in *scanf()*!

EXERCISE 5A: Run floating-point I/O.

✳ **STARTER FILE:** EX04-5A.C

```
#include <stdio.h>
void main()
{
    float anyNumber;

    printf( "\nEnter a real number: " );
    scanf( "%f", &anyNumber );
    printf( "Here's what you entered: %f", anyNumber );
}
```

✳ **DO:** Type in the above program, then run it twice and type the distance in miles to the sun as a fixed-decimal number, 93000000. (ENTER), and as an exponent 93e6 (ENTER).

✳ **RESULT:**

```
Enter a real number: 93000000.
Here's what you entered: 93000000.000000

Enter a real number: 93e6
Here's what you entered: 93000000.000000
```

✳ **DISCUSSION:** Notice that the default for the *%f* conversion specifier displays six digits after the decimal point.

EXERCISE 5B: Use another floating-point conversion specifier.

✳ **DO:** Replace conversion specifier *%f* with *%E* then run the program twice and type the same numbers.

✳ **SOLUTION FILE:** EX04-5B.C

✳ **RESULT:**

```
Enter a real number: 93000000.
Here's what you entered: 9.300000E+07

Enter a real number: 93e6
Here's what you entered: 9.300000E+07
```

✳ **DISCUSSION:** Notice the precision and placement of the decimal point in the output. As a default, the *%E* conversion specifier displays seven significant digits and puts the decimal point after the first digit.

EXERCISE 6:   Use conversion modifiers.

✳ **STARTER FILE:** EX04-6.C

✳ **DO:** Copy the starter file from the companion disk then run the program.

✳ **RESULT:**

```
Minimum width:/    abcdef/      123/-45.599998/
    Precision:/    abcde/     00123/ -45.60000/
 Left justify:/abcdef   /123      /-45.599998/
Space prefix:/       123/ -45.60000/
  Zero prefix:/0000000123/-045.60000/
  Sign prefix:/+123/-45.599998/
   Alternates:/0173/0x7b/123.000000/
```

✳ **DISCUSSION:** This exercise illustrates the effect of most of the conversion modifiers on three data types.

EXERCISE 7A: Convert formatted output to a buffer.

✳ STARTER FILE: EX04-7A.C

```
#include <stdio.h>
void main()
{
    unsigned hours   = 0;
    unsigned minutes = 0;
    unsigned seconds = 0;
    char time[9];

    sprintf( time, "%u:%u:%u", hours, minutes, seconds );
    printf( "%s\n", time );
}
```

✳ DO: Type in the above program and run it.

✳ RESULT:

```
0:0:0
```

✳ DISCUSSION: The program initializes all the integer variables to zero, which *sprintf()* converts to character zeros displayed as a string.

EXERCISE 7B: Enter time from the keyboard.

✳ DO: Add one *scanf()* statement to accept the hours, minutes, and seconds from the keyboard (see the RESULT below for the format). Also add conversion modifiers to the *printf()* statement to always display two digits with leading zeros.

✳ SOLUTION FILE: EX04-7B.C

✳ RESULT:

```
Enter the time as hh-mm-ss: 10-2-4
10:02:04
```

✳ DISCUSSION: In addition to typing the three numbers (if you are familiar with soft drink advertising, maybe you'll recognize this as Dr. Pepper time) separated by hyphens, try typing them with some other separator such as a comma or (SPACE).

EXERCISE 7C: Parse time back to its individual components.

✳ **DO:** Add an s*scanf()* statement to extract the integers *hours, minutes,* and *seconds* out of the string *time* and display them with another *printf().*

✳ **SOLUTION FILE:** EX04-7C.C

✳ **RESULT:**

```
Enter the time as hh-mm-ss: 10-2-4
10:02:04
hours = 10, minutes = 2, seconds = 4
```

✳ **DISCUSSION:** It's just as easy to convert strings to numbers as it is to build strings. You just need to include punctuation characters from the data in the format string.

SUMMARY

At this point, you know how to read text, integers, and floating-point numbers from the keyboard and how to display them on the screen in the desired format. You have used the specialized functions *getchar()*, *gets()*, *putchar()*, and *puts()* to read and display characters and strings. You know the the syntax of *scanf()*, *printf()*, *sscanf()*, and *sprintf()* statements, and by working the exercises you have seen how various modifications of conversion specifiers alter formatted data. Now you have the skills to create custom format specifications suitable for particular program requirements.

OPERATORS, EXPRESSIONS, AND STATEMENTS

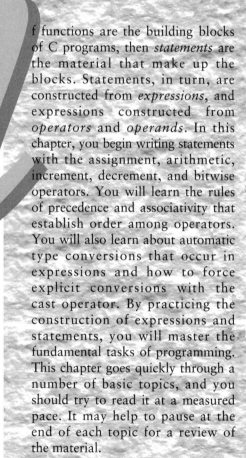

f functions are the building blocks of C programs, then *statements* are the material that make up the blocks. Statements, in turn, are constructed from *expressions*, and expressions constructed from *operators* and *operands*. In this chapter, you begin writing statements with the assignment, arithmetic, increment, decrement, and bitwise operators. You will learn the rules of precedence and associativity that establish order among operators. You will also learn about automatic type conversions that occur in expressions and how to force explicit conversions with the cast operator. By practicing the construction of expressions and statements, you will master the fundamental tasks of programming. This chapter goes quickly through a number of basic topics, and you should try to read it at a measured pace. It may help to pause at the end of each topic for a review of the material.

LECTURE

An *operator* is a symbol that uses values of constants, variables, or expressions to produce a result. Any value that an operator uses to perform its work is called an *operand*. An *expression* is a collection of operators and operands that evaluates to a single result. A *statement* in C is a collection of expressions, operators, operands, key words, and punctuation, ending with a semicolon. Armed with these basic definitions, let's look at some specific operators, expressions, and statements.

Expressions

Here are three expressions that use the familiar operators for addition and subtraction (+ and -):

```
2500.00 + interest
income + dividends - taxes
-profit
```

Notice that even a single operator and operand *(-profit)* constitutes an expression. After your program applies the operators to the operands, each of these expressions yields a single value. This is true of any expression, no matter how many operators and operands it has.

Simple Statements

An expression becomes a statement when you add a semicolon to the end. Here are three examples of statements:

```
netIncome = revenue - expenses - taxes;
;
2500.00 + interest;
```

The first statement above uses the *assignment operator* (=) to set the variable on the left to the result of the expression on the right. Notice the semicolon all by itself on the second line—this is the simplest statement of all, the *null statement*. The null statement does nothing, yet it is a valid statement and has a real purpose. You can use it to complete the syntax of a loop statement that performs processing in the loop expression (more on this in Chapter 7). The third statement is valid, but it is not of much use—it performs an addition but doesn't do anything with the result.

Compound Statements

A *compound statement* contains one or more statements between braces.

```
{
    /* Place any number of statements here */
}
```

A compound statement is also called a *block*. The statements within a block can either be simple statements or they can be other compound statements. Here is an example of a compound statement:

```
{
    int numChildren, numSons, numDaughters;
    int numParents, familySize;

    numChildren = numSons + numDaughters;
    familySize = numParents + numChildren;
}
```

Both the lines that define the variables and the lines that use them in expressions are statements. As you learned in Chapter 3, the scope of variables defined inside a block is limited to that block. Compound statements are a basic ingredient of C programs, providing a mechanism for you to group statements that need to be executed together. They form the bodies of all C functions and are essential for looping and branching statements.

Assignment Operators

C has several assignment operators. The most elementary is the equal symbol (=) that separates an *lvalue* on the left from an expression on the right.

```
lvalue = expression;
```

The assignment operator takes the result of the expression and assigns it to the *lvalue*. The term *lvalue* means "left value"; it is an expression that refers to an element of storage. An *lvalue* usually is the name of a variable. Here are several assignment statements that you might use in a program that keeps track of a basketball score:

```
fieldGoals = 2 * numGoals;
threePointers = 3 * numThrees;
totalScore = freeThrows + fieldGoals + threePointers;
```

Each of these three statements evaluates the expression on the right and assigns the result to the variable on the left. The order in which a program applies operators is determined by the rules of *precedence*. Table 5-1 lists the C operators in order of precedence, with the highest at the top of the table.

Operators	Category	Associativity
() [] ->	Membership	Left to Right
sizeof() (Size) ! (Logical Not) ~ (Bitwise Not) + - (Arithmetic Sign) & * (Address and Indirection) ++ - - (Increment and Decrement) (type)(Typecast)	Unary Operators	Right to Left
* / %	Arithmetic	Left to Right
+ -	Arithmetic	Left to Right
<< >>	Shift	Left to Right
< > <= >=	Relational	Left to Right
== !=	Relational	Left to Right
&	Bitwise	Left to Right
^	Bitwise	Left to Right
|	Bitwise	Left to Right
&&	Logical	Left to Right
||	Logical	Left to Right
?:	Conditional	Right to Left
= += -= *= /= %= &= |= ^= <<= >>=	Assignment	Right to Left
,	Sequence	Left to Right

Table 5-1   Precedence and associativity of operators

There are quite a few operators and you'll learn them all, but this chapter covers only the assignment, arithmetic, increment, and bitwise operators. To evaluate an expression, you find the operator with the highest precedence and apply it first, then you apply the operator with the next highest precedence, and so on. The assignment operator (=) has low precedence; therefore C applies all other operators (thereby evaluating the expression on the right) before making the assignment.

You can use more than one assignment operator in a statement, such as:

```
totalScore = fieldGoals = freeThrows = 0;
```

This statement assigns the same value to three variables—first it assigns zero to *freeThrows*, then it assigns the value of *freeThrows* to *fieldGoals*, then the value of *fieldGoals* to *totalScore*. This assignment order is regulated by the rules of *associativity* that govern left-right evaluation of operators with equal precedence. The right-hand column of Table 5-1 shows the associativity of operators. The assignment operator has right-to-left associativity, so C makes multiple assignments in a single statement progressing from right to left. It's tempting to wonder what would happen with a statement like this:

```
totalScore = fieldGoals = 0 = freeThrows;
```

The compiler will reject this statement with an error—you can't assign a value (*freeThrows*) to a constant because the constant is not an *lvalue* (capable of receiving a new value).

C provides ten other forms of the assignment operator that combine a simple assignment with another operator (see the last three lines in Table 5-1). For example, the += operator adds the result of an expression on the right to the *lvalue* on the left. If you need a statement to accumulate points for field goals in a game, you could write:

```
fieldGoals += 2;
```

This is the same as writing:

```
fieldGoals = fieldGoals + 2;
```

These two statements are entirely equivalent—the first, a combined form of the assignment operator, is a convenient shorthand notation. You haven't yet learned all ten of these operators, but the principle is the same for all of them—first apply the operator, then assign the result to the *lvalue*.

Arithmetic Operators

C has a total of seven arithmetic operators in two categories, unary and binary. Unary operators have one operand and binary operators have two. Table 5-2 lists the unary and binary arithmetic operators available in C.

Unary Arithmetic Operatiors	Binary Arithmetic Operators
+ (positive sign)	+ (addition)
- (negation)	- (subtraction)
	* (multiplication)
	/ (division)
	% (modulus or remainder)

Table 5-2   **Arithmetic operators**

Unary Arithmetic Operators

The unary plus (+) and unary minus (-) operators have only one operand. Anytime a + or - does not have a constant or variable in front of it, the C compiler knows it is a unary operator. For example:

```
forward = 9;
reverse = -forward;
ahead = +forward;
```

These statements will assign the value -9 to *reverse* and the value 9 to *ahead*. You will probably never need to use the plus unary operator—you can leave it out of any expression without affecting the result.

Binary Arithmetic Operators

Binary operators have two operands; C syntax requires that one operand precede the operator and one follow it. Four of the binary arithmetic operators (+, -, *, /) need little explanation—here is an example of each:

```
sum = x + y;
difference = x - y;
product = x * y;
dividend = x / y;
```

The fifth binary arithmetic operator is the *modulus* operator (%). The result of modulus is the remainder after the first operand is divided by the second. If you divide 11 by 4 you get 2 with a remainder of 3; therefore, the expression 11 % 4 yields a value of 3. Table 5-3 shows the result of several modulus expressions.

Modulus expression	Result
1776 % 10	6
1776 % 100	76
1776 % 2	0
23 % 5	3
23 % 7	2
5 % 100	5

Table 5-3   **Modulus arithmetic**

The modulus operator is good for determining the number of remaining or leftover items. Suppose you need to display a group of data values in a fixed number of columns; you could use the modulus operator to find out how many values are left over after dividing them into an even number of columns.

Referring to Table 5-1, you can see that multiplication, division, and modulus have higher precedence than addition and subtraction. Also, unary plus and minus have higher precedence than any of the other arithmetic operators. Therefore the following expression (which contains one of each of the five arithmetic operators) evaluates to 14:

```
-5 + 2 * 11 - 3 / 5 % 2
```

The unary minus has highest precedence, so you first evaluate -5, but because it is a constant, the result is still -5. Then operator precedence says to evaluate 5 % 2, yielding

```
-5 + 2 * 11 - 3 / 1
```

The * and / operators have equal precedence and left-to-right associativity, so evaluate 2 * 11 next, yielding

```
-5 + 22 - 3 / 1
```

Now evaluate 3 / 1, yielding

```
-5 + 22 - 3
```

Plus and minus have left-to-right associativity, so evaluate -5 + 22, yielding

```
17 - 3
```

and finally subtract 3 to get 14.

Parentheses Operators

In the C language, left and right parentheses are operators that force evaluation of an enclosed expression. If you look at Table 5-1, you will see that the parentheses have the highest precedence, so you can use them to control the evaluation of an expression explicitly. This is especially important when the default operator precedence conflicts with how you need the evaluation to proceed. Suppose you want to calculate the tax on net income of a business (which is revenue minus expenses). Without parentheses the equation looks like this:

```
tax = taxRate * revenue - expense;
```

Operator precedence dictates that multiplication occur before subtraction; therefore if *taxRate* is .34, *revenue* is $200,000, and *expense* is $100,000, the statement calculates *tax* to be negative $32,000. This is a nice result, where the IRS pays you to make a profit, but unfortunately it is wrong. To make it correct you need to insert parentheses to force the subtraction to occur first:

```
tax = taxRate * ( revenue - expense );
```

Now the statement will correctly calculate *tax* as $34,000.

You can use multiple parentheses in an expression, and even nest parentheses inside one another. The compiler always evaluates nested parentheses from the inside out; that is, it evaluates expressions within the innermost parentheses first. This occurs because of the left-to-right associativity of parentheses; the compiler evaluates an expression when it encounters the closing, right parenthesis. Figure 5-1 illustrates the sequence of evaluations of an expression with nested parentheses—spend some time reviewing this example.

You should make liberal use of parentheses. It is sometimes difficult to remember precedence and associativity of a particular operator, and you can easily specify priority by inserting parentheses. Inserting parentheses is good practice also because it makes statements easier to read and clarifies the intended order of calculations.

Type Conversion and the Cast Operator

Because there are different data types, C compilers can encounter interesting situations while applying operators to operands. Consider the case of assigning a floating-point number (type *float)* to an integer variable (type *int*). The floating-point number is 4 bytes in size, too large to fit in the 2-byte integer. Even if it were small enough, the floating-point number is not compatible because it has a fractional part. What is the compiler to do? As usual, C has some rules to cover situations like this, rules called type *conversions*.

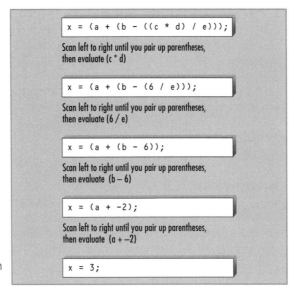

```
x = (a + (b - ((c * d) / e)));
```
Scan left to right until you pair up parentheses,
then evaluate (c * d)

```
x = (a + (b - (6 / e)));
```
Scan left to right until you pair up parentheses,
then evaluate (6 / e)

```
x = (a + (b - 6));
```
Scan left to right until you pair up parentheses,
then evaluate (b − 6)

```
x = (a + -2);
```
Scan left to right until you pair up parentheses,
then evaluate (a + −2)

```
x = 3;
```

FIGURE 5-1   Order of evaluation of an expression with parentheses

Type Conversions During Assignment

If you assign an arithmetic data type to an *lvalue* having a different data type, the C compiler will convert the value to the type of the *lvalue*. For example:

```
int roughAmount;
double exactAmount = 5.71;
roughAmount = exactAmount;
```

The last statement assigns the integer value of 5 to *roughAmount*. This is called *demotion* because some data (the fraction .71) is discarded. When the compiler converts a smaller data type to one that is larger, it is called *promotion*. Figure 5-2 shows the ranking of data types; promotion is the conversion of a lower-ranking data type to one higher in rank, and demotion is the opposite. Promotion does not affect a data value—the program just expands the value to fit in the larger storage area. Demotion necessarily eliminates some data because the target storage area is smaller. C programs demote floating-point data types to integers by truncating the fraction; they demote larger floating-point types to smaller ones by reducing the precision and range; and they demote larger integers to smaller ones by reducing the range. You need to be aware that automatic conversion takes place and avoid statements that trigger demotion unless that is what you intend.

Type Conversion in Expressions

For all other operators (except assignment) in an expression, C handles type conversion by promotion. Thus, the compiler will promote all operands in an expression to be the same type as the highest ranking operand present, and the result of the expression will also be that higher ranking type. For instance, if you write a calculation having variables of types *int, float,* and *double,* the compiler will convert them all to *double* before performing the calculation. Then if you assign the result to another variable, it will be either promoted or demoted, depending on the type of the *lvalue.*

Cast Operator

You can explicitly force type conversion with the *cast operator.* The syntax of this operator is a data type enclosed by parentheses preceding a constant or variable:

```
( type )variable
```

The effect of a cast operator is to change the data type of the constant or variable temporarily within the context of the expression. For example, the last statement in the following code fragment converts both the value of *x* and the value of *y* to integer and yields an integer result, regardless of the original data types of *x* and *y:*

```
float x = 1.1;
float y = 2.2;
float answer;
answer = (int)x * (int)y;
```

The above calculation assigns a value of 3 to *answer.* However, automatic conversion would still occur if you introduced another variable into the calculation, like this:

```
float x = 1.1;
float y = 2.2;
float answer;
double z = 3.3;
answer = (int)x * (int)y + z;
```

Even though *z* is type *double,* the compiler will first honor your cast and convert *x* and *y* values to integers (because cast has higher precedence than multiply or add), then it will promote all three values to *double* (because of the presence of the *double* value *z*), and report the answer as type *double.* This last statement assigns a value of 6.3 to *answer.* The original declared type of a typecast operand remains unchanged and the cast does not affect its use anywhere else in the program. If you use *x* and *y* again in the above example, the original types and values are still valid:

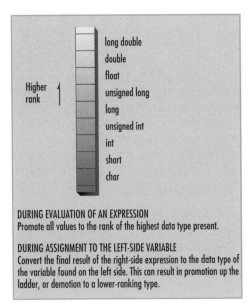

DURING EVALUATION OF AN EXPRESSION
Promote all values to the rank of the highest data type present.

DURING ASSIGNMENT TO THE LEFT-SIDE VARIABLE
Convert the final result of the right-side expression to the data type of the variable found on the left side. This can result in promotion up the ladder, or demotion to a lower-ranking type.

FIGURE 5-2   Rank ordering of data types on the ladder of promotion

```
float x = 1.1;
float y = 2.2;
float answer;
double z = 3.3;
answer = (int)x * (int)y + z;
answer = x + y;
```

The last statement assigns a result of 3.3 to *answer*.

Increment and Decrement Operators

Increment and decrement are two unary operators that you will use a lot. Increment (++) adds one to the value of its operand and decrement (- -) subtracts one. The following three expressions are all equivalent:

```
i = i + 1
i += 1
++i
```

You can use increment and decrement operators with any numeric operand, including floating-point types, but they are most often used to change the value of integer indexing variables in looping control expressions. Here is an example of a *for* expression that you will become more familiar with in Chapter 7:

```
for ( i=0; i<10; ++i )
```

The index variable *i* takes on values between the limits of the *for* loop (0 and 10), and each time the loop executes, the increment operator increases the value of *i* by one. Increment and decrement apply only to variables—you cannot increment or decrement constants or expressions.

```
--3;          /* Illegal - you cannot decrement a constant */
++(i / 2);    /* Illegal - you cannot increment an expression */
```

When you put the operator in front of the variable, it is called *prefix* increment or decrement, and when you put it behind the variable it is called *postfix* increment or decrement. Used in an expression with other operators, prefix increment or decrement causes the value of the variable to change before it is used in the expression, whereas postfix increment or decrement changes the value only after the expression is evaluated. Here is a statement with such an expression:

```
time = ++hour - 2;
```

If *hour* is 10 prior to this statement, *time* becomes 9 after it executes; first the prefix increment operator adds one, then the expression subtracts two. However, if you modify the statement to use postfix increment:

```
time = hour++ - 2;
```

it will then assign a value of 8 to *time* because *hour* does not increment until after it is used to evaluate the expression.

INCORRECT USE OF INCREMENT AND DECREMENT

You should not increment or decrement variables in the argument list of a function call.

```
printf( "%d", ++hour );    /* Don't do this! */
```

This is bad practice because C does not specify whether the compiler should pass the value to the function before or after applying the increment operator. Another word of caution for increment and decrement operators—use parentheses to avoid ambiguous expressions when using increment operators with other arithmetic operators. The following expression:

```
time---hour
```

could mean either

```
(time- -) - hour
```

or

```
time - (- -hour )
```

These two interpretations yield different values.

Bitwise Operators

Bitwise operators are sometimes called Boolean operators because Boolean algebra, invented by George Boole, is the study of logical operations expressed as binary numbers. C has six bitwise operators that change the values of individual bits of integer operands (types *char*, *short*, *int*, and *long*). Integers have a fixed number of bits and each bit can be either *set* to a value of one or *reset* to a value of zero. Figure 5-3 shows the bits in a *signed char* variable and an *unsigned char* variable. The *least significant* bit contributes zero or one to the integer value; the second bit contributes zero or two to the integer value; the third bit contributes zero or four; and so on. Take particular notice of the last bit on the left; this is the *most significant* bit of an unsigned integer or the *sign* bit for a signed integer.

Left Shift and Right Shift Operators

You can simultaneously change the position of all bits of an integer with a shift operator. The syntax of a left shift operation is:

```
operand << amount
```

and a right shift is:

```
operand >> amount
```

In these expressions *amount* is an integer specifying the number of bit positions to move. You cannot shift a negative distance; that is, *amount* cannot be negative. A shift operator moves all bits in unison to a new location, so no values are lost except at the end of the integer in the direction of the shift. Figure 5-4 illustrates left and right shift of an *unsigned* integer. Notice that shifting discards the end bits in the direction of the shift, and notice that it moves zeros into the new bits at the other end. Figure 5-5 shows left and right shift of a *signed* integer, which is the same as for an *unsigned* integer unless the value is negative. C does not specify the values of new most-significant bits during right shift of a negative integer—some systems will replicate the sign bit and others will set the new values to 0. Turbo C++ replicates the sign bit—you can verify this by running a program with the following two statements:

```
int x = -100;
printf( "Original: %X, Shifted result: %X", x, x >> 4 );
```

The displayed output will be:

```
Original: FF9C, Shifted result: FFF9
```

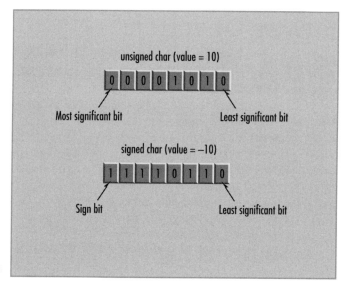

FIGURE 5-3   Integer bits

You will observe that the most significant bits in both the original and the result are set (a hex value of F corresponds to 4 bits that are 1).

Shifting does not affect the value of the original operand, so you can apply shift operands to constants as well as variables. The compiler puts the shifted result in a temporary location and changes the value of a variable only if you explicitly use an assignment operator. For example, this expression does not change the value of *kibbles:*

```
kibbles << 5
```

But the following expression does:

```
kibbles <<= 5
```

Left shifting by one is equivalent to multiplying by two and right shifting by one is equivalent to dividing by two. Shifting is much faster than performing arithmetic, so you can use the shift operators as a fast way of multiplying or dividing by powers of two. However, unless there is a significant performance advantage from a very large number of such operations, you should avoid using shift to accomplish arithmetic because it obscures the intent of the statements. Another programmer will clearly understand the expression:

```
total *= 8
```

but the intent of the equivalent shift expression is not obvious:

```
total <<= 3
```

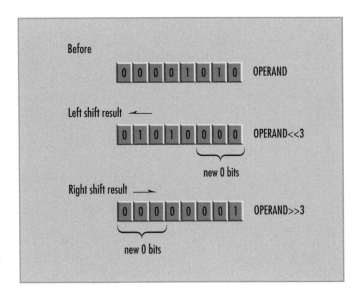

Before

OPERAND

Left shift result

OPERAND<<3

new 0 bits

Right shift result

OPERAND>>3

new 0 bits

FIGURE 5-4 Unsigned bitwise shift

You can use shifting in connection with other bitwise operators to insert and extract successive data fields within integer variables. This is one of the main applications for shift operations, and in the lab exercises you will have a chance to do this.

Bitwise AND, OR, and Exclusive OR Operators

The bitwise AND (&), OR (|), and exclusive OR (^) operators combine bit values from corresponding positions in two operands. The syntax for these operators is:

```
operand1 operator operand2
```

If both operands are not the same type, C will promote the one with the lower type. The operator determines the first bit of the result from the first bit of *operand1* and the first bit of *operand2*; likewise it determines the second bit of the result from the second bits of the two operands, and so on for each of the bit positions.

The AND operator returns a bit value of one only if the corresponding bits in both operands have values of one. The OR operator yields a one for any bit position where either operand has a value of one. The exclusive OR operator returns one if one operand has a value of one and the other has a value of zero. Table 5-4 is a *truth table* of all possible values for 2 bits combined with these three operators.

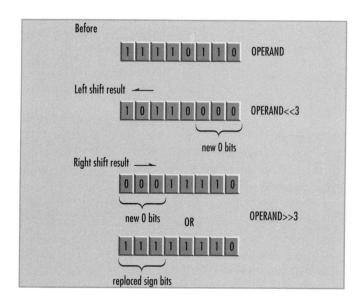

FIGURE 5-5 Signed bitwise shift

Operand1	Operand2	AND	Operand1 OR	Operand 2 Exclusive OR
0	0	0	0	0
0	1	0	1	1
1	0	0	1	1
1	1	1	1	0

Table 5-4   Truth table for bitwise operators

A *mask* is an integer value where the position of a data field within a variable is identified by bits that are set (to one). The bitwise AND and OR operators are frequently used with masks to insert and extract data fields. You can insert data into a variable by ORing it, and you can extract data from a field by ANDing a variable with a mask. Figure 5-6 shows an example of these operations. Masking is often important when working with CPU hardware registers or peripheral devices.

The exclusive OR operator finds specialized applications, primarily in graphics programming. If you take the exclusive OR between an original value and a second operand, then take the exclusive OR between the result and the same second operand, the final result is the same as the original value. This is useful for animated graphics, where exclusive OR alternately inserts and erases a foreground figure against a background scene.

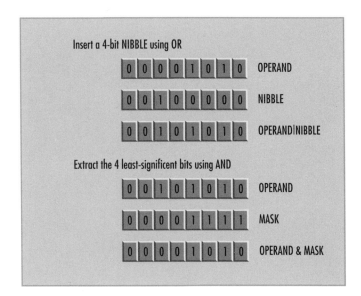

FIGURE 5-6   Bitwise access to data fields

Complement Operator

The *complement* is a unary operator that inverts the value of each bit in the operand. Figure 5-7 shows the result of a complement operation. Like other bitwise operators, the complement does not change the value of its operand unless you use an assignment operator to do so. You can use complement to invert a mask in order to clear all bits of a field of data. For example:

```
data &= ~mask;
```

This statement clears all bits in *data* that correspond to the field defined by 1s in *mask*; it leaves the remaining bits unchanged. Table 5-5 shows values of variables *mask* and *data* before and after this statement.

Variable	Before	After
data	10110110	10110000
mask	00000111	
~mask	11111000	

Table 5-5   **Operation of expression data &= ~mask**

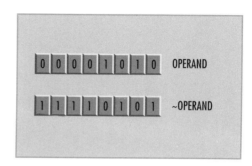

FIGURE 5-7   Bitwise complement

LAB

Exercise 1:   Implement a compound assignment.

✳ STARTER FILE: EX05-1A.C

```c
#include <stdio.h>
void main()
{
    float inputValue = 0.;

    do
    {
        /* Place statements to read and accumulate values here */
    } while ( inputValue > .009 );
}
```

✳ DO: The above program contains a loop that continues as long as variable *inputValue* has a value of at least 1 cent (.01)—the loop ends when the value is 0. Your job is to add statements in the *do while* block to read dollar amounts into *inputValue* and accumulate them in a new floating-point variable called *checksOutstanding*. Display the accumulated total when the loop ends (after you enter 0). In the next two chapters, we'll develop this into a complete program to help balance your checkbook. Run the program and type:

1.10<Enter> 2.20<Enter> 3.30<Enter> 0<Enter>

✳ SOLUTION FILE: EX05-1B.C

✳ RESULT:

```
Enter an outstanding check amount (zero when done): 1.10
Enter an outstanding check amount (zero when done): 2.20
Enter an outstanding check amount (zero when done): 3.30
Enter an outstanding check amount (zero when done): 0
checksOutstanding = 6.60
```

✳ DISCUSSION: Compare your implementation with EX05-1B.C. The *printf()* conversion modifier of .2 displays the total with only two decimal digits (because it is dollars and cents). The easiest way to accumulate the total checks outstanding is with the += operator.

Exercise 2A: Use arithmetic operators.

✳ DO: Write a program to accept two floating-point operands from the keyboard and display the product of the numbers. Run the program and enter values of 1.1 and 2.2.

✳ SOLUTION FILE: EX05-2A.C

✳ RESULT:

```
Enter two operands (op1 * op2): 1.1 * 2.2
op1 * op2 = 2.420000
```

✳ DISCUSSION: You might have handled the *scanf()* format differently, but the program EX05-2A.C includes the character * in the entry sequence.

Exercise 2B: Use unary arithmetic operators.

✳ DO: Modify the previous program to multiply by the negative of the second operand (use a unary minus).

✳ SOLUTION FILE: EX05-2B.C

✳ RESULT:

```
Enter two operands (op1 * op2): 1.1 * 2.2
op1 * -op2 = -2.420000
```

✳ DISCUSSION: The result is the negative of the previous result.

Exercise 3:   Use arithmetic divide and modulus operators.

✳ **DO:** Write a program that accepts the value of a weight in ounces from the keyboard and then converts the value to pounds and remaining ounces (there are 16 ounces per pound). Use integer values throughout and use the divide (/) and modulus (%) operators. Run the program and enter 350 ounces.

✳ **SOLUTION FILE:** EX05-3.C

✳ **RESULT:**
```
Enter a weight in ounces: 350
350 ounces = 21 lbs, 14 ozs
```

✳ **DISCUSSION:** The modulus operator is useful for deriving the remainder for any quantity.

Exercise 4A: Experiment with operator precedence.

✳ **DO:** Write a program that, in a single statement, calculates the difference between 128 pounds and 121 pounds and converts the difference to ounces. Use integers and do not use parentheses. There are 16 ounces per pound.

✳ **SOLUTION FILE:** EX05-4A.C

✳ **RESULT:**
```
128 lbs - 121 lbs = 112 ounces
```

✳ **DISCUSSION:** This calculation is awkward without parentheses.

Exercise 4B: Insert parentheses.

✳ **DO:** Use parentheses to simplify the previous calculation.

✳ **SOLUTION FILE:** EX05-4B.C

✳ **RESULT:** Same as Exercise 4A.

✳ **DISCUSSION:** The result is the same with a simpler expression. This small example shows the importance of parentheses.

Exercise 5: Accomplish automatic type conversion.

✳ DO: You can round a real number to the nearest integer by adding one-half (.5) to the real number and truncating the result to an integer. Write a program to accept a real number from the keyboard and then round it to the nearest integer. Use the automatic conversion that accompanies assignment of a floating-point value to an integer to truncate. Run the program twice and type 2.5 (ENTER) then 2.49 (ENTER) Experiment with other values—particularly, see how the program behaves with negative values.

✳ SOLUTION FILE: EX05-5.C

✳ RESULT:

```
Enter a real number: 2.5
Rounded number = 3
Enter a real number: 2.49
Rounded number = 2
```

✳ DISCUSSION: You can use an integer cast to display the truncated value without assigning to an integer variable as follows:

```
printf( "Rounded number = %d\n", (int)(originalNumber + .5) );
```

Exercise 6A: Practice more automatic type conversion.

✳ STARTER FILE: EX05-6A.C

```
#include <stdio.h>
void main()
{
    int celsius;
    int fahrenheit;
    double degreesFperC;

    degreesFperC = 9 / 5;
    printf( "Enter a Celsius temperature: " );
    scanf( "%d", &celsius );
    fahrenheit = degreesFperC * celsius + 32;
    printf( "%d degrees Celsius = %d degrees Fahrenheit\n",
        celsius, fahrenheit );
}
```

✳ DO: Type and run the above program that converts a Celsius temperature to Fahrenheit. In response to the prompt, type the Celsius boiling point of water, 100 degrees.

✳ RESULT:

```
Enter a Celsius temperature: 100
100 degrees Celsius = 132 degrees Fahrenheit
```

✳ DISCUSSION: The result is wrong—the boiling point of water is 212 degrees Fahrenheit! Do you know why the result is wrong? See if you can figure out a way to correct the program, then go to the next exercise.

Exercise 6B: Use floating-point cast.

✳ DO: Fix the problem with the calculation of *degreesFperC* in the previous program.

✳ SOLUTION FILES: EX05-6B.C and EX05-6C.C

✳ RESULT:

```
Enter a Celsius temperature: 100
100 degrees Celsius = 212 degrees Fahrenheit
```

✳ DISCUSSION: The original statement to calculate the number of Fahrenheit degrees per Celsius degrees uses integer arithmetic to divide 9 by 5, yielding a value of 1 for *degreesFperC*. You can force a floating-point result either by casting one of the constants (9 or 5) to *double* (EX05-6B.C) or by adding a decimal point (EX05-6C.C).

Exercise 7A: Use a prefix increment operator.

✳ STARTER FILE: EX05-7A.C

```c
#include <stdio.h>
void main()
{
    float inputValue = 0.;
    float checksOutstanding = 0.;
    float serviceCharge;
    int numChecks = 0;

    do
    {
        printf( "Enter an outstanding check amount (zero when done): " );
        scanf( "%f", &inputValue );
        checksOutstanding += inputValue;
        serviceCharge = .01 * ++numChecks;
        printf( "Number of checks = %d\nService charge = %.2f\n",
```

```
            numChecks, serviceCharge );
    } while ( inputValue > .009 );

    printf( "checksOutstanding = %.2f\n", checksOutstanding );
}
```

✳ **DO:** Start with the program from EX05-1B.C and add four new statements as shown above to calculate a service charge based on the number of checks entered. Run the program and enter values of 1.10, 2.20, and 3.30.

✳ **RESULT:**

```
Enter an outstanding check amount (zero when done): 1.10
Number of checks = 1
Service charge = 0.01
Enter an outstanding check amount (zero when done): 2.20
Number of checks = 2
Service charge = 0.02
Enter an outstanding check amount (zero when done): 3.30
Number of checks = 3
Service charge = 0.03
Enter an outstanding check amount (zero when done): 0
Number of checks = 4
Service charge = 0.04
checksOutstanding = 6.60
```

✳ **DISCUSSION:** The statement

```
serviceCharge = .01 * ++numChecks;
```

calculates the service charge and, at the same time, uses prefix increment to count the number of checks. The program mistakenly counts the ending entry of 0 as check number 4, but that is of no consequence.

Exercise 7B: Use a postfix increment operator.

✳ **DO:** Change the prefix increment to postfix, then rerun the program and enter the same data.

✳ **SOLUTION FILE:** EX05-7B.C

✳ **RESULT:**

```
Enter an outstanding check amount (zero when done): 1.10
Number of checks = 1
Service charge = 0.00
Enter an outstanding check amount (zero when done): 2.20
Number of checks = 2
Service charge = 0.01
```

```
Enter an outstanding check amount (zero when done): 3.30
Number of checks = 3
Service charge = 0.02
Enter an outstanding check amount (zero when done): 0
Number of checks = 4
Service charge = 0.03
checksOutstanding = 6.60
```

✳ **DISCUSSION:** The number of checks is the same as before, but the service charge is less. This is because postfix increment does not change *numChecks* until after its value is used in the expression that calculates *serviceCharge*.

Exercise 8A: Use bitwise operators.

✳ **STARTER FILE:** EX05-8A.C

```c
#include <stdio.h>
void main()
{
    char inputChar;
    int position;
    unsigned long packedChars = 0L;

    printf( "Enter a character and position (1-4): " );
    scanf( "%c %d", &inputChar, &position );

    packedChars |= (unsigned long)inputChar << (8 * (position - 1));
    printf( "packedChars = %08lX\n", packedChars );
}
```

✳ **DO:** Type in the above program that packs up to four character values into an *unsigned long* integer. Run the program four times and type A 1 (ENTER) A 2 (ENTER) A 3 (ENTER) A 4 (ENTER).

✳ **RESULT:**

```
Enter a character and position (1-4): A 1
packedChars=00000041
Enter a character and position (1-4): A 2
packedChars=00004100
Enter a character and position (1-4): A 3
packedChars=00410000
Enter a character and position (1-4): A 4
packedChars=41000000
```

✳ **DISCUSSION:** The first *printf()* statement prompts you for a character value and an integer to specify where to put the value. The last two statements contain some interesting details. Variable *inputChar* must be cast to *unsigned* *long* so that there is room for the 8 bits of character data to shift left by 0, 8, 16, or 24 bits. The expression (8 * (position - 1)) calculates one of these four shift amounts—notice the need for parentheses. The last *printf()* statement displays the 4-byte result using the conversion specifier *%08lX;* the *08* specifies eight digits with leading zeros, and *lX* specifies an uppercase hexadecimal format for a *long* integer.

Exercise 8B: Use more bitwise operators.

✳ **DO:** Using the previous program, initialize *packedChars* with a hex constant (0x04030201L) to place the values 1, 2, 3, 4 in each of the 4 bytes. Then add a statement to clear the selected byte before inserting the input character. Hint: Use a mask and the complement operator. Run the program four times and type the same input sequence as before.

✳ **SOLUTION FILE:** EX05-8B.C

✳ **RESULT:**

```
Enter a character and position (1-4): A 1
packedChars=04030241
Enter a character and position (1-4): A 2
packedChars=04034101
Enter a character and position (1-4): A 3
packedChars=04410201
Enter a character and position (1-4): A 4
packedChars=41030201
```

✳ **DISCUSSION:** The program initializes *mask* with 8 bits set in the first byte. Then it shifts the 8 set bits into the selected byte position and inverts all *mask* bits so that it contains zeros in the selected position and ones everywhere else. Finally, it clears the selected position by ANDing the mask with *packedChars.*

SUMMARY

You now have a good grasp of C operators and how to construct expressions and statements using them. You understand the rules that govern how programs evaluate expressions, and you know how data types and type conversions affect the results of expressions. You are now ready to progress to the next chapter and incorporate expressions into statements that will control the flow of a C program.

*Average time to
complete this chapter
(including lab and
quiz) is 6 hours.*

BRANCHING CONTROL STATEMENTS

he C language was designed in the tradition of procedural programming—this means that the flow of events in a program goes mainly in a straight line from beginning to end. Branching allows you to alter program flow and execute different statements based on data values, so your program can effectively "make decisions." In this chapter, you will learn how to control the decision-making process of programs with the few, but powerful, branching statements in C, and you will see the factors that determine the advantage of one statement over another for different situations. You will also learn how to avoid some common problems associated with branching statements.

LECTURE

C has three primary branching statements, *if, if else,* and *switch,* two related statements, *break* and *goto,* and a branching operator, the *conditional operator.* Although their syntax differs, these statements all test some data value(s) and cause another statement to execute based on the result. Let's start with the simplest conditional statement, *if.*

The *if* Statement

An *if* statement has the following syntax:

```
if ( control expression )
    target statement
```

The key word *if* and the parentheses are essential elements; you complete the syntax by adding any control expression and target statement. You should indent the target statement underneath the *if* clause. Figure 6-1 shows the effect of an *if* statement.

If the value of the control expression is TRUE, the program executes the target statement (which may be a compound statement); otherwise the program skips the target statement and proceeds directly to the next statement in sequence. Because it determines what happens next, the control expression is important—it is also an essential ingredient in looping statements, the topic of the next chapter.

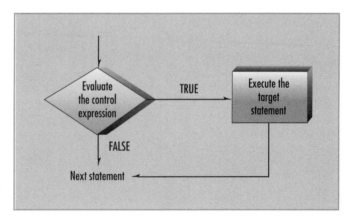

FIGURE 6-1   Flow of an *if* statement

Control Expressions

A control expression is any expression that evaluates to a single value of TRUE or FALSE. This includes virtually all C expressions, because any of the basic data types (*char, int, float, double)* can yield TRUE or FALSE values.

TRUE and FALSE

The terms TRUE and FALSE have specific meanings in C. Any nonzero value is TRUE, and, conversely, a value of exactly zero is FALSE. Given these definitions:

```
#define YES 1
#define NO  0
int i = 2;
float f = 3.5;
```

here are some examples of expressions that evaluate to TRUE:

```
i / 2
f - 1.
i + f
1
YES
```

here are some examples of expressions that evaluate to FALSE:

```
i % 2
0.
NO
```

And here is an example of an expression that will probably evaluate to FALSE, but you should not rely on this outcome because of the uncertainty of floating-point precision:

```
f - 3.5
```

TRUE and FALSE values are important for both relational and logical operators.

Relational Operators

C has six relational operators that you can use to compare two values:

Operator	Operation
<	Less Than
>	Greater Than
==	Equal To
!=	Not Equal To
>=	Greater Than or Equal To
<=	Less Than or Equal To

The result of an expression using any of these operators is type *int* with a value of either one (TRUE) or zero (FALSE). The TRUE value of one is consistent with the definition of nonzero being TRUE.

The syntax of a relational expression is:

```
operand1 relational_operator operand2
```

The following statement:

```
overTheLimit = catch > limit;
```

will compare the values of *catch* and *limit* and assign a value of one (TRUE) to *overTheLimit* if *catch* is greater than *limit*; otherwise it will assign zero (FALSE). If the operands are different types, C promotes one of them (following the rules of promotion discussed in Chapter 5) so that they are both the same type. The operands can be constants, variables, or expressions, and the six relational operators provide the means to make whatever comparisons you might need.

You will use relational expressions primarily to control branching statements like this one:

```
if ( catch > limit )
    fine = 100.00;
```

Variable *fine* is assigned a value of 100.00 only if the value of *catch* exceeds the value of *limit*, that is, only if *catch* > *limit* is TRUE. Notice that if *catch* is merely equal to *limit*, the statement is FALSE and the assignment does not occur.

Logical Operators

You can make several comparisons within one control expression by connecting them with *logical operators*. Actually, you can use logical operators in any expression, but they are most useful in control expressions. C has three logical operators, AND (&&), OR (||), and NOT(!), that yield TRUE or FALSE results. Operators AND and OR are binary—you insert them between two operands. The NOT operator is unary—you use it in front of one operand. Table 6-1 is a truth table of values resulting from the application of these logical operators.

Op1	Op2	Op1 && Op2	Op1 || Op2	!Op1
0	0	0	0	1
0	nonzero	0	1	1
nonzero	0	0	1	0
nonzero	nonzero	1	1	0

Table 6-1   A truth table for logical operators

The AND operator returns TRUE (one) only if both operands have TRUE (nonzero) values; the OR operator returns TRUE (one) if either operand is TRUE (nonzero). The NOT operator returns the opposite value of its single operand—if the operand is TRUE (nonzero), NOT returns FALSE (zero) and if the operand is FALSE, it returns TRUE (one). Like the relational operators, logical operators accept nonzero operand values as being TRUE, and they return a value of one for TRUE. Here is an example of how you can combine relational operators with logical operators in a control expression:

```
if ( ( catch > limit ) && ( numOffenses == 0 ) )
    fine = 50.00;
```

This control expression says that your fine is $50.00 for going over the limit if it is your first offense. Here is another way of expressing the same logic:

```
if ( ( catch > limit ) && !numOffenses )
    fine = 50.00;
```

In this case the NOT operator (!) returns TRUE allowing the entire expression to be TRUE only if *numOffenses* is zero.

Notice the parentheses in both of the above examples—they help clarify the statements even though they are not necessary because operator precedence would maintain the same order of evaluation.

Early Termination of Expression Evaluation

C allows programs to take shortcuts during the evaluation of expressions. Sometimes a program will determine the outcome of an expression without evaluating all of the terms. This causes the program to run faster, but it can also cause problems for poorly written control expressions. For example, suppose you had written the following *if* statement to specially process luggage when the weight exceeds a limit:

```
if ( ( luggageWeight > limit ) ||
     ( totalWeight += luggageWeight ) > totalLimit ) )
{
    /* Special processing */
}
```

The intent of this statement is to perform special processing if either the individual luggage weight or the total luggage weight exceeds a limit. However, in reality, if the value of *luggageWeight* alone exceeds *limit*, the program knows that the expression is TRUE and it doesn't need to evaluate the second part. This is a problem because the program can take the shortcut and skip the calculation of *totalWeight* in the second part of the expression. Therefore, the value of *totalWeight* is wrong, and this value may be needed later in the program. You can easily prevent these kinds of errors by avoiding the use of operators that change the values of variables in control expressions. In the above example, the problem is solved by placing the *totalWeight* calculation above the *if* statement:

```
totalWeight += luggageWeight;
if ( ( luggageWeight > limit ) ||
     ( totalWeight > totalLimit ) )
{
    /* Special processing */
}
```

The *if else* Statement

You can extend the *if* statement with key word *else* so that a program executes a separate target statement when the control expression is FALSE. Here is the syntax of an *if else* statement:

```
if ( control expression )
    TRUE target statement
else
    FALSE target statement
```

Figure 6-2 illustrates how an *if else* statement executes; it's the same as an *if* statement except that, when the control expression is FALSE, the program executes the FALSE target statement before going on. For example, you can change the value of *fine* like this:

```
if ( catch > limit )
    fine = 100.00;
else
    fine = 0.00;
```

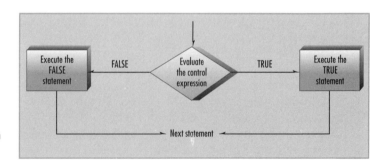

FIGURE 6-2 Flow of an *if else* statement

You can chain several *if else* statements together to accomplish a multiway branch. This takes the form:

```
if ( control expression 1 )
    target statement 1
else if ( control expression 2 )
    target statement 2
else if ( control expression 3 )
    target statement 3
```

A chain of *if else* statements is good for performing alternative processing based on different conditions. For instance, you could assign different gates to airline flights:

```
if ( flight == 761 )
    gate = 3;
else if ( flight == 710 )
    gate = 10;
else if ( flight == 406 )
    gate = 11;
```

Because C is free form, you could write a confusing chain of *if* and *if else* statements, like:

```
if ( flight == 761 ) gate = 3;
else
if ( flight == 710 )
if ( weekDay == 6 ) gate = 10;
else gate = 11;
```

If you are taking flight 710 on the first day of the week, can you tell for sure which gate is yours? The above code is perfectly valid and a C compiler has no trouble sorting it out because of the following rule:

Pair an *else* with the closest preceding *if*.

The best programming style is to make the logic of branching statements clear by indenting *if else* statements according to the above rule.

```
if ( flight == 761 )
{
    gate = 3;
}
else if ( flight == 710 )
{
    if ( weekDay == 6 )
    {
        gate = 10;
    }
    else
    {
```

continued on next page

continued from previous page

```
                gate = 11;
        }
    }
```

By indenting and consistently using the recommended layout guidelines, you can preserve the pairings and write clear *if else* statements.

Programming Style for *if* Statements

A target statement always comes immediately after the closing parenthesis of an *if* clause or immediately after the *else* key word. If the target is a single statement (not compound) it is generally acceptable to keep it on the same line as the *if* or *else*. However, we strongly recommend that you put target statements on lines of their own and indent them under the *if* or *else* clauses. Further, we recommend that you write target statements as compound statements with braces even when there is only one statement. You probably noticed the compound statement blocks in the previous example, and you will frequently see them in the lab exercises. Following this recommendation can save you from one of the common and very troublesome errors in C programming. When you enhance a program by adding features, it is very easy to expand a target statement to multiple statements and forget to insert the compound braces. If you always insert them with the original code, you will never forget them. Compound braces have no effect on the efficiency of program execution, so use them liberally. The same is true of parentheses—the compiler has to work a little harder, but this is of little consequence. The important result is clear, correct lines of source code.

The *switch* Statement

As you have seen, multiple *if else* statements can become quite elaborate. Even with our recommended format, they can be hard to read or revise. C provides an alternative called *switch* that makes some kinds of multiple tests easier to write. The *switch* statement is good for multiway branching on the result of an integer expression. Integer expressions are necessary so that accurate branching can occur on discrete values—this means that you cannot use a floating-point expression in a *switch* statement (although you can use type *char*). The syntax of a *switch* statement is:

```
switch ( expression )
{
    case value1:
        statement(s)1
        break;
```

```
case value2:
    statement(s)2
    break;
.
.
.

default:
    default statement(s)
    break;
}
```

Required punctuation for this statement is the key word *switch,* the parentheses around the expression, the opening and closing braces, and the *case* key words and associated colons (:). Although they are not punctuation, the *break* statements are also important. The effect of a *switch* statement is shown in Figure 6-3. The program evaluates the expression, then compares the result with each *case value* until it finds an exact match (the compiler will not allow you to insert duplicate *case values*). When the program finds a match, it executes the statement(s) located immediately after the *case.* You can place one or more statements there. You should usually end these statements with a *break* statement that guides the program to the closing brace of the *switch* syntax. Thus a *break* statement has the effect of terminating the *switch* processing, causing the program to continue with the next statement. If the program finds no match among the *case* values, it executes the *default* statement(s) and goes to the closing brace upon encountering a *break.* You should indent the *case* clauses, and under each *case* also indent the statements and associated *break* as shown below.

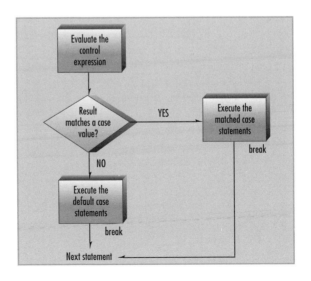

FIGURE 6-3 Flow of a *switch* statement

Imagine that you have the task of processing a list of names and that each name requires a different procedure depending on the first letter of the last name. A *switch* statement like the one below would be a good mechanism to support this processing:

```
switch ( letter )
{
    case 'A':
        /* Processing for the 'A' names */
        break;

    case 'B':
        /* Processing for the 'B' names */
        break;

        .
        .
        .

    default:
        /* Processing for all remaining instances */
        break;
}
```

You should normally end each *case* with a *break*, and you should always include a *default* even when you have no *default* statements to execute. Including the *default* assures that every possible value of the *switch* expression is accounted for, and it prevents you from overlooking values that you have not made explicit. You can place the *default* anywhere in the list of *case* clauses, but it usually is the last item in the list.

Occasionally, you will find a reason to omit a break intentionally. This causes the program to "fall through" and execute the statements associated with the next *case* (even though the value does not match that *case*). In the above example, you could add *case* values for lowercase letters that fall through to share the uppercase processing:

```
switch ( letter )
{
    case 'a':     /* fall through */
    case 'A':
        break;

        .
        .
        .
}
```

You could also insert a separate statement following the first *case* that would execute before the fall through. In this instance, you might want to convert the letter to uppercase before continuing:

```
switch ( letter )
{
    case 'a':
        letter -= 32;      /* Convert to uppercase, then fall through */
    case 'A':
        break;
    .
    .
    .
}
```

ASCII codes for uppercase characters are 32 less than the lowercase codes, so subtracting 32 accomplishes the conversion. It's a good idea to denote with a comment that a fall through is intentional so that later on someone won't misinterpret your code and incorrectly add a break statement.

if else vs *switch*

When should you use an *if else* construction rather than a *switch* to accomplish a multiway branch? A *switch* statement is restricted to branching on a single, integer value; thus you should use *if else* whenever you need to test floating-point values. Also, any branching situation that depends on separate testing of two or more values calls for an *if* or *if else* statement. For instance, it is impossible to accomplish the following in a reasonable manner with a *switch* statement:

```
if ( ( temperature < 10.5 ) || ( temperature > 120.7 ) )
{
    warningLight = ON;
}
else
{
    warningLight = OFF;
}
```

The *if else* is also a better choice when you have only a few branches because the syntax is simpler. A *switch* statement is suited for circumstances involving a large number of *case* values. There is no hard rule on this, but somewhere beyond three or four branches it becomes easier to add *case* clauses than additional *if else* clauses. A *switch* statement is better for such things as processing alphabetic lists and handling keyboard input. For keyboard input, you can *switch* on the value of a key code and include the proper processing for different keys under *case* values.

The Conditional Operator

C has a unique operator that acts much like an *if else* statement. The *conditional operator* has three operands in the following syntax:

```
control expression ? TRUE expression : FALSE expression
```

Figure 6-4 shows the effect of a conditional operator. If the control expression is TRUE, the conditional operator evaluates the TRUE expression; otherwise it evaluates the FALSE expression. For example, you can find the minimum of two values with a conditional operator:

```
minValue = ( oneValue < otherValue ) ? oneValue : otherValue;
```

This is equivalent to the following *if else* statement:

```
if ( oneValue < otherValue )
{
    minValue = oneValue;
}
else
{
    minValue = otherValue;
}
```

It seems the conditional operator is just a shorthand method of writing a simple *if else;* however, the fact that it returns the value of one of the expressions makes it particularly useful for *macros*. Macros are not discussed until Chapter 14, but it is interesting to note that your C header file, STDLIB.H, contains the macros *max()* and *min()* which use the conditional operator to return maximum and

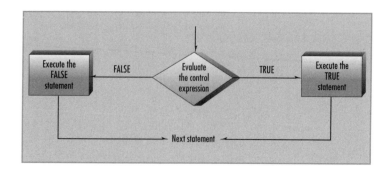

FIGURE 6-4 Flow of a conditional operator

minimum values of two numbers. (Take a look in file STDLIB.H in directory \TCLITE\INCLUDE.)

The *goto* Statement

Learning the *goto* statement can be compared to purchasing a new gun. You should learn all about it, then you should use it sparingly. A *goto* statement causes a program to branch immediately and unconditionally to another location. The syntax of *goto* is in two parts:

```
goto label;
other statements
label:
```

The *label* is any unique C identifier (as discussed in Chapter 3). You must have a label following the *goto* key word and a matching label with an ending colon (:) at the desired branch location in the program. Figure 6-5 illustrates the operation of a *goto* statement. When the program reaches the *goto*, it jumps to the location of the matching label. You can use each label only once to identify a transfer location, but any number of *goto* statements can refer to that label. You can place a goto either ahead of or following a matching label; that is, you can jump backward or forward in a program.

The reason you should use *goto* sparingly is that it can easily cause a program to be confusing. Use too many *gotos* and you create what is commonly called "spaghetti code." Notice that, in Figure 6-5, there is no way for the program to get to the statements between the *goto* and the label. Executing these statements would require another *goto* and label, creating unnecessarily complicated program flow. You can almost always write clearer, more readable programs by using other branching and looping statements.

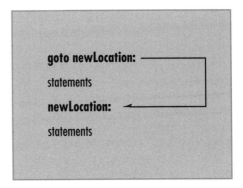

FIGURE 6-5   Flow of a *goto* statement

LAB

Exercise 1A: Run an adder program.

✳ STARTER FILE: EX06-1A.C

```
#include <stdio.h>
void main()
{
    char  arithOp;        /* Arithmetic operator  */
    float op1;            /* First operand        */
    float op2;            /* Second operand       */
    float answer;         /* Result               */

    printf( "Enter a calculation: " );
    scanf( "%f %c %f", &op1, &arithOp, &op2 );

    answer = op1 + op2;
    printf( " = %.1f\n", answer );
}
```

✳ DO: Type in and run the above program that adds two numbers, then type 6.3 + 15.7 (ENTER).

✳ RESULT:

```
Enter a calculation: 6.3 + 15.7
= 22.0
```

✳ DISCUSSION: Other exercises below will ask you to modify this program with branching statements.

Exercise 1B: Develop a four-function calculator.

✳ DO: Add *if else* statements to make the program a four-function calculator capable of addition, subtraction, multiplication, and division. Run the program four times to apply each operator to the numbers 6.3 and 15.7.

✳ SOLUTION FILE: EX06-1B.C

✳ RESULT:

```
Enter a calculation: 6.3 + 15.7
= 22.0
Enter a calculation: 6.3 - 15.7
= -9.4
```

```
Enter a calculation: 6.3 * 15.7
= 98.9
Enter a calculation: 6.3 / 15.7
= 0.4
```

✳ **DISCUSSION:** A chain of four *if else* statements can accomplish the four operations, and the final *else* can display an error message when you enter an illegal operator.

Exercise 1C: Program a four-function calculator with *switch* statement.

✳ **DO:** Convert the *if else* statements in Exercise 1B to a *switch* statement. Run the program four times, entering each operator and the numbers 6.3 and 13.7 to verify that it works.

✳ **SOLUTION FILE:** EX06-1C.C

✳ **RESULT:** Same as Exercise 1B.

```
Enter a calculation: 6.3 + 15.7
= 22.0
Enter a calculation: 6.3 - 15.7
= -9.4
Enter a calculation: 6.3 * 15.7
= 98.9
Enter a calculation: 6.3 / 15.7
= 0.4
```

✳ **DISCUSSION:** Do you think the *switch* statement is better than *if else* for this program? Actually, for this number of branches (four), neither is a clear choice over the other. However, the next exercise shows an interesting advantage of *switch*.

Exercise 1D: Insert a fall through.

✳ **DO:** An alternate way of subtracting is to add a negative number. Modify the calculator so that subtraction applies the unary minus operator to the second operand, then falls through to the plus operator. Run the program and subtract 15.7 from 6.3.

✳ **SOLUTION FILE:** EX06-1D.C

✳ **RESULT:**

```
Enter a calculation: 6.3 - 15.7
= -9.4
```

✳ **DISCUSSION:** Don't forget to mark the fall-through line with a comment to make the intent clear.

Exercise 1E: Program a four-function calculator with continuous operation.

✳ **DO:** Use a *goto* statement to modify Exercise 1D so that you can enter new calculations without having to restart the program. Use an *if* statement to end the program when the operator is Q. Run the program and apply each operator to the numbers 6.3 and 15.7, then end by typing: 0 Q 0.

✳ **SOLUTION FILE:** EX06-1E.C

✳ **RESULT:**

```
Enter a calculation: 6.3 + 15.7
= 22.0
Enter a calculation: 6.3 - 15.7
= -9.4
Enter a calculation: 6.3 * 15.7
= 98.9
Enter a calculation: 6.3 / 15.7
= 0.4
Enter a calculation: 0 Q 0
illegal operator   = 0.4
```

✳ **DISCUSSION:** The method for quitting (with a Q operator) works, but it is awkward—it leaves undesirable output on the screen. Can you propose other methods for stopping the program?

Exercise 2A: Develop a keyboard handler.

✳ **STARTER FILE:** EX06-2A.C

```
#include <stdio.h>
#include <conio.h>
void main()
{
    int ext;    /* 0 = Normal key, 1 = Extended key */
    int key;    /* Key code */

    ext = 0;
    if ( ( key = getch() ) == 0 )
    {
        ext = 1;
        key = getch();
    }
```

```
        printf( "ext = %d, key = %d\n", ext, key );
}
```

✳ **DO:** Type in the above program that accepts normal or extended-code keystrokes from the keyboard. Run the program eight times, pressing each of the following keys, and observe the displayed data: (A), (PAGEUP), (PAGEDOWN), (CURSORLEFT), (CURSORRIGHT), (CURSORUP), (CURSORDOWN), (ESC).

✳ **RESULT:**

```
ext = 0, key = 65
ext = 1, key = 73
ext = 1, key = 81
ext = 1, key = 75
ext = 1, key = 77
ext = 1, key = 72
ext = 1, key = 80
ext = 0, key = 27
```

✳ **DISCUSSION:** This program uses the non-ANSI function *getch()* with a prototype in header file CONIO.H. The ANSI character function *getchar()* won't capture extended character codes. Most keys on a PC keyboard (letters and punctuation) generate a single nonzero code, but certain keys place two codes in the keyboard buffer: an *extended* code of zero, followed by a nonzero key code. Here we use *getch()* to capture both codes when they occur. The program notes the existence of the extended code by setting variable *ext* to one; notice which keys have an extended code.

Exercise 2B: Implement a keyboard handler with branching.

✳ **DO:** Add an *if* statement to the branch on the extension code, and add *switch* statements to the branch on each of the key codes in the previous exercise. At each branch, display the name of the key; for example, display "Escape" in response to pressing (ESC). Also display any of the alphabetic or numeric keys that might be pressed (hint: use *default*). Optionally, you can provide for continuous operation by inserting a *goto* statement. Run the program and press all of the same keys as for the previous exercise.

✳ **SOLUTION FILE:** EX06-2B.C

✳ **RESULT:**
```
ext = 0, key = 65
A
ext = 1, key = 73
PageUp
ext = 1, key = 81
PageDown
ext = 1, key = 75
```

continued on next page

121

continued from previous page

```
CursorLeft
ext = 1, key = 77
CursorRight
ext = 1, key = 72
CursorUp
ext = 1, key = 80
CursorDown
ext = 0, key = 27
Escape
```

✳ DISCUSSION: You can extend this program to customize the response to any key on the keyboard.

Exercise 3A: Use a conditional operator.

✳ DO: Write a program to accept a floating-point number from the keyboard and display its absolute value—use a conditional operator. The absolute value of a number is the number without a sign. Run the program twice and type -2.5 then +2.5.

✳ SOLUTION FILE: EX06-3A.C

✳ RESULT:

```
Enter a number: -2.5
Absolute value is 2.500000

Enter a number: +2.5
Absolute value is 2.500000
```

✳ DISCUSSION: The conditional operator is particularly good for returning the result of a two-way conditional branch.

Exercise 3B: Use multiple conditions without parentheses.

✳ STARTER FILE: EX06-3B.C

```c
#include <stdio.h>
void main()
{
    float x, y;

    printf( "Enter two numbers: " );
    scanf( "%f %f", &x, &y );

    printf( "Product is %f\n",
        x*y < 0. && x > -1. && x < 1. || y > -1. && y < 1. ? -x*y : x*y );
}
```

✳ **DO:** The above program is supposed to display the absolute value of the product of two numbers if either of them is in the range of -1 to +1; outside of that range it is supposed to display the signed product. In words, the above conditional statement says: "If x times y is less than 0 and x is between -1 and +1 or y is between -1 and +1, then return negative x times y; otherwise return x times y." Enter this program and run it twice—type -.5 .5 in response to the first prompt, and .5 .5 the second time.

✳ **RESULT:**

```
Enter two numbers: −.5 .5
Product is .250000
Enter two numbers: .5 .5
Product is −.250000
```

✳ **DISCUSSION:** The program doesn't quite work correctly. It reports the correct absolute value the first time, but if you enter .5 for both numbers, the program displays -.25 for the product.

Exercise 3C: Use multiple conditions with parentheses.

✳ **SOLUTION FILES:** EX06-3C.C and EX06-3D.C

✳ **DO:** Spot the problem in Exercise 3B, then insert parentheses to correct the error. Run the program twice to verify the correction—type -.5 .5 in response to the first prompt, and .5 .5 the second time.

✳ **RESULT:**

```
Enter two numbers: −.5 .5
Product is .250000
Enter two numbers: .5 .5
Product is .250000
```

✳ **DISCUSSION:** File EX06-3C.C shows the minimum solution, which is to insert one set of parentheses. File EX06-3D.C contains a better solution—it uses parentheses for each relational and logical operator to control the order of evaluation explicitly.

SUMMARY

Now you have the tools to control the flow of a program based on data values. You know how to use *if* and *if else* statements to accomplish branching from conditions involving several data values or values of floating-point numbers. You know how to use a *switch* statement when you need a large number of branches from an integer value. You've mastered the shorthand of the conditional statement, and you know the wisdom of using *goto* statements sparingly. The next chapter increases your ability to affect program flow by introducing looping control statements.

7

Average time to complete this chapter (including lab and quiz) is 6 hours.

LOOPING CONTROL STATEMENTS

ooping is the process of repeating a sequence of operations. Computers are very good at performing repetitive tasks, so looping control statements are at the heart of what computers do best. In this chapter, you will learn how to set up loops and you will see that looping statements are specialized for certain purposes. You will also learn the different ways to stop loops.

LECTURE

There are two principal statements in C for looping: *while* and *for*. There is also a variation of *while* called *do while,* and two statements, *break* and *continue,* that assist with looping control. As you saw in Chapter 6, *goto* can jump backward and cause a program to repeat statements, so it can also serve as a looping statement, although it is not recommended for that purpose.

The *while* Statement

The simplest looping control statement is *while*; it executes a target statement as long as the control expression is nonzero, or TRUE. Here is the syntax of *while*:

```
while ( control expression )
   target statement
```

The key word *while* and the parentheses are necessary, and to accomplish something you also need to include a control expression and target statement. You should always indent the target statement under the *while* line, and we recommend that you always make the target a compound statement (use braces even when the target is a single statement). Figure 7-1 shows how a *while* statement works. It evaluates the control expression and, if the result is FALSE (or zero), the *while* statement ends and the program proceeds to the next statement. However, if the result is TRUE, the program executes the target statement, then loops back to evaluate the control expression again.

You determine when a *while* loop ends by setting up the control expression. You can make a loop repeat a fixed number of times by counting:

```
n = 0;
while ( ++n <= 100 )
{
   /* This will repeat 100 times */
}
```

Or you can make the control expression test for a specific condition that ends the loop no matter how many times it must repeat—this is the best way to use a *while* statement. The code fragment below repeatedly subtracts $100.00 from variable *moneyInTheBank* as long as it is greater than zero:

```
moneyInTheBank = 1555.00;
while ( moneyInTheBank > 0. )
{

   moneyInTheBank -= 100.00;
}
```

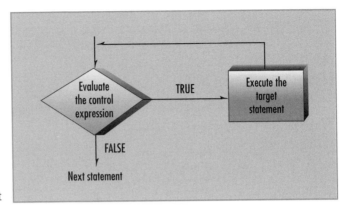

FIGURE 7-1 Program
flow of a *while* statement

This loop repeats 16 times, and when it ends the value of *moneyInTheBank* will
be -45. If you initialize *moneyInTheBank* to a different value, the number of loop
cycles will change accordingly.

The Null Statement

A semicolon by itself is a *null statement*. Even though a null statement does
nothing, it is perfectly valid and it has a purpose in connection with loops. You
can write loops where there is no need for a target statement—all the processing is
included in the control expression. However, loop statements require a body, or
target statement, and the null statement fills this need. You could rewrite the
previous example as:

```
moneyInTheBank = 1555.00;
while ( ( moneyInTheBank -= 100.00 ) > 0. )
{
    ;
}
```

A more practical example is the need to read input values until a particular
value occurs. Here is a statement that repeatedly takes characters from the
keyboard until a 'Y' occurs:

```
while ( getchar() != 'Y' )
{
    ;
}
```

Obviously you could put all this on one line:

```
while ( getchar() != 'Y' );
```

but the null statement is hardly noticeable. Another programmer modifying the code could easily overlook the semicolon, misinterpret the intent of the statement, and introduce an error. It is important that a null statement be on a separate line; the compound braces make it even more visible.

Indefinite Loop

You can cause a *while* loop to execute indefinitely by using a nonzero constant for the control expression. The following loop never ends:

```
#define TRUE 1
while ( TRUE )
{
}
```

This may seem kind of silly, but the *break* statement makes it a very useful construction. You can stop this loop after one cycle by inserting *break*:

```
#define TRUE 1
while ( TRUE )
{
    break;
}
```

The *break* statement makes the program jump to the end of the current loop (to the closing brace). You can exercise control over when the ending occurs by using *break* with a conditional expression. For instance, you could use *break* to stop when a bank balance drops below zero:

```
#define TRUE 1
moneyInTheBank = 1555.00;
while ( TRUE )
{
    if ( ( moneyInTheBank -= 100.00 ) <  0. )
    {
        break;
    }
}
```

You no doubt noticed the symbolic constant, TRUE, in the above examples. We could have directly inserted a numeric constant (one in this case), but it is better programming technique to use the symbolic name.

The indefinite loop is well suited for setting up a repeating process that depends on data values for stopping. You might use it for reading all the data from a file of unknown size. Or you might use it to take a variable amount of data from the keyboard. Here's how you can total the amounts of a variable number of bank deposits, stopping the loop with a deposit of zero or less:

```
#define TRUE 1
```

```
moneyInTheBank = 0.;
while ( TRUE )
{
    scanf( "%f", &deposit );
    if ( deposit > 0. )
    {
        moneyInTheBank += deposit;
    }
    else
    {
        break;
    }
}
```

Another way of setting up an indefinite loop is to use a *flag* variable in the control expression. You initialize the flag to TRUE before entering the loop, then after a statement inside the loop sets the flag to FALSE, the loop will end.

```
#define TRUE 1
#define FALSE 0
int processingFlag = TRUE;
moneyInTheBank = 0.;
while ( processingFlag )
{
    scanf( "%f", &deposit );
    if ( deposit > 0. )
    {
        moneyInTheBank += deposit;
    }
    else
    {
        processingFlag = FALSE;
    }
}
```

Instead of stopping with a *break* statement, this program assigns FALSE (or zero) to *processingFlag*, which causes the loop to end on the very next cycle. The method of using a flag variable to end a loop is better when the number of statements is large—the connection between a *while* and a *break* statement gets lost in a large section of code. The flag technique is also very good for ending nested loops, as you will see later in this chapter.

The *do while* Statement

The only difference between the *while* and the *do while* statements is when the control expression is evaluated. The *do while* evaluates its control expression at the end of the loop rather than at the beginning. The syntax of the *do while* statement is:

```
do
    target statement
while ( control expression );
```

The essential elements are the key words *do* and *while*, the parentheses, and the ending semicolon. You can insert any target statement and control expression. Figure 7-2 shows what happens within a *do while* statement.

The program first executes the target statement, then it evaluates the control expression to see whether to repeat the loop or move on to the next statement. This means that a *do while* statement always executes the target statement at least one time. In contrast, *a while* statement can end without ever executing the target statement.

You can display a bank balance each time a check is posted against it with the following code fragment:

```
moneyInTheBank = 1555.00;
do
{
    printf( "Bank balance = %.2f", moneyInTheBank );
    scanf( "%f", checkAmount );
} while ( ( moneyInTheBank -= checkAmount ) > 0. );
```

You could also do this with a *while* statement:

```
moneyInTheBank = 1555.00;
while ( moneyInTheBank > 0. )
{
    printf( "Bank balance = %.2f", moneyInTheBank );
    scanf( "%f", checkAmount );
    moneyInTheBank -= checkAmount;
}
```

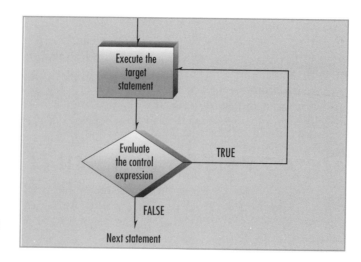

FIGURE 7-2   Flow of a
do while statement

These two pieces of code accomplish the same thing with a subtle difference—if the initial bank balance were not positive (if you initialized *moneyInTheBank* = 0.) the *while* loop would never display the amount; whereas the *do while* executes at least one time and displays the initial value of *moneyInTheBank*. Many circumstances call for the guaranteed execution of a loop at least one time. Certain card games require a player to draw from the deck until finding a specific card. You can easily simulate this process with a *do while* statement:

```
do
{
    /* Draw a card */
} while ( draw != neededCard );
```

We recommend you always use a compound target statement with *do while* and, even though it adds an extra line, vertically align the opening and closing braces rather than put the opening brace on the first line with the key word *do*.

Just as with *while,* you can write indefinite *do while* loops. Insert a TRUE constant for the control expression and use a *break* statement to end the loop.

The *for* Statement

The *for* syntax has three control expressions: one that initializes control variables, one that tests for an ending condition, and one that updates the variables:

```
for ( initialize; test; update )
    target statement
```

Essential ingredients are the key word *for,* the parentheses, the semicolons, and a target statement. Figure 7-3 shows the operation of a *for* statement.

The order of processing is important here: a *for* statement executes the initialize expression only once, then it begins the first loop cycle by evaluating the test expression. If the result is FALSE, the loop ends and the program goes to the next statement in sequence. If the test expression is TRUE, the program executes the target statement, then executes the update expression and starts the next cycle by re-evaluating the test expression.

You can leave out any or all three of the control expressions of a *for* statement. Therefore the smallest *for* statement is:

```
for ( ; ; )
    ;
```

This statement does nothing, but it does it for a very long time because there is no ending condition. In the absence of a test expression, a *for* statement defaults to a TRUE condition and continues executing. The only way you can stop it is by putting a *break* in the body of the target statement (or a *goto*).

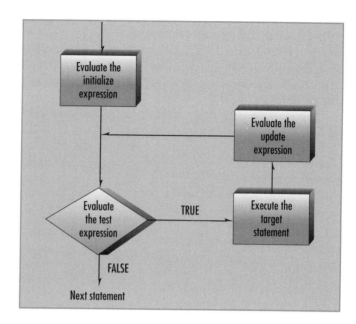

FIGURE 7-3   Flow of a
for statement

A typical use of the *for* statement is to operate a loop over a fixed number of cycles; here's a classic example:

```
int i;
float interest, principal, rate;
principal = 1000.;
rate = .04 / 12;
for ( i=0; i<12; ++i )
{
    interest = principal * rate;
    principal += interest;
}
```

This loop calculates the compound interest on a monthly basis for one year in a savings account yielding 4 percent annually. The initialize control expression sets the index variable *i* to zero, the test expression ends the loop after 12 cycles (when *i* reaches 12), and the update expression increments *i* by one each time. You could move the initialize expression above the *for* statement and move the update expression into the *for* block without affecting the outcome:

```
i = 0;
for ( ; i<12; )
{
    interest = principal * rate;
    principal += interest;
    ++i;
}
```

However, this is a misuse of the *for* syntax—it is not as straightforward and clear as the first example. Sometimes you will find good cause to omit one or more of the control expressions, but this is infrequent. This might be justified when the index variable is already set by a previous statement, or when the target statement performs the update task.

Comma Operator

C allows more than one initialize or update expression in a *for* statement. The *comma operator* makes this possible; it separates two or more expressions, as shown below:

```
for ( init1, init2; test; update1, update2 )
```

Only one test expression is allowed; this is reasonable because ending the *for* loop is based on a single TRUE/FALSE value. The C compiler evaluates multiple expressions separated by commas from left to right, and the final value is the value of the last expression on the right (the final value is of no significance here). In the example of calculating compound interest, you could initialize and update variable *principal* in the *for* statement along with the index *i*:

```
for ( principal=1000., i=0; i<12; principal+=interest, ++i )
{
    interest = principal * rate;
}
```

You can place any kind of initialization and update in the control expressions of *for,* but it is best to restrict them to variables that control the actual looping. This is discretionary and you should choose expressions that make the program more understandable.

for vs *while*

A complete *for* statement is equivalent to the following *while* construction:

```
initialize;
while ( test )
{
    target statement
    update;
}
```

Therefore, you can set up any loop using either *for* or *while* statements. However, a *for* is more suited for loops controlled by index variables because you can initialize and update the index right there in the first line. A *while* statement is a better choice for looping an indefinite number of cycles or for situations where there are no simple index values.

Interrupting Loops with *break* and *continue*

There are three ways to end a loop. The best method is to allow the control statement to end the loop normally. The next best method is to end with a *break* statement. The least desirable method is to jump out with a *goto* because this can lead to confused "spaghetti" code. Figure 7-4 illustrates the action of *break* and *goto* from inside a loop.

In the banking example, here's how you can stop the interest calculation after nine months:

```
for ( i=0; i<12; ++i )
{
    if ( i == 9 )
    {
        break;
    }
    interest = principal * rate;
    principal += interest;
}
```

The *continue* statement gives you a way to skip processing in a loop selectively. As Figure 7-5 shows, it causes the program to jump to the beginning of the next loop cycle.

If you withdraw your money from the bank just for the month of June and then redeposit it, you would need to skip the interest rate calculation for that month—here's how to do this with a *continue* statement:

```
for ( i=0; i<12; ++i )
{
    if ( i == 6 )
    {
        continue;
    }
    interest = principal * rate;
    principal += interest;
}
```

Here, when *i* is equal to 6, the *continue* statement causes the program to skip the interest and principal calculations and take them up again at the beginning of the loop. Of course, you can also use *continue* in *while* or *do while* loops. In a *while* or *do while* loop, *continue* goes directly to the test expression; in a *for* loop it goes to the update expression.

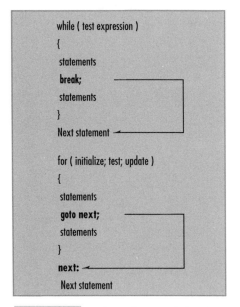

FIGURE 7-4   Ending a loop with *break* or *goto*

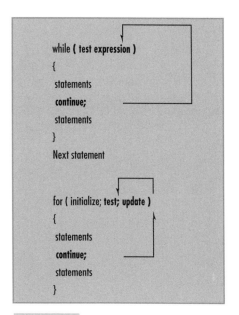

FIGURE 7-5   Action of a *continue* statement

Nested Loops

If you put a loop inside another loop it is called a *nested loop*. Each time the outer loop performs a cycle, the inner loop runs from beginning to end, completing all of its cycles. Figure 7-6 diagrams a nested loop.

Using our banking example, to calculate five years of interest, you could nest the 12-month loop inside another loop:

```
int year;
for ( year=1; year<=5; ++year )
{
    for ( i=0; i<12; ++i )
    {
        if ( i == 9 )
        {
            break;
        }
        interest = principal * rate;
        principal += interest;
    }
    printf( "Principal at the end of year %d = %.2f",
            year, principal );
}
```

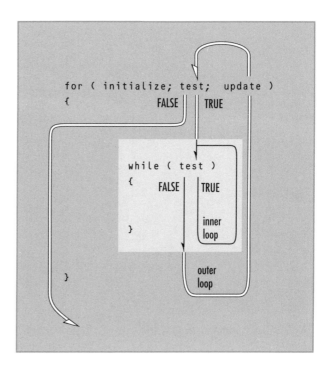

FIGURE 7-6   A nested loop

The *printf()* executes once for each cycle of the outer loop—it reports the principal amount available at the end of each year.

When you nest loops, be sure to indent so that each loop and its nesting level is clear.

You can nest loops to any depth, and you can place any type of loop inside any other (*for* inside *while*, *while* inside *for,* etc.). A *break* or *continue* affects only the loop where it is located. In the above example, the *break* does not end the outer *for* loop, which makes five complete cycles. Each time the inner loop ends after nine cycles, the outer loop initiates another inner cycle.

As you know from Chapter 6, *break* also causes a program to jump to the end of a *switch* statement. Thus you cannot use *break* within a *switch* statement to end a loop. This is a minor annoyance that you can easily overcome with a separate flag variable that signals when to end the loop (see Exercise 1).

LAB

Exercise 1:   Develop a looping calculator.

✳ **STARTER FILE:** EX06-1E.C

✳ **DO:** Make a copy of file EX06-1E.C (from the Chapter 6 lab) that contains the calculator program. Replace the *goto* statement (which causes the program to repeat until you enter Q for an operator) with a loop that has the same effect. See if you can also get rid of the undesirable output that previously occurred after entering Q. Run the program, add 6.3 to 15.7, then quit by entering Q for the operator.

✳ **SOLUTION FILE:** EX07-1.C

✳ **RESULT:**

```
Enter a calculation: 6.3 + 15.7
= 22.0
Enter a calculation: 0 Q 0
```

✳ **DISCUSSION:** The undesirable output was eliminated, not by the loop, but by the new case 'Q': clause and by moving the *printf()* statement that displays the answer inside the *switch* statement.

Exercise 2A: Perform continuous keyboard input using *while*.

✳ **STARTER FILE:** EX06-2B.C

✳ **DO:** Make a copy of file EX06-2B.C (from the Chapter 6 lab). Add a *while* loop to repeat keyboard input until the (ESC) key is pressed. Run the program and type (A) (PAGEUP) (PAGEDOWN) (CURSORLEFT) (CURSORRIGHT) (CURSORUP) (CURSORDOWN) (ESC).

✳ **SOLUTION FILE:** EX07-2A.C

✳ **RESULT:**

```
ext = 0, key = 65
A
ext = 1, key = 73
PageUp
ext = 1, key = 81
PageDown
ext = 1, key = 75
CursorLeft
ext = 1, key = 77
```

```
CursorRight
ext = 1, key = 72
CursorUp
ext = 1, key = 80
CursorDown
ext = 0, key = 27
Escape
```

✳ **DISCUSSION:** To cover all input possibilities, you should include a test for the extended code value of zero in the ending condition. You should also initialize variable *key* to zero (any value other than 27) to guarantee that the *while* loop will execute at least once.

Exercise 2B: Perform continuous keyboard input using *do while*.

✳ **DO:** Substitute a *do while* for the *while* loop in the previous exercise. Run the program and press the same keys as in Exercise 2A.

✳ **SOLUTION FILE:** EX07-2B.C

✳ **RESULT:** Same as Exercise 2A.

✳ **DISCUSSION:** You can eliminate the initialization of *key* because it is assigned a value before the test at the end of the loop.

Exercise 2C: Perform continuous keyboard input with indefinite loop.

✳ **DO:** Change *do while* to an indefinite *while* loop and use the ESCAPE case to end the loop. Hint: You will have to use a separate flag variable. Run the program and press the same keys as for Exercise 2B.

✳ **SOLUTION FILE:** EX07-2C.C

✳ **RESULT:** Same as Exercise 2B.

✳ **DISCUSSION:** You can use a flag named *notDone,* initialized to TRUE, as the control expression, and end by assigning FALSE to it. Or you can name it *done* and apply the opposite logic, ending by assigning a value of TRUE—in this case the control expression would have to be *!done.*

Exercise 3A: Balance your checkbook.

✳ **DO:** Write a program to help balance your checkbook. The program should prompt for a series of outstanding checks (checks not reported on your bank statement) and accumulate the amounts you enter. It should do the same for outstanding deposits. Then the program should ask for the latest balance from your checkbook and the balance reported on the bank statement. Finally, it should calculate a trial balance as the checkbook balance plus outstanding checks minus outstanding deposits and report the difference between the trial balance and the bank statement balance. Use a copy of the program in EX05-1B.C (from the Chapter 5 lab) to start—it already accumulates the total of outstanding checks. Run the program and enter the amounts shown below.

✳ SOLUTION FILE: EX07-3A.C

✳ RESULT:

```
Enter an outstanding check amount (zero when done): 12.95
Enter an outstanding check amount (zero when done): 111.11
Enter an outstanding check amount (zero when done): 98.99
Enter an outstanding check amount (zero when done): 0
Enter an outstanding deposit (zero when done): 250.00
Enter an outstanding deposit (zero when done): 80.50
Enter an outstanding deposit (zero when done): 0
Enter your latest checkbook balance: 543.21
Enter the statement balance: 435.76
Congratulations, your checkbook balances!
```

✳ DISCUSSION: You can tailor this program to suit your own needs and taste by changing the order of data input or the appearance of the display.

Exercise 3B: Balance your checkbook.

✳ DO: Instead of ending the outstanding check loop with the expression (inputValue > .009), use a *break* statement to end the loop on the same condition. (The value of .009 is less than one cent, but it avoids a test for exactly zero.) Run the program and enter some data similar to Exercise 3A.

✳ SOLUTION FILE: EX07-3B.C

✳ RESULT: Same as Exercise 3A if you use the same input data; otherwise you should get the message that shows the difference between your trial balance and the bank statement balance.

✳ DISCUSSION: Placement of the *break* is important here. Can you explain why it would matter whether the *break* occurs before or after assignment of the input value? If it were placed after, and if the input were not exactly zero, the spurious input value would accumulate in the outstanding checks.

Exercise 3C: Balance your checkbook.

✳ **DO:** In the above program, you can end the loop that prompts for outstanding checks by entering a negative amount. Modify your program from Exercise 3B to use a *continue* to ignore a negative amount without stopping the loop. Run the program and enter the same data as Exercise 3B, except insert -1.00 in the check amounts.

✳ **SOLUTION FILE:** EX07-3C.C

✳ **RESULT:**

```
Enter an outstanding check amount (zero when done): 12.95
Enter an outstanding check amount (zero when done): -1.00
Enter an outstanding check amount (zero when done): 111.11
Enter an outstanding check amount (zero when done): 98.99
Enter an outstanding check amount (zero when done): 0
Enter an outstanding deposit (zero when done): 250.00
Enter an outstanding deposit (zero when done): 80.50
Enter an outstanding deposit (zero when done): 0
Enter your latest checkbook balance: 543.21
Enter the statement balance: 435.76
Congratulations, your checkbook balances!
```

✳ **DISCUSSION:** A negative check amount would never occur except by mistake, which is precisely the point of this exercise. It shows one method of protecting an input stream against erroneous data.

Exercise 4A: Report a savings account balance.

✳ **STARTER FILE:** EX07-4A.C

```c
#include <stdio.h>
void main()
{
    int n = 0;
    float balance = 100.;

    while ( ++n < 12 )
    {
        balance += balance * .04;
        printf( "Balance at the end of month %d is %.2f\n",
                n, balance );
    }
}
```

✳ **DO:** This program calculates the balance at the end of each month for a savings account that pays interest. It is supposed to repeat the balance for 12 months, but displays only 11 lines of data. Find the error in the program and correct it. There are three ways to make the program calculate and display 12 months of savings balances easily.

✳ **SOLUTION FILES:** EX07-4B.C, EX07-4C.C, and EX07-4D.C

✳ **RESULT:**

```
Balance at the end of month 1 is 104.00
Balance at the end of month 2 is 108.16
Balance at the end of month 3 is 112.49
Balance at the end of month 4 is 116.99
Balance at the end of month 5 is 121.67
Balance at the end of month 6 is 126.53
Balance at the end of month 7 is 131.59
Balance at the end of month 8 is 136.86
Balance at the end of month 9 is 142.33
Balance at the end of month 10 is 148.02
Balance at the end of month 11 is 153.95
Balance at the end of month 12 is 160.10
```

✳ **DISCUSSION:** For the starter program (EX07-4A.C), the last line of output will be absent because of the prefix increment of *n* in the *while* control expression. The three solutions involve changing to postfix increment, changing the control expression, and changing to a *do while* loop.

Exercise 5A: Report a savings account balance.

✳ **DO:** Write a program to calculate and display the monthly balance in a savings account for one year. The account pays 4 percent annual interest and you deposit $100 in the account at the beginning of each month. Here's the basic calculation: given that the balance for any month is variable *balance*, then the next month's balance is *(balance + deposit) * (1. + interest)*. Run the program and compare the output with the result below.

✳ **SOLUTION FILE:** EX07-5A.C

✳ **RESULT:**

```
Balance at the end of month 1 is 104.00
Balance at the end of month 2 is 212.16
Balance at the end of month 3 is 324.65
Balance at the end of month 4 is 441.63
Balance at the end of month 5 is 563.30
```

```
Balance at the end of month 6 is 689.83
Balance at the end of month 7 is 821.42
Balance at the end of month 8 is 958.28
Balance at the end of month 9 is 1100.61
Balance at the end of month 10 is 1248.64
Balance at the end of month 11 is 1402.58
Balance at the end of month 12 is 1562.68
```

✳ **DISCUSSION:** A *for* loop is best here because it repeats a fixed number of times.

Exercise 5B: Vary the deposit for a savings account.

✳ **DO:** Use a nested loop to display monthly balances for deposits of $100, $150, and $200 at the beginning of each month.

✳ **SOLUTION FILE:** EX07-5B.C

✳ **RESULT:**

```
Monthly deposit of $100.00

Balance at the end of month 1 is 104.00
Balance at the end of month 2 is 212.16
Balance at the end of month 3 is 324.65
Balance at the end of month 4 is 441.63
Balance at the end of month 5 is 563.30
Balance at the end of month 6 is 689.83
Balance at the end of month 7 is 821.42
Balance at the end of month 8 is 958.28
Balance at the end of month 9 is 1100.61
Balance at the end of month 10 is 1248.64
Balance at the end of month 11 is 1402.58
Balance at the end of month 12 is 1562.68
Press <Enter> to continue

Monthly deposit of $150.00

Balance at the end of month 1 is 156.00
Balance at the end of month 2 is 318.24
Balance at the end of month 3 is 486.97
Balance at the end of month 4 is 662.45
Balance at the end of month 5 is 844.95
Balance at the end of month 6 is 1034.74
Balance at the end of month 7 is 1232.13
Balance at the end of month 8 is 1437.42
Balance at the end of month 9 is 1650.92
Balance at the end of month 10 is 1872.95
Balance at the end of month 11 is 2103.87
```

```
Balance at the end of month 12 is 2344.03
Press <Enter> to continue

Monthly deposit of $200.00

Balance at the end of month 1 is 208.00
Balance at the end of month 2 is 424.32
Balance at the end of month 3 is 649.29
Balance at the end of month 4 is 883.26
Balance at the end of month 5 is 1126.60
Balance at the end of month 6 is 1379.66
Balance at the end of month 7 is 1642.85
Balance at the end of month 8 is 1916.56
Balance at the end of month 9 is 2201.22
Balance at the end of month 10 is 2497.27
Balance at the end of month 11 is 2805.16
Balance at the end of month 12 is 3125.37
Press <Enter> to continue
```

✳ **DISCUSSION:** The number of deposits is fixed, so it makes sense to use another *for* loop. It is OK to use a floating-point variable *(deposits)* in the control expressions of the loop. You have to be sure to initialize the *balance* to zero each time the inner loop begins.

Exercise 5C: Vary the interest for a savings account.

✳ **DO:** Use a triple nested loop to display monthly balances for deposits of $100, $150, and $200, for each interest rate of 4 percent, 6 percent, and 8 percent.

✳ **SOLUTION FILE:** EX07-5C.C

✳ **RESULT:**

```
Interest rate of 0.04

Monthly deposit of $100.00

Balance at the end of month 1 is 104.00
Balance at the end of month 2 is 212.16
Balance at the end of month 3 is 324.65
Balance at the end of month 4 is 441.63
Balance at the end of month 5 is 563.30
Balance at the end of month 6 is 689.83
Balance at the end of month 7 is 821.42
Balance at the end of month 8 is 958.28
Balance at the end of month 9 is 1100.61
Balance at the end of month 10 is 1248.64
Balance at the end of month 11 is 1402.58
```

```
Balance at the end of month 12 is 1562.68
Press <Enter> to continue

Monthly deposit of $150.00

Balance at the end of month 1 is 156.00
Balance at the end of month 2 is 318.24
Balance at the end of month 3 is 486.97
Balance at the end of month 4 is 662.45
Balance at the end of month 5 is 844.95
Balance at the end of month 6 is 1034.74
Balance at the end of month 7 is 1232.13
Balance at the end of month 8 is 1437.42
Balance at the end of month 9 is 1650.92
Balance at the end of month 10 is 1872.95
Balance at the end of month 11 is 2103.87
Balance at the end of month 12 is 2344.03
Press <Enter> to continue

Monthly deposit of $200.00

Balance at the end of month 1 is 208.00
Balance at the end of month 2 is 424.32
Balance at the end of month 3 is 649.29
Balance at the end of month 4 is 883.26
Balance at the end of month 5 is 1126.60
Balance at the end of month 6 is 1379.66
Balance at the end of month 7 is 1642.85
Balance at the end of month 8 is 1916.56
Balance at the end of month 9 is 2201.22
Balance at the end of month 10 is 2497.27
Balance at the end of month 11 is 2805.16
Balance at the end of month 12 is 3125.37
Press <Enter> to continue

Interest rate of 0.06

Monthly deposit of $100.00

Balance at the end of month 1 is 106.00
Balance at the end of month 2 is 218.36
Balance at the end of month 3 is 337.46
Balance at the end of month 4 is 463.71
Balance at the end of month 5 is 597.53
Balance at the end of month 6 is 739.38
Balance at the end of month 7 is 889.75
Balance at the end of month 8 is 1049.13
Balance at the end of month 9 is 1218.08
Balance at the end of month 10 is 1397.16
Balance at the end of month 11 is 1586.99
Balance at the end of month 12 is 1788.21
```

```
Press <Enter> to continue

Monthly deposit of $150.00
Balance at the end of month 1 is 159.00
Balance at the end of month 2 is 327.54
Balance at the end of month 3 is 506.19
Balance at the end of month 4 is 695.56
Balance at the end of month 5 is 896.30
Balance at the end of month 6 is 1109.08
Balance at the end of month 7 is 1334.62
Balance at the end of month 8 is 1573.70
Balance at the end of month 9 is 1827.12
Balance at the end of month 10 is 2095.75
Balance at the end of month 11 is 2380.49
Balance at the end of month 12 is 2682.32
Press <Enter> to continue

Monthly deposit of $200.00

Balance at the end of month 1 is 212.00
Balance at the end of month 2 is 436.72
Balance at the end of month 3 is 674.92
Balance at the end of month 4 is 927.42
Balance at the end of month 5 is 1195.06
Balance at the end of month 6 is 1478.77
Balance at the end of month 7 is 1779.49
Balance at the end of month 8 is 2098.26
Balance at the end of month 9 is 2436.16
Balance at the end of month 10 is 2794.33
Balance at the end of month 11 is 3173.99
Balance at the end of month 12 is 3576.43
Press <Enter> to continue

Interest rate of 0.08

Monthly deposit of $100.00

Balance at the end of month 1 is 108.00
Balance at the end of month 2 is 224.64
Balance at the end of month 3 is 350.61
Balance at the end of month 4 is 486.66
Balance at the end of month 5 is 633.59
Balance at the end of month 6 is 792.28
Balance at the end of month 7 is 963.66
Balance at the end of month 8 is 1148.76
Balance at the end of month 9 is 1348.66
Balance at the end of month 10 is 1564.55
Balance at the end of month 11 is 1797.71
Balance at the end of month 12 is 2049.53
Press <Enter> to continue
```

```
Monthly deposit of $150.00

Balance at the end of month 1 is 162.00
Balance at the end of month 2 is 336.96
Balance at the end of month 3 is 525.92
Balance at the end of month 4 is 729.99
Balance at the end of month 5 is 950.39
Balance at the end of month 6 is 1188.42
Balance at the end of month 7 is 1445.49
Balance at the end of month 8 is 1723.13
Balance at the end of month 9 is 2022.98
Balance at the end of month 10 is 2346.82
Balance at the end of month 11 is 2696.57
Balance at the end of month 12 is 3074.29
Press <Enter> to continue

Monthly deposit of $200.00

Balance at the end of month 1 is 216.00
Balance at the end of month 2 is 449.28
Balance at the end of month 3 is 701.22
Balance at the end of month 4 is 973.32
Balance at the end of month 5 is 1267.19
Balance at the end of month 6 is 1584.56
Balance at the end of month 7 is 1927.33
Balance at the end of month 8 is 2297.51
Balance at the end of month 9 is 2697.31
Balance at the end of month 10 is 3129.10
Balance at the end of month 11 is 3595.43
Balance at the end of month 12 is 4099.06
Press <Enter> to continue
```

✳ **DISCUSSION:** It makes sense that the inner loop must control the months, but you could choose either the deposits or the interest rate for the outer loop. Because we're building on the previous exercise, it's easier to make the interest rate the outer loop. This is a small program, but it generates quite a lot of output, illustrating the power of loops.

Exercise 5D: Reformat savings account output.

✳ **DO:** You can dramatically reduce the amount of output from Exercise 5C by displaying several monthly balances on one line instead of devoting a separate line to each one. Modify formatting of the *printf()* statements to make the display output more compact.

✳ **SOLUTION FILE:** EX07-5D.C

✳ **RESULT:**

```
Deposit: $100.00, Interest rate: 0.04
   1:  104.00  2:  212.16  3:  324.65  4:  441.63  5:  563.30  6:  689.83
   7:  821.42  8:  958.28  9: 1100.61 10: 1248.64 11: 1402.58 12: 1562.68

Deposit: $150.00, Interest rate: 0.04
   1:  156.00  2:  318.24  3:  486.97  4:  662.45  5:  844.95  6: 1034.74
   7: 1232.13  8: 1437.42  9: 1650.92 10: 1872.95 11: 2103.87 12: 2344.03

Deposit: $200.00, Interest rate: 0.04
   1:  208.00  2:  424.32  3:  649.29  4:  883.26  5: 1126.60  6: 1379.66
   7: 1642.85  8: 1916.56  9: 2201.22 10: 2497.27 11: 2805.16 12: 3125.37
Press <Enter> to continue

Deposit: $100.00, Interest rate: 0.06
   1:  106.00  2:  218.36  3:  337.46  4:  463.71  5:  597.53  6:  739.38
   7:  889.75  8: 1049.13  9: 1218.08 10: 1397.16 11: 1586.99 12: 1788.21

Deposit: $150.00, Interest rate: 0.06
   1:  159.00  2:  327.54  3:  506.19  4:  695.56  5:  896.30  6: 1109.08
   7: 1334.62  8: 1573.70  9: 1827.12 10: 2095.75 11: 2380.49 12: 2682.32

Deposit: $200.00, Interest rate: 0.06
   1:  212.00  2:  436.72  3:  674.92  4:  927.42  5: 1195.06  6: 1478.77
   7: 1779.49  8: 2098.26  9: 2436.16 10: 2794.33 11: 3173.99 12: 3576.43
Press <Enter> to continue

Deposit: $100.00, Interest rate: 0.08
   1:  108.00  2:  224.64  3:  350.61  4:  486.66  5:  633.59  6:  792.28
   7:  963.66  8: 1148.76  9: 1348.66 10: 1564.55 11: 1797.71 12: 2049.53

Deposit: $150.00, Interest rate: 0.08
   1:  162.00  2:  336.96  3:  525.92  4:  729.99  5:  950.39  6: 1188.42
   7: 1445.49  8: 1723.13  9: 2022.98 10: 2346.82 11: 2696.57 12: 3074.29

Deposit: $200.00, Interest rate: 0.08
   1:  216.00  2:  449.28  3:  701.22  4:  973.32  5: 1267.19  6: 1584.56
   7: 1927.33  8: 2297.51  9: 2697.31 10: 3129.10 11: 3595.43 12: 4099.06
Press <Enter> to continue
```

✳ **DISCUSSION:** You can reformat the data in any number of ways—the solution file shows just one way. This solution combines and relocates the *printf()* statements for the deposits and interest rates. Notice the use of the modulus operator (%) to determine when to issue a newline (at the first and sixth months).

SUMMARY

This chapter concludes your lessons on control statements. In summary: use *while* and *do while* when you need to create a loop that repeats indefinitely or when exit conditions are not based on simple index values. The *while* statement tests the exit condition at the beginning of each loop cycle, whereas the *do while* statement tests at the end and executes at least one time. Use *for* to create a loop that repeats a fixed number of times or to create a loop controlled by index values. You can end a loop with a *break* statement, and you can skip to the next cycle of a loop with a *continue* statement.

Average time to complete this chapter (including lab and quiz) is 12 hours.

FUNCTIONS

t this point you have enough C under your belt to begin writing more complex programs. Functions allow you to do this without becoming overwhelmed by complexity. You will begin this chapter by reading an explanation of the advantages of using functions. Then you will learn how to write functions, how to call and pass data values to functions, and how to return data values from functions. You will also learn methods for writing functions that allow the compiler to help you minimize errors. Following that, you'll see some techniques for designing programs with functions; finally, you will see how to place functions in a library and access them from different files and programs.

LECTURE

A function is an entity that performs a task or returns one or more values. When you think about what goes into a C program, you should think in terms of functions—the step-by-step process of writing a C program amounts to writing functions. Whether you realize it or not, you have been writing functions, because each program titled *main()* is a function. You have also been calling functions, because I/O operations like *printf()* and *scanf()* are functions linked from the Turbo C++ library.

Reasons for Using Functions

The advantages of encapsulating the basic operations of a program into functions are many:

- Functions are reusable. You can write a function once and use it as many times as necessary without having to rewrite the same source code.

- Programs become smaller with functions. You eliminate lines of code by calling functions instead of replicating source lines.

- Programs are easier to write when segmented into functions. With functions, you can organize programs into manageable sections.

- Functions are easier to read than one big program. Functions provide a logical structure, suggesting natural divisions for improved commenting and readability. Well-chosen function names are important for describing which processes are occurring.

- Programs are easier to maintain with functions. You will find it easier to understand and modify smaller entities.

Functions have only one significant disadvantage: program execution is sometimes slower. Calling a function takes some additional time that would not be necessary if the code were *inline* with the program, that is, repeated wherever needed. Most programs are not noticeably slower than they would be without functions. But occasionally a program calls a function a great many times (perhaps within a loop), and the associated overhead can make an important difference in the execution time. Normally, however, the advantages of using functions far outweigh the disadvantages and you will want to use them liberally.

Defining a Function

When you write the source code for a function, you have *defined* it. The compiler allocates memory for variables and executable statements found in function definitions; it also translates the statements into code that is suitable for execution and arranges links for entry to and exit from the function. The basic form of a function definition is:

```
type name( parameter list )
{
    statements
}
```

Figure 8-1 labels the parts of a function.

The work of a function is accomplished by the statements in the body; the name is used to call, or execute, the function; the parameter list provides for receiving data values from a calling function; and the type designates the data type that the function can return as a value.

Function Body

The body of a function consists of a compound statement that includes the two braces and enclosed statements. Variables defined in the body of a function are limited in scope to the function—the program creates them on entry and destroys them upon leaving the function. Normally, you should left-justify the braces and indent the statements by one level (four spaces). Here is a function where the body displays the name of the function:

```
void message( void )
{
    printf( "This is a function named message." );
}
```

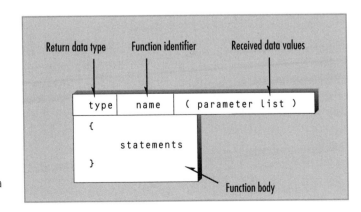

FIGURE 8-1   Parts of a function

Function Name

A function name is a normal C identifier (a series of letters, digits, and underscores beginning with a letter). The maximum length of a function name is 31 characters; you can use more, but an ANSI compiler will ignore characters beyond the 31st. You should avoid beginning a function name with an underscore (_) because this is often used for functions in the system libraries. The name serves as the means for calling the function and for returning a value when the function ends. Here are some examples of both legal and illegal function names:

```
doubleTheArea       /* OK */
areaX2              /* OK */
display_sales       /* OK */
displaySalesData    /* OK */
displaySalesDataFromRegionalOffice1
                    /* OK, but the compiler will recognize only
                       the first 31 characters, or
                       displaySalesDataFromRegionalOff. Beware!
                       Don't try to write another function named
                       displaySalesDataFromRegionalOffice2. */
_display     /* OK, but not recommended: The leading underscore
                usually signifies a system library function. */
function     /* OK, but not recommended: The name function is not
                very unique. */
max          /* OK, but not recommended: This is a common name
                that will likely be a duplicate of a library
                function and cause a link error. */
2xArea       /* ILLEGAL: Can't begin with a number */
double       /* ILLEGAL: double is a key word */
```

We will use the same naming convention for functions as for variables (an example is the first function name above, *doubleTheArea* (capitalize only the first letter of each word beyond the first). Other naming conventions have particular advantages. You are free to choose any convention that you prefer.

Function Return Type

A function can return a value to the function name; therefore, you need to declare a data type by preceding the function name with a type. You can use any of the C data types available for any other variable, including data types that you declare with *typedef*. If you omit the type, the compiler will assume a return type of *int*, but you should always explicitly declare a type. Type *void* signifies that the function has no return value. Here are some examples:

```
void displayData()    /* No return value */
int average()         /* Return an integer that is the average
                         calculated by the function. */
average()             /* No return type specified, so it is int
```

```
                               by default */
    typedef unsigned char BYTE;
    BYTE search()           /* Return the results of a search as the
                               value of an unsigned char. */
```

Function Parameter List

A parameter list provides for receiving values of variables from a calling function. The parameter list is optional (you don't have to receive any parameters), but the parentheses are necessary in any case. If there are no parameters, you can leave the parentheses empty, but this is the pre-ANSI style and it is better to insert the key word *void* to signify the absence of parameters. Here is a function definition that accepts no parameters.

```
    int nothing( void )
    {
    }
```

A parameter list, when it exists, includes variables (types and names) separated by commas. Here is a function that receives an integer, a character, and a floating-point number:

```
    void something( int anIndex, char aLetter, float aValue )
    {
    }
```

This is the form of an ANSI function parameter list.

OLD-STYLE FUNCTION DEFINITIONS

The older, Common C form (called the "old style") of function definition looks like this:

```
    void something( anIndex, aLetter, aValue )
    int    anIndex;
    char   aLetter;
    float  aValue;
    {
    }
```

The old style of function definition gives a list of variable names inside the parentheses, then declares the data types just before the opening brace. The old style is still recognized by ANSI compilers for the sake of compatibility with old programs, but you should always use the new ANSI style.

Calling a Function

Functions cause other functions to execute by *calling* them. C programs are made up of functions that execute in an order that you determine by placing function calls within other functions. A function call is simply the function name attached to parentheses containing arguments (arguments in a function call correspond to parameters in the function definition). Suppose you write a function that averages three integer weights:

```
int average( int weight1, int weight2, int weight3 )
{
    /* Statements to calculate and return the average */
}
```

Here is a call to that function from a *main()* program:

```
void main()
{
    average( 13, 456, 82 );
}
```

The ending semicolon is not part of the call; it is only necessary to make this a valid C statement. This particular call ignores the returned average. To make use of the return value, you can use the name of a function much like the name of any other variable (although you cannot assign a value to a function name). For instance, you can assign the result of the average to another variable:

```
aveWeight = average( 13, 456, 82 );
```

or you can insert it into an expression:

```
if ( 16 * ( average( 13, 456, 82 ) + 500 ) > weightLimit )
```

When the program evaluates this expression, it calls function *average()* in order to obtain the return value to use as an operand for the + operator.

If you want to calculate an average then display the result, you could do it with two function calls. Figure 8-2 illustrates the sequence of events involved in calling the two functions from the following program:

```
void main()
{
    int aveWeight;

    aveWeight = average( 13, 456, 82 );
    printf( "Average weight = %d", aveWeight );
}
```

After calling a function, a program does not continue processing statements until the function completes its task and returns. You could also display the average value in one statement like this:

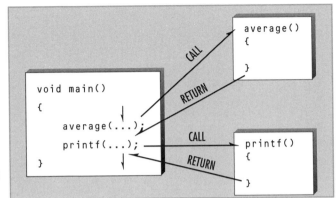

FIGURE 8-2 Calling and
returning from functions

```
printf( "Average weight = %d", average( 13, 456, 82 ) );
```

Here you are using the return value of one function as one of the arguments to another function, *printf()*. Figure 8-3 shows the sequence of events associated with the above statement. In order to pass argument values to *printf()*, the program must first call *average()*.

The *return* Statement

A function returns when it encounters the closing brace of the body or when it executes a *return* statement. You can use *return* statements to end a function for any number of reasons. Perhaps there are alternate processing paths, each with a separate ending, or perhaps you need to end prematurely because of an error. In this example, the *average* function returns if any of the parameters is zero:

```
int average( int weight1, int weight2, int weight3 )
{
    if ( ( weight1 == 0 ) || ( weight2 == 0 ) || ( weight3 == 0 ) )
    {
        return(0);
    }
    /* Statements to calculate and return the average */
}
```

If none of the parameters received by the function is zero, the return will occur at the last closing brace of the body.

Returning a Value from a Function

The *return* key word also allows you to pass a value back to the calling function. You can use either of two forms:

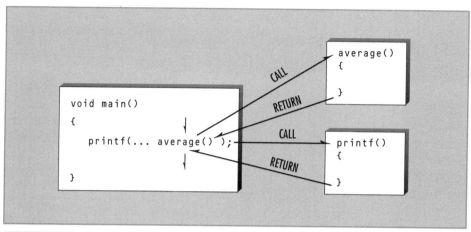

FIGURE 8-3   A nested function call

```
    return( expression );
```
or
```
    return expression;
```

The first form is preferable because the parentheses make it easier to read—they connect the expression with the *return* key word. The effect of either of these statements is to cause the program to evaluate the expression and assign the result to the name of the function. Let's complete function *average* by filling in a statement to calculate and return the average weight:

```
int average( int weight1, int weight2, int weight3 )
{
    if ( ( weight1 == 0 ) || ( weight2 == 0 ) || ( weight3 == 0 ) )
    {
        return( 0 );
    }
    return( ( weight1 + weight2 + weight3 ) / 3 );
}
```

Notice that the first *return* also needs a value—we have chosen to return zero for an error. The value of the *return* expression should be the same type as the function return type. If not, the compiler will convert the expression value by promotion or demotion, whichever is necessary to match the declared function type. If the types don't match, the compiler may also issue a warning—you can avoid such warnings by explicitly converting return values with the cast operator.

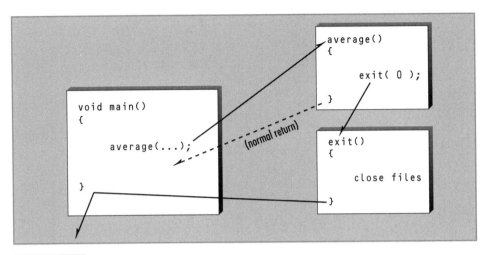

FIGURE 8-4   The *exit( )* function

Exiting and Returning from *main()*

You can use a return statement to pass an integer value from the *main()* function to the operating system (or whatever program called *main())*. Usually a zero (0) return value from *main()* signals normal completion and nonzero (or 1) signals an error. To return one of these values, you need to declare *main ()* to be type *int;* if there is no exit value, you should declare *main ()* to be type *void.*

There is a system library function called *exit()* that performs a similar role to *return*. The *exit()* function has one integer argument that also signals success (0) or failure (1) to the caller of *main()*. Calling *exit()* from any function causes the main program to cease execution; thus you can make the program end from any function, not just *main()*. A call to *exit()* also has the effect of closing any open files. A *return* from *main()* is the same as calling *exit()*. Figure 8-4 illustrates what happens when you call *exit()* from a function.

Passing Values to a Function

You've already learned the basics about how to pass values to a function, but now let's fill in the details. Figure 8-5 shows the correspondence between arguments from a function call and parameters received by a function.

The terms *argument* (sometimes called *actual argument*) and *parameter* (also known as *formal argument*) refer to the same values in different places—arguments in a function call become parameters received by the function. C passes arguments *by value,* which means that the program makes

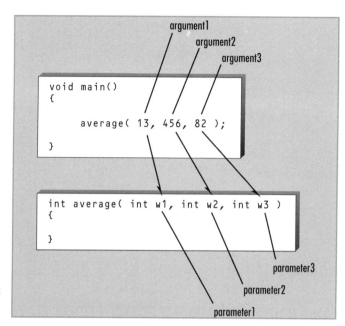

FIGURE 8-5 Arguments
and parameters

a copy of the value before passing it to the function. Thus, a function does not have direct access to the original values in the calling function. This is in contrast to calling *by reference* in other languages like FORTRAN and C++, where a function can alter the original value of an argument. The only way a C function can change the values of variables in other functions is via *pointer* arguments— pointers are the topic of Chapter 11, so we will not discuss this mechanism here. Arguments can be constants, variables, or expressions, but parameters must be variables because they have to receive a single value passed from the caller. The arguments in a call must agree, both in number and type, with the parameters of a function. If they do not, serious errors can occur. The section below titled "Declaring a Function" discusses methods for assuring that arguments and parameters match.

The names of parameters don't have to be the same as the corresponding arguments. But as a matter of convenience, we recommend that you make them the same. It is easier to keep track of variables in different functions if corresponding values have the same name. You can give separate items the same name if they have different scopes—automatic variables in separate functions satisfy this requirement. Thus, you can define arguments in one function (like in *main()* below) with the same names as parameters in a called function (like in *average()* below).

```
void main()
{
    int weight1, weight2, weight3;
```

```
      /* The scope of arguments weight1, weight2, weight3
         is limited to the body of main(), here
         between the braces of the main program. */

      average( weight1, weight2, weight3 );
   }
   int average( int weight1, int weight2, int weight3 )
   {
      /* The scope of parameters weight1, weight2, weight3
         is limited to the body of average(), here
         between the braces of the function. */
   }
```

Even though the two sets of variables have the same names and values, they are different because they are defined in separate functions. If you change the values of the parameters in *average()*, you do not affect the values of the arguments in *main()*.

A program has a very precise way of passing arguments to a function that involves sequential memory locations called a *stack*. When a function call occurs, the program evaluates the arguments and places the results on a call stack in sequential order along with a number that tells how many arguments exist. The function can then retrieve the correct number of values (copies) in the correct order. Figure 8-6 illustrates how a stack serves as an intermediary between a caller and a function.

In addition to the argument values, the program places the location of the calling statement on the stack so that it can remember where to resume processing when the function ends.

PARAMETER STACK VARIATIONS

The normal C ordering for arguments is to put the values on the stack from right to left so that the last (rightmost) argument is on the bottom and the first (leftmost) is on the top. This facilitates functions with a variable number of arguments, which C allows. If you add an ellipsis (...) to the end of the parameter list in the function definition, you can pass a variable number of extra arguments. However you must keep careful track of the order and data types because the compiler cannot make any checks.

Most compilers (including Turbo C++) provide an option to specify the PASCAL calling convention, which reverses the order of values on the stack, but does not allow a variable number of arguments. A PASCAL call is usually faster than the normal C call.

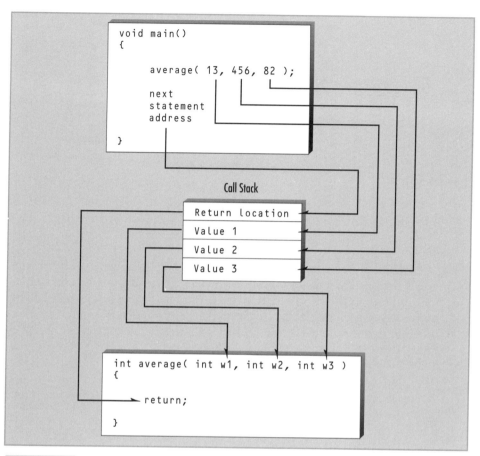

FIGURE 8-6   Passing values to a function

Recursion

C functions have the interesting ability to call themselves—this is called *recursion*. You will probably not often use recursion, but it is a very powerful technique for solving certain problems. You implement recursion by inserting a call to a function inside its own definition:

```
void repeat( void )
{
    repeat();
}
```

This function will call itself over and over again and it will not stop until your computer runs out of memory (each call uses memory storage for the parameter stack). The trick to recursion is in getting it to stop. None of the call instances in the above function ever reaches the closing brace. You can remedy this by adding a conditional statement (such as an *if*) to force the function to return eventually:

```
void repeat( void )
{
    if ( done )
    {
        return;
    }
    repeat();
}
```

When one call instance returns, it can trigger a return of all previous instances. Thus, the call process unwinds back to the initial call from the main program.

A practical example of recursion is a function that calculates the square root of a number to a certain accuracy. The algorithm for computing square root is given in Figure 8-7.

This procedure makes an initial rough guess at the answer, then refines the result through successive approximation until the result is within the requested accuracy. Successive approximation uses an equation that guarantees that you get closer to the correct answer after each calculation. You can implement the successive approximation procedure shown in Figure 8-7 as a loop, but you can also implement it as a recursive function. In Figure 8-7, if the amount of error is unacceptable, the process starts again by adjusting the number and recalculating the error. You can start the process over again by jumping to the start with a loop, or you can start it over by calling the same function again (which is recursion). You will develop a recursive version of this program in the lab exercises.

Declaring a Function

We need to make a clear distinction between a function *definition* and a function *declaration*. The definition (explained above) is the working function itself; whereas the declaration does not allocate memory or do anything—it just describes qualities of the function. The ANSI specification for C introduced the mechanism of a *prototype* for declaring a function. A prototype contains all the same information as the first line of a function definition: the return type, the name, and the parameter list. But the prototype does not need to have identifiers for the parameters, and it ends with a semicolon. You can include parameter identifiers if you wish, but the compiler will ignore them. It is generally a good idea to insert identifiers for the parameters because they enhance the readability of the prototype. Below is a prototype for the average function:

```
int average( int value1, int value2, int value3 );
```

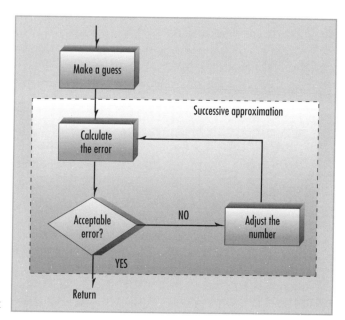

FIGURE 8-7 Algorithm for computing square root

Over time, one of the major causes of errors in C programs has been mismatched data types between function definitions and function calls. The sole purpose of a prototype is to allow the compiler to check for consistency of data types and the number of arguments between function calls and function definitions. In this instance, the compiler will generate a warning if the definition or a call has anything but *int* data types for arguments, parameters, or return values. It will also alert you if the number of arguments in a function call or definition does not match the number of parameters in the prototype. You place a prototype near the top of a program, before the function definition or any calls. This way, each time the compiler encounters a reference to the function it can verify that the return data type and argument or parameter data types are correct.

Functions in Separate Files

With larger programs it is often more efficient to organize functions into different files. This reduces the bulk of material for editing and makes compiling more efficient. You can often group functions according to application (I/O, math calculations, conversions, etc.) and deal with only one file at a time. You can also collect prototypes for functions into one or more *header* files. Then you can insert the prototypes into any of the source files with a single preprocessor *#include* directive. Figure 8-8 illustrates this process.

For example, you could put the prototype for *average* in a file named MYPROTOS.H along with prototypes for other functions, then include MYPROTOS.H in each source file with the single directive:

```
#include <myprotos.h>
```

This has the effect of inserting all the prototypes into each source file. The first line of most of the exercise programs in previous chapters has been:

```
#include <stdio.h>
```

This directive inserts the contents of header file STDIO.H at the beginning of the program. This header file, which comes with the compiler, contains prototypes for the standard I/O functions, such as *printf()* and *getchar()*. If you open this file with the TC editor and browse through it (it's in directory \TCLITE\INCLUDE), you will see a rich variety of prototypes for I/O functions in the system libraries. You probably won't recognize most of them, but you will learn more I/O functions in Chapter 12.

If you declare a function to be static (with key word *static)*, you limit its scope to the file where the function is defined. That is, a static function is not recognized outside of its file and you can call it only from other functions in the same file. This is useful for hiding or restricting access to certain kinds of processing. If a function has a purpose that is meaningful only in the context of functions of a single file, or if you want to limit access to a function, you would declare it to be *static*. Here is an example of a *static* function intended to decode some encrypted data:

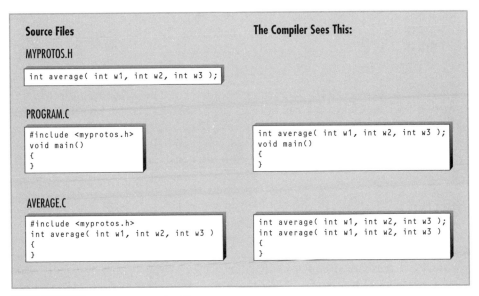

FIGURE 8-8   Including a header file

```
static int decode( void *pData );    /* Function prototype */

static int decode( void *pData )     /* Function definition */
{
    /* Body of decoding statements */
}
```

The static designation limits interaction with this specialized function to other functions in the same file so that widespread access is not possible.

Libraries

An object library is a collection of compiled object files. You can link a single library with a program instead of specifying all the individual object files that it holds. The following paragraphs explain how you can link with the Turbo C++ system libraries and discuss designing personal libraries of your own.

System Libraries

Compiler systems (Turbo C++ included) supply precompiled libraries of functions. The I/O functions in system libraries are particularly important because all I/O in C occurs via functions. In directory \TCLITE\LIB, there are four library files: MATHS.LIB, GRAPHICS.LIB, EMU.LIB, and CS.LIB. When you *Make* or *Link* a program, Turbo C++ links your object files with one or all of these libraries to form the executable file. Directory \TCLITE\INCLUDE has header files that contain prototypes for all of the functions in the system libraries. Most linkers know where to find these libraries by referring to environment variables. You can set the LIB environment variable by inserting the following line in your AUTOEXEC.BAT file:

```
LIB = C:\TCLITE\LIB
```

Or you can accomplish the same thing within the IDE by selecting *Directories...* from the *Options* menu and typing C:\TCLITE\LIB in the *Library Directories* dialog box. When you use any of these system library functions, you must include the appropriate header files in your function (you can look up a system function in the *Help* menu and it will tell you which header file contains the prototype for that function).

Personal Libraries

You can also build personal libraries of object files compiled from functions that you write. Typically, you will place functions into a library if you use them repeatedly, if they are utility functions, or if they share a common application (such as graphics). Once you have written and tested such functions, you can get them out of the way by placing them in a library to make the rest of the development process more efficient. Many PC compiler systems have an executable program called *LIB.EXE* that you can use to insert object modules into a single file with the extension *.LIB*. The Turbo C++ project file serves much the same purpose; it does not create a separate library file, but you enter names of functions that are needed for a program into a *.PRJ* file and the system will automatically link the specified object modules.

Designing a Program with Functions

Before you write a program you should develop a clear design that describes both the purpose and the operation of the program. You might do this with any combination of the following methods:

- Make a flow diagram of the process
- Lay out file structures and other data requirements
- Formulate equations
- Describe operator interaction
- Determine peripheral device actions
- Draw a timing diagram

Using any of these devices (or others), you can break the problem down into logical components, then identify functions that apply to these components. Here are some criteria for identifying functions:

- Use a function for any operation that is needed in more than one place in a program, or when the operation is common to more than one program. For example, if you read or display the same data in more than one place, make that operation a function. Or if you repeatedly make a calculation that uses different data, write a function for that.

- Any calculation or process that returns a single value is a candidate for a function. For example, if you need the area of a plot of land calculated from the perimeter values, return it from a function. Or if you need the average of a group of numbers, write a function for it.

- If an operation can be described as a distinct task, it should be a function. For example, if you need to display a list of items on the screen it would make sense to put this in a function (even if you call it only once). Or if you want to search a list of names to extract social security numbers, you could accomplish this with a function.

Let's go through the process of designing a program. Suppose you are wrestling with a decision whether or not to refinance a home loan. A program that makes financial calculations might help. To design such a program, you need to decide which calculations are important and how you will make use of the results. You might rely on the first three of the above methods to design this program (flow diagram, data requirements, and equations). First, state the criteria for a refinance decision—you might base the decision on any of these four factors:

1. Amount of monthly payment for a new loan versus your current loan
2. Total cost of your current loan versus a new one for the time period you hold the loan
3. Net cost difference between the loans, taking into account accumulated equity
4. Time required to break even for a new loan

You want to interact with the program by entering data for the current loan and a new loan, and then by selecting one or more of the four decision criteria. Basic financial equations for these criteria are:
Monthly payment for a loan of m months at interest rate r:

```
payment = (principal * r) / ( 1 - ( 1/(1+r) ) pow m )
(pow m means raise the preceding quantity to the power m)
```

Total cost of loan for m months:

```
totalCost = payment * m
```

Net cost of loan for m months:

```
netCost = totalCost - equity
```

You accumulate the equity month by month by subtracting interest paid from the payment:

```
equity(m) += payment - ( principal - equity(m-1) ) * r
```

Notice that the equity for each month is dependent on the equity for the previous month (*equity(m-1)*—this calculation will require a loop. Break-even occurs when the difference between the net costs of the two loans equals the total fees for the new loan:

```
netCost1 - netCost2 = fees
```

For data requirements, you might establish that all data be entered from the keyboard and reported to the screen, and that the program be able to calculate the above factors for different interest rates, loan periods, loan fees, and principal amounts.

Figure 8-9 shows a flow diagram that integrates the above factors and requirements.

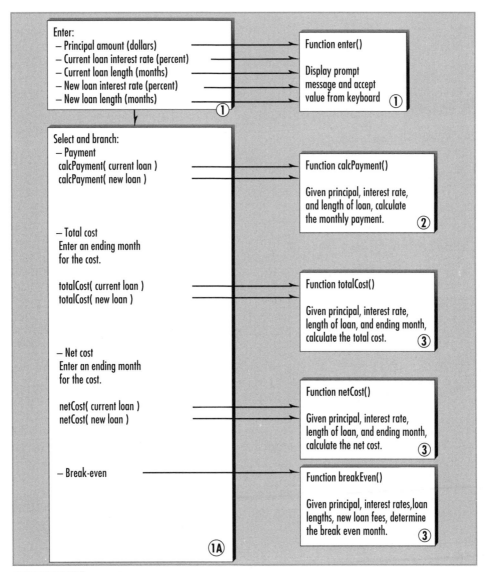

FIGURE 8-9   Flow diagram for home loan decision

Armed with this design information, you should be able to develop the program. In the lab section, you will do just that.

LAB

EXERCISE 1A: Develop new keyboard and screen I/O function.

✳ STARTER FILE: EX08-1A.C

```
#include <stdio.h>
double enter( char * );

void main()
{
    enter( "Here is a message string" );
}

double enter( char *message )
{
    printf( "%s\n", message );

    /* Enter new statements here */

    return( 0 );
}
```

✳ **DO:** In previous exercises, whenever you needed something from the keyboard, you had to write two I/O statements to prompt and get the value. You can do this with one function call instead. Write a utility function called *enter()* to both prompt for and accept a value from the keyboard. Pass a prompt message to the function as a character pointer and return the entered value as type *double*. We won't cover the topics of character strings and pointers until Chapters 10 and 11, so the starter file shows how to pass a character string to a function.

Write a main program that calls function *enter()* to get the following information from the keyboard:

1. Principal loan amount (dollars)

2. Interest rate of the current loan (percent)

3. Length of the current loan (months)

4. Interest rate of a new loan (percent)

5. Length of a new loan (months)

Insert a temporary *printf()* statement at the end of the main program to display the entered values. Run the program and type the values shown below in response to the prompts.

✳ SOLUTION FILE: EX08-1B.C

✳ RESULT:

```
Enter the principal loan amount: 100000
Enter the current loan rate (percent): 10.5
Enter the current loan period (months): 360
Enter the new loan interest rate (percent): 8
Enter the new loan period (months): 360
100000.00
10.50
360
8.00
360
```

✳ **DISCUSSION:** This *main()* program implements the boxes labelled (1) in Figure 8-9. Even though the *enter()* utility returns a floating-point data type, you can use it to get integer values (use *cast*).

EXERCISE 1B: Program a numbered selection menu.

✳ **DO:** Delete the temporary *printf()* display statement from your program from Exercise 1A. Add a prompt to the *main()* program to get a value from the keyboard that will select one of four criteria for making a loan decision: payment, total cost, net cost, or break-even (see box 1A in Figure 8-9). Add a branching statement that displays which selection was typed. Repeat the selection process until you type some value that ends the loop. Run the program and type each possible selection.

✳ SOLUTION FILE: EX08-1C.C

✳ RESULT:

```
Enter the principal loan amount: 100000
Enter the current loan rate (percent): 10.5
Enter the current loan period (months): 360
Enter the new loan interest rate (percent): 8
Enter the new loan period (months): 360

0. Quit
1. Payment
2. Total cost
3. Net cost
4. Break-even

Select a number: 1
Payment
```

continued on next page

continued from previous page

```
0. Quit
1. Payment
2. Total cost
3. Net cost
4. Break-even

Select a number: 2
Total cost

0. Quit
1. Payment
2. Total cost
3. Net cost
4. Break-even

Select a number: 3
Net cost

0. Quit
1. Payment
2. Total cost
3. Net cost
4. Break-even

Select a number: 4
Break-even

0. Quit
1. Payment
2. Total cost
3. Net cost
4. Break-even

Select a number: 0
```

✳ **DISCUSSION:** You can use either an *if else* statement or a *switch* statement for branching—it's an open choice here. You can use any symbols you like for the selection value; we used numbers 1 through 4 (with 0 to end) as a matter of convenience. Also, any reasonable choice of words for the prompts is acceptable—your choices might be better than those above.

Exercise 2:   Develop a payment function.

✳ **DO:** Write the function shown in box (2) of Figure 8-9 to calculate and return the monthly payment for a loan. Name the function *calcPayment()*. The equation for calculating the monthly payment is listed at the end of the lecture section above. You will need to call library function *pow()* to raise quantity

(1/(1+r)) to the power *m*. The prototype for *pow()* is in header file MATH.H. The first argument is a value that is raised to the power of the second argument, and the function returns the answer as data type *double*. Add two calls to *calcPayment()* under the appropriate branch in the *main()* program (one call for the current loan and one for a new loan) and display the returned values. Run the program, enter the same data values as in Exercise 1A, then select the *payment* criterion from the menu.

✳ **SOLUTION FILE:** EX08-2.C

✳ **RESULT:**

```
Enter the principal loan amount: 100000
Enter the current loan rate (percent): 10.5
Enter the current loan period (months): 360
Enter the new loan interest rate (percent): 8
Enter the new loan period (months): 360

0. Quit
1. Payment
2. Total cost
3. Net cost
4. Break-even

Select a number: 1
currentPayment = $914.74
newPayment = $733.76

0. Quit
1. Payment
2. Total cost
3. Net cost
4. Break-even

Select a number: 0
```

✳ **DISCUSSION:** The solution file implements the body of function *calcPayment()* with one statement. Correct placement of parentheses is crucial in this case.

Exercise 3:   Program cost functions.

✳ **DO:** Write functions for the remaining three criteria (named *totalCost()*, *netCost()*, and *breakEven()*). These functions implement the boxes labelled (3) in Figure 8-9. Refer to the discussion under "Designing a Program with Functions" for details about how to write these functions.

Add two calls to *totalCost()* (one for the current loan and one for a new loan) in the appropriate branch of the *main()* program, and two other calls to *netCost()*. Display the returned values. Be sure to prompt for the ending month and pass this value to these two functions along with other needed values (principal, interest rate, and loan length).

In the *break-even* branch, prompt for the total fees required to start a new loan, then call the function *breakEven()* to calculate the break-even time and display the result. Run the program, enter the same data values as for Exercise 2, then select each of the criteria in turn.

✳ SOLUTION FILE: EX08-3.C

✳ RESULT:

```
Enter the principal loan amount: 100000
Enter the current loan rate (percent): 10.5
Enter the current loan period (months): 360
Enter the new loan interest rate (percent): 8
Enter the new loan period (months): 360

0. Quit
1. Payment
2. Total cost
3. Net cost
4. Break-even

Select a number: 1
currentPayment = $914.74
newPayment = $733.76

0. Quit
1. Payment
2. Total cost
3. Net cost
4. Break-even

Select a number: 2
Cost ending in what month: 180
Total cost of current loan = $164653.07
Total cost of new loan = $132077.62

0. Quit
1. Payment
2. Total cost
3. Net cost
4. Break-even

Select a number: 3
Cost ending in what month: 180
```

```
Net cost of current loan = $147405.03
Net cost of new loan = $108859.18

0. Quit
1. Payment
2. Total cost
3. Net cost
4. Break-even

Select a number: 4
Enter total fees for the new loan: 2000
You will break even in month 10

0. Quit
1. Payment
2. Total cost
3. Net cost
4. Break-even

Select a number: 0
```

✳ DISCUSSION: Congratulations! You have completed a complex program that can interactively provide information about a home loan decision. Notice that the calculations even work for loans of different periods (180 and 360 months).

Exercise 4A: Pass values via static variables.

✳ DO: Another way to communicate values between functions is via static variables. Eliminate the arguments from function *totalCost()* and replace them with static variables having a scope that includes the entire file. Review Chapter 3 if you need more information on static variables and scope. Run the program to verify that you made the right changes. Enter the same loan data as for Exercise 3 and select the total cost calculation from the menu.

✳ SOLUTION FILE: EX08-4A.C

✳ RESULT:

```
Enter the principal loan amount: 100000
Enter the current loan rate (percent): 10.5
Enter the current loan period (months): 360
Enter the new loan interest rate (percent): 8
Enter the new loan period (months): 360

0. Quit
1. Payment
2. Total cost
```

```
3. Net cost
4. Break-even

Select a number: 2
Cost ending in what month: 180
Total cost of current loan = $164653.07
Total cost of new loan = $132077.62

0. Quit
1. Payment
2. Total cost
3. Net cost
4. Break-even

Select a number: 0
```

✳ **DISCUSSION:** Generally it is advisable to pass values to functions via arguments. Arguments are attached directly to functions, whereas static variables tend to be hidden from sight, making program maintenance more difficult.

Exercise 4B: Return values via static variables.

✳ **DO:** Use the same method as in Exercise 4A to eliminate the return value for function *totalCost()*. In other words, declare *totalCost()* to be type *void*. Run the program and type the same values as for Exercise 4A.

✳ **SOLUTION FILE:** EX08-4B.C

✳ **RESULT:** Same as Exercise 4A.

✳ **DISCUSSION:** You should normally use a *return* statement to pass a value back from a function—it is more explicit than a static variable. You might consider static variables when you have more than one value to return. However, pointers and structures (Chapters 11 and 13) provide a better alternative for returning multiple values.

Exercise 5A: Separate source files.

✳ **DO:** Put the main program and function *enter()* in one file (EX08-5A.C), and put the four functions, *calcPayment()*, *totalCost()*, *netCost()*, and *breakEven()*, in another (EX08-5B.C). You can use the *Copy* and *Paste* operations on the *Edit* menu to do this easily. Be sure to copy prototypes into both files along with the function definitions. Hint: you will need some new statements in file EX08-5B.C in order to give the *totalCost()* function access to the static values it needs. Refer to Chapter 3 if you need information about accessing variables from separate files.

Create a project file (EX08-5.PRJ) by selecting the *Project* menu item, then add the two new files to the project and run the program. Repeat the keyboard input from Exercise 3 to check out the program.

✳ SOLUTION FILES: EX08-5A.C and EX08-5B.C

✳ RESULT: Same as Exercise 3.

✳ DISCUSSION: You need prototypes for all functions in the main program file so the compiler can check both the function calls and function definitions. But in file EX08-5B.C you only need the prototypes for functions defined there. Try leaving out one or more prototypes to see the compiler reaction.

Exercise 5B: Use a header file.

✳ DO: Create a new file named EX08-5.H and copy all the function prototypes into this header file from the two source files. Delete the prototypes from the source files, then insert the header in their place with a *#include* directive. You will need to use the *Options/Directories* menu to make sure the *#include* path refers to your current source directory (where EX08-5.H resides). You can add your directory after the \TCLITE\INCLUDE directory if you separate them with a semicolon. Run the program and check out its operation by repeating the keyboard input from Exercise 3.

✳ SOLUTION FILES: EX08-5.H, EX08-5C.C, and EX08-5D.C

✳ RESULT: Same as Exercise 3.

✳ DISCUSSION: It doesn't matter if a *#include* header file contains more prototypes than you call or define in a function. The compiler processes all the prototypes, but unused prototypes have no effect on your executable program.

Exercise 6A: Determine square root by recursion.

✳ DO: Write a recursive function named *squareRoot()* to calculate the square root of any number. Refer to Figure 8-10 for the algorithm. You will need a *main()* program that prompts for a number and the desired accuracy for the answer, makes an initial guess at the answer, then calls the recursive function. Test the program several times by entering the numbers under RESULT below.

SELECT A NUMBER AND ACCURACY

Enter any positive real number and the desired
accuracy of the square root answer.

MAKE AN INITIAL GUESS

Any number will do for an initial guess of the square root, but
a closer guess is better.

Here's one way of guessing: Repeatedly divide the original
number by 100 until you get a value, x, that is less than 100.
Count the number of times you divided and call this n. The
initial guess is (x / 2.5) * 10 exp n. (Divide x by 2.5, then n
times, multiply the result by 10).

Beginning with the initial guess as an approximation of the
square root, make the following calculations:

CALCULATE SQUARE ROOT BY SUCCESSIVE APPROXIMATION
(This is the recursive function)

A. Error=original number-approximation*approximation
B. If the absolute value of the error (ignore the sign) is less
   than the selected accuracy, then return the approximation
   as the correct answer.
C. Adjustment=original number / approximation
   New approximation = (adjustment + old approximation)
D. Repeat steps A-D (call the function).

FIGURE 8-10 Detailed
algorithm for computing
square root

✳ **SOLUTION FILE:** EX08-6A.C

✳ **RESULT:**

```
Enter a real number: 4
Enter desired accuracy of the square root: .1
Square root of 4 is 2.004558

Enter a real number: 1210000
Enter desired accuracy of the square root: .1
Square root of 1210000.000000 is 1100.000000

Enter a real number: .04
Enter desired accuracy of the square root: .0001
Square root of .040000 is .200014
```

✳ **DISCUSSION:** The function works for all except negative numbers. You can
choose any value at all for an initial guess—if it is closer to the final answer the
program will make fewer recursive calls.

Exercise 6B: Observe recursion.

✳ **DO:** Add a *printf()* statement at the beginning of the recursive function in order to display the value of the approximate square root answer, and another that displays the answer just before the *return* statement. Run the program and request the square root of 4 to an accuracy of .1.

✳ **SOLUTION FILE:** EX08-6B.C

✳ **RESULT:**

```
Enter a real number: 4
Enter desired accuracy of the square root: .1
Approximation = 0.800000
Approximation = 2.900000
Approximation = 2.139655
Approximation = 2.004558
Returning root = 2.004558
Returning root = 2.004558
Returning root = 2.004558
Returning root = 2.004558
Square root of 4.000000 is 2.004558
```

✳ **DISCUSSION:** From the output you can see that four recursive calls occur before the answer is within the required accuracy. Notice particularly that four calls take place before the first return occurs, and then all four returns happen in quick succession.

Exercise 6C: Use the *exit()* function.

✳ **DO:** Replace the *return* statement in the square root function with a call to *exit()*. To do this, you will have to declare *squareRoot()* to be type *void*. Run the program and request the square root of 4 to an accuracy of .1.

✳ **SOLUTION FILE:** EX08-6C.C

✳ **RESULT:**

```
Enter a real number: 4
Enter desired accuracy of the square root: .1
Approximation = 0.800000
Approximation = 2.900000
Approximation = 2.139655
Approximation = 2.004558
Returning root = 2.004558
```

✳ **DISCUSSION:** Now there is only one return from function *squareRoot()*. The program does not unwind in normal fashion; instead the call to *exit()* causes the program to end immediately.

SUMMARY

This chapter covers functions—a topic that is centrally important to writing C programs. If you didn't read the lecture thoroughly or didn't work through all the exercises, you should take the time to do so now. From this chapter you should acquire a good understanding of these techniques:

- How to use a program design to identify functions to be written
- How to define (or write) functions
- How to pass values to functions
- How to return values from functions
- How to use functions in separate files

9

Average time to complete this chapter (including lab and quiz) is 8 hours.

ARRAYS

omputers perform repetitive tasks well; they can easily handle large quantities of data. Up until now you have defined only small amounts of storage. If you need to define storage for the hundreds or thousands of characters and numbers that computers demand, how would you do it? By defining hundreds or thousands of individual variables? No, of course not. You can easily make storage for very large quantities of variables by defining *arrays*. This chapter covers the methods for defining arrays, for initializing values in arrays, and for accessing data in arrays. It also shows you how to store strings of character data in one-dimensional arrays, and it discusses storing data in multidimensional arrays.

LECTURE

An array is more than just a mass of memory space. It is a connected group of individual storage elements, all of the same data type. You specify the number of elements and the data type when you define an array.

Defining Arrays

A statement that defines an array is similar to the statements you previously used to define single variables. It consists of a data type followed by an identifier and one new syntax element: square brackets that enclose an integer constant to specify the size of the array:

```
type name[SIZE];
```

The following statement defines an array named *inventory* that has space for 100 integer values:

```
int inventory[100];
```

Each member of an array is called an *element* and each element has the same data type; thus *inventory* has 100 elements, each capable of storing a 2-byte integer. When the compiler allocates storage for an array, it places all the elements together in one contiguous block of memory. Figure 9-1 illustrates the array *inventory* in memory.

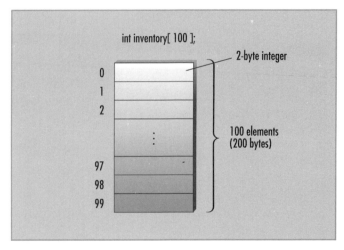

FIGURE 9-1   An array in memory

You can only use integers to specify the size of arrays; you can use any type of integer (*int*, *short*, *or long*), but it must be an integer. Arrays are made of discrete numbers of elements—you can never have a fraction of an element. Furthermore, you must use only integer constant expressions, not variables. A constant expression is a constant that is the result of operators with constant operands. For instance, both of these statements define arrays with 50 elements:

```
int inventory[ 50 ];
int inventory[ 20 + 30 ];
```

The latter form might be helpful when an array holds two kinds of items—it shows that the size is the sum of the two kinds. The best way to declare the size of an array is with symbolic constants or values declared with the *const* qualifier. Not only is a symbolic constant more descriptive, but it can be a great time saver during program maintenance. The following statements tell you that the size of the array is determined by the number of items in a store:

```
#define NUM_ITEMS 50
int inventory[ NUM_ITEMS ];
```

The symbolic constant can be used elsewhere in the program (perhaps to control a *for* loop to access all the elements in the array); you can universally change the number of items by modifying the one *#define* directive.

All the same rules and considerations for type, class, and scope that apply to other variables also apply to arrays. You can declare an array to be any standard data type or any type declared with *typedef.* You can declare an array to be *automatic* or *static,* and you can control the scope of an array by placing its declaration inside or outside a function definition.

Accessing Array Elements

You can do anything with an array element that you can do with a separate variable. You can assign values to array elements, and you can use array elements as individual variables. You refer to an array element by placing an integer *index* value between the square brackets. Here's how you would assign values to the first two elements of the *inventory* array and put their sum into the third element:

```
inventory[ 0 ] = 10;
inventory[ 1 ] = 5;
inventory[ 2 ] = inventory[ 0 ] + inventory[ 1 ];
```

After executing these statements, the value of *inventory[2]* would be 15. Notice that the index of 0 refers to the first element of the array. C uses *zero-based indexing* for arrays, so that 0 specifies the first element, 1 specifies the second element, and so on. Thus, if you define an array with a size of NUM_ITEMS, the index for the last element is NUM_ITEMS - 1.

You can use integer variables to access array elements. It is acceptable to use short, nondescriptive names for index variables because they are frequently used and generic in nature. The letter *i* is a favorite for this purpose:

```
#define NUM_ITEMS 100
int i = 2;
inventory[ NUM_ITEMS ];
inventory[ i ] = 6;
```

The above statements assign the value of 6 to the third element in *inventory*. Here is a *for* statement that sets all of the elements in the array to 6:

```
for ( i=0; i<NUM_ITEMS; ++i )
{
    inventory[ i ] = 6;
}
```

COMMON INDEXING ERRORS

You need to be aware of the hazard commonly known as *array overrun* or *blowing an index*. In C (as with many other programming languages) it is very easy to specify an index that is out of bounds (less than zero or greater than the size of the array minus one). Unfortunately, this is a frequent error, and it can cause horrible problems when it occurs. If you assign a value to an array element that is beyond the limits of the array, the program will obediently do so, but the assignment will destroy some other value or executable statement of the program. Few compilers (Turbo C++ included) automatically check for illegal index values because this is a complex task, although some offer an option to perform this service. So it is up to you to keep your indexes in bounds. This is not difficult; just think twice about the limits of an array any time you use an index value. Troublesome situations usually occur only when you calculate indexes, so you should take some extra time to analyze such calculations for potential limit violations.

Initializing Arrays

There are three ways of getting data into arrays:

1. by reading data from files,
2. by assignment, and
3. by initializing.

The first method is good for moving massive amounts of data into an array—file I/O will be covered in Chapter 12. The second method is appropriate for setting the values of small numbers of array elements, unless the values are all the same. The third method is useful for small to medium amounts of data.

Using the second method, you can set values in an array by assigning within a loop. For example, you can set all elements of a large array of floating-point numbers to zero as follows:

```
#define NUM_ELEMENTS 1000
float numbers[ NUM_ELEMENTS ];
for ( i=0; i<NUM_ELEMENTS; ++i )
{
    numbers[ i ] = 0.;
}
```

Another way to accomplish this is with the library function, *memset()*. This function fills an area of memory with a byte value. It has three arguments: a pointer to the beginning of memory, the number of bytes to fill, and the value to place in each byte. The name of an array is a pointer to the first element, so a call to *memset()* to set the entire array of *numbers* to zero would look like this:

```
memset( numbers, 0, sizeof( numbers ) );
```

Notice how you can obtain the number of bytes in an array with the *sizeof()* operator. The prototype for *memset()* is in header file MEM.H in directory \TCLITE\INCLUDE. This function is short and sweet; it is a compact statement that can fill large or small memory blocks, and it has been optimized to execute very fast. The header file MEM.H also contains the prototype for a companion function named *memcpy()* that efficiently copies bytes from one area of memory to another. The arguments are a pointer to the target memory, a pointer to the source data, and the number of bytes to copy. If *target* and *source* are names of arrays, the following statement will copy *size* bytes from the source array to the target array:

```
memcpy( target, source, size );
```

You can initialize an array at the same time you define it (the third method mentioned above) by assigning a list of values separated by commas and enclosed by braces:

```
type name[ size ] = { value1, value2, ... };
```

Each value must be a constant expression, that is, a constant or an expression using only constant operands. The number of initializer values must be less than or equal to the size of the array (the number of elements). If the number of initializers is less than the array size, the compiler will set the remaining, unspecified elements to zero. Here are three valid examples of array initialization:

CERTIFIED COURSE IN C

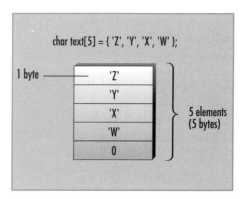

char text[5] = { 'Z', 'Y', 'X', 'W' };

1 byte —— 'Z'

'Y'

'X'   5 elements
       (5 bytes)
'W'

0

FIGURE 9-2 Array values for an incomplete initialization list

```
int digit[5] = { 1, 2, 3, 4, 5 };
float number[3] = { 9.8, 7.6, 5.4 };
char text[5] = { 'Z', 'Y', 'X', 'W' };   /* text[4] is 0 */
```

Figure 9-2 shows the initialized values in the third array.
Here are three illegal initializations that will cause compiler errors:

```
int digit[5] = 1, 2, 3, 4, 5;            /* Illegal! No braces */
float number[3] = { 9.8, digit[0] };  /* Illegal! The second
                                         initializer is not a constant. */
char text[5] = { 'a', 'b', 'c', 'd', 'e', 'f' };  /* Illegal! Too many
                                         initializer values */
```

Under the older, Common C standard you could not initialize automatic arrays (nonstatic arrays), but the ANSI standard allows you to initialize either static or automatic arrays. If you do not explicitly initialize an array, the compiler follows the normal rules for variables regarding default initialization: If the array is static, it is initialized to zero, otherwise no initialization occurs.

If you initialize an array, you can leave out the size specification and the compiler will infer the size from the length of the initializer list. This is a convenience allowed by both the older, Common C standard and the ANSI standard. The compiler will allocate four elements for the following array:

```
int array[] = { 99, 88, 77, 66 };
```

You can use an array to implement a look-up table for fetching predetermined information. Look-up tables have been used since the dawn of computing to convert reference values efficiently into some other form of information. If you have a list of values that correspond to other values, you have the makings of a look-up table. You are probably all too familiar with the IRS tax tables in the instructions for 1040 individual income tax forms. This is an example of a look-up table that converts your taxable income into an amount of tax due. Look-up tables are particularly good for values that cannot be calculated (like names derived from social security numbers). Or they can speed up processes that frequently need values that are hard to calculate—extracting a value from a table is faster than almost any calculation. It can take some effort to set up a look-up table, but once it is complete, it is a very efficient way to access data. Suppose you were writing a program that calculates transit time and customer charges based on distance for a delivery service. The company has repeat customers with ten heavily travelled delivery routes. You might want to incorporate a look-up table by initializing a floating-point array with those ten distances:

```
float distances[] = { 20.6,  4.3,  8.1, 15.7, 24.4,
                      72.0,  9.2, 18.7, 33.3, 12.8 };
```

If you assign codes of 0 through 9 to the routes, you can look up any of the frequently used distances. For example, the distance of route 6 is:

```
distances[ 6 ]
or 9.2 miles.
```

Character Strings in Arrays

Character strings are sequences of characters ending with a null character ('\0'). You can store a string in a character array, that is, an array of type *char*. To avoid confusion, let's make a clear distinction between character arrays and strings. A character array is a contiguous block of bytes of memory, and a string is a sequence of character values ending with a null. A string is data, not the storage for the data. A string can be stored in a character array, but a character array can hold data other than strings.

The length of a string is the number of characters up to, but not counting, the terminating null. Thus the maximum length string that an array of size NUM_ELEMENTS can hold is NUM_ELEMENTS - 1. You can initialize an array with a string in three ways. The first is to put the string values in an initializer list:

```
char quotation[] = { 'T', 'i', 'm', 'e', ' ', 'f', 'l', 'i', 'e', 's', '\0'
};
```

This defines an array with 11 elements, and fills it with the phrase "Time flies." Figure 9-3 shows the array after initialization.

The second way is to initialize with a different syntax:

```
char quotation[] = "Time flies";
```

This syntax was not available under the older, Common C, but it is allowed by ANSI C. A sequence of characters enclosed by double quotes is a *string constant*. This statement takes the sequence of characters from the string constant, including

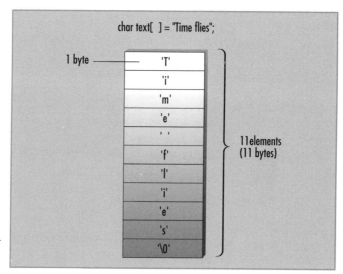

char text[ ] = "Time flies";

1 byte

'T'
'i'
'm'
'e'
' '
'f'
'l'
'i'
'e'
's'
'\0'

11 elements
(11 bytes)

FIGURE 9-3   A character
array with string data

a terminating null, and places them in the array elements. It accomplishes exactly the same thing as the first example, but it is certainly easier to write.

The third way is to copy a string with the library function *strcpy()*:

```
strcpy( quotation, "Time flies" );
```

This call copies the string given by the second argument into the array specified by the first argument. You must first define the array and be sure that it is large enough to hold the string. The prototype for *strcpy()* is in header file STRING.H found in directory \TCLITE\INCLUDE.

Accessing Array Data Between Functions

You will often use functions to process array data, so you will need to access arrays in other functions. The only way to do this is with pointers. Chapter 12 gives a full explanation of pointers, but we'll provide a brief introduction here that will give you an understanding of array access.

In C you do not directly pass array values between functions; instead you pass a pointer to the array that allows access to the original data. A pointer to an array is simply the name of the array; therefore you can use the name of an array as an argument. A receiving function gets a copy of the pointer value (the address of the array) in the matching parameter. It can then use the parameter name to refer to the original array elements. Let's look at an example. Below is a program that initializes an array with a string and calls a function that modifies an element of the array before displaying the string:

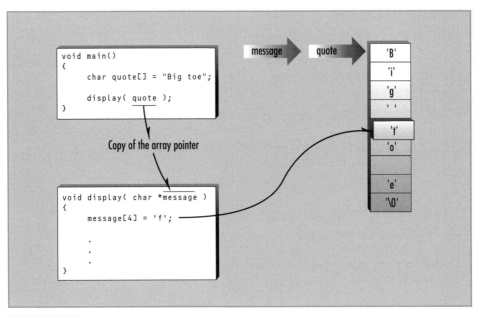

FIGURE 9-4   Array access via function arguments

```c
#include <stdio.h>

void share( char *message );    /* Function prototype */

void main()
{
    char quote[] = "Big toe";   /* Array definition and initialization */

    share( quote );             /* Function call */
}

void share( char *message )     /* Function definition */
{
    message[4] = 'f';
    printf( "%s\n", message );
}
```

Notice the parameter in both the prototype declaration and function definition for *share()*—the asterisk following data type *char* signifies that the parameter is a pointer to a character array. Therefore parameter *message* is the name of an array, and *printf()* uses the name to display the string data. Function *share()* also accesses the array to assign the letter *'f'* to the fifth element before displaying the result "Big foe." Figure 9-4 depicts the array access from function *share()*.

This program uses different names for the calling argument and the function parameter, but the values of these two items are both pointers to the same array.

Now let's access array data in the opposite direction, that is, have the main function use data defined in the called function. We'll do this by moving the array pointer from the parameter to the return value of function *share()*. We'll also switch roles so that function *share()* defines the array and function *main()* modifies and displays the string.

```c
#include <stdio.h>
char *share( void );            /*  Function prototype */
void main()
{
    char *quote;                /*  Pointer variable */

    quote = display();          /*  Function call with assignment of returned value */
    quote[4] = 'f';
    printf( "%s\n", quote );
}
char *share( void )             /*  Function definition */
{
    static char message[] = "Big toe";  /* Array definition and initialization */
    return( message );      /* Return of array pointer */
}
```

Figure 9-5 illustrates how the reverse access occurs.

Now function *share()* merely initializes the array and returns the pointer to the array. Notice that it declares *message* to be of the *static* storage class; otherwise the program would release storage for the array after the function returns and *main()* could not reliably access the data. The *main* program must define pointer variable *quote* to accept the returned pointer value, and it can then use this variable to access the array data.

Multidimensional Arrays

Up to this point, we have discussed one-dimensional arrays that require only one index to access any element. You can define two-, three-, and higher dimensional arrays in C. It is possible to store all the data you need in an array with one dimension, but a multidimensional array can fit the data organization more accurately and provide easier access.

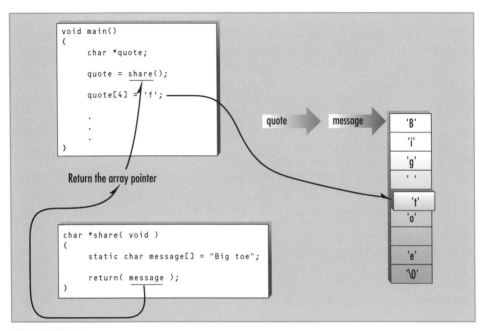

```
void main()
{
    char *quote;

    quote = share();

    quote[4] = 'f';
        .
        .
        .
}
```

Return the array pointer

```
char *share( void )
{
    static char message[] = "Big toe";

    return( message );
}
```

quote ⟹ message ⟹ 'B' 'i' 'g' ' ' 't' 'o' 'e' '\0'

FIGURE 9-5   Array access via function return value

Defining Multidimensional Arrays

The number of square brackets that you attach to an array definition determines the number of dimensions for the array. One pair of brackets specifies one dimension, two pair specifies two dimensions, and so on. At the beginning of this chapter we defined a one-dimensional array to hold in-stock quantities of inventory items:

```
#define NUM_ITEMS 100
int inventory[ NUM_ITEMS ];
```

You can add a second dimension to track inventories in several stores:

```
#define NUM_STORES 5
int inventory[ NUM_STORES ][ NUM_ITEMS ];
```

This array has 500 elements, 100 for each of 5 stores. The inventory quantity of the first item in the first store is:

```
inventory[ 0 ][ 0 ]
```

The quantity of the tenth item in the second store is:

```
inventory[ 1 ][ 9 ]
```

And the quantity of the last item in the fifth store is:

```
inventory[ 4 ][ 99 ]
```

Computer memory is one-dimensional in nature, so the compiler lays out a two-dimensional array in memory as a one-dimensional block of storage. Figure 9-6 shows the layout for the above inventory array.

The compiler places five 100-element sections end-to-end in memory. You could define a one-dimensional array of size 500 and the compiler would allocate the same memory layout.

```
int oneD[ 500 ];
```

However, you would have to access the data differently in your program because you would be limited to one index. You would have to compute an index with the following calculation:

```
index = store * 100 + item;
```

where *store* is the zero-based index of the store number and *item* is a zero-based index of the desired item. The index of the tenth item in the second store is:

```
index = 1 * 100 + 9;
```

The inventory for the tenth item in the second store in a one-dimensional array is:

```
oneD[ 109 ];
```

It is simpler to deal with two-dimensional data by defining a two-dimensional array. Your compiler handles all the details of computing the location of desired elements in the one-dimensional memory layout from any two indexes that you give it. The advantage of matching an array structure to data organization increases when you go to three or more dimensions. By declaring three dimensions, you can expand the inventory array to hold a reorder quantity for items (the minimum inventory level below which more items should be ordered) in addition to the current inventory quantity.

```
#define NUM_VALUES 2
int inventory[ NUM_STORES ][ NUM_ITEMS ][ NUM_VALUES ];
```

Now the array has 1000 elements (5 * 100 * 2), and it can store two values for each item in each store. The inventory quantity for the tenth item in the second store is:

```
inventory[ 1 ][ 9 ][ 0 ]
```

And the reorder quantity for the same item is:

```
inventory[ 1 ][ 9 ][ 1 ]
```

Figure 9-7 shows how this three-dimensional array is laid out in memory.

The C compiler will lay out elements for the first dimension (farthest from the array name) in memory, then it will repeat the layout a number of times equal to

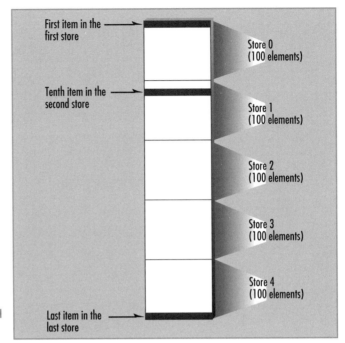

First item in the
first store

Store 0
(100 elements)

Tenth item in the
second store

Store 1
(100 elements)

Store 2
(100 elements)

Store 3
(100 elements)

Store 4
(100 elements)

Last item in the
last store

FIGURE 9-6 Memory
layout of a two-dimensional
array

the size of the second dimension, and then repeat that whole layout a number of times equal to the third dimension (closest to the array name). However, you will not normally be concerned about the internal memory layout of an array. Only if you use pointer arithmetic as discussed in Chapter 11 will the memory allocation order of multidimensional arrays become important.

Initializing Multidimensional Arrays

You can initialize a multidimensional array in the definition statement just as you would a one-dimensional array—assign a list of values separated by commas and enclosed by braces. You can initialize the first ten elements of a two-dimensional inventory array like this:

```
int inventory[ NUM_STORES ][ NUM_ITEMS ] =
    { 2, 4, 6, 8, 10, 12, 14, 16, 18, 20 };
```

An initialization list starts at the beginning of an array and assigns values to elements in sequential order until the list is exhausted. The above statement assigns values to the first ten items of the first store. The list is far short of the total number of elements, so the remaining 490 elements are initialized to 0 by default. You can use additional sets of braces to group the initializer values according to level in the array. If the list has fewer values than elements at any level, the

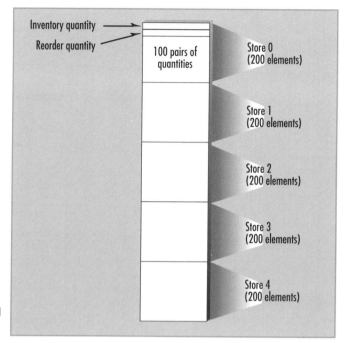

FIGURE 9-7   Memory layout of a three-dimensional array

remaining elements are initialized to zero. For example, you could force values into the first two items of each store with this initialization:

```
int inventory[ NUM_STORES ][ NUM_ITEMS ] =
    { { 2, 4 }, { 6, 8 }, { 10, 12 }, { 14, 16 }, { 18, 20 } };
```

All other array elements not specified in these initializer lists are set to 0 by default; thus the last 98 items of each store are initialized to 0. Figure 9-8 shows the values in memory.

You must separate initializer values with commas even when there is an intervening brace.

LAB

Exercise 1:   Define an array.

✳ **DO:** Define a floating-point array of size 5; read a price (dollars and cents) into each element of the array from the keyboard. Display the entire array after each input. Run the program and enter the values 3.33, 7.77, 1.11, 9.99, 5.55.

✳ SOLUTION FILE: EX09-1.C

✳ RESULT:

```
Enter a price: 3.33
Price 0 = $3.33
Price 1 = $0.00
Price 2 = $0.00
Price 3 = $58446449622150350700000000000000.00
Price 4 = $-0.00
Enter a price: 7.77
Price 0 = $3.33
```

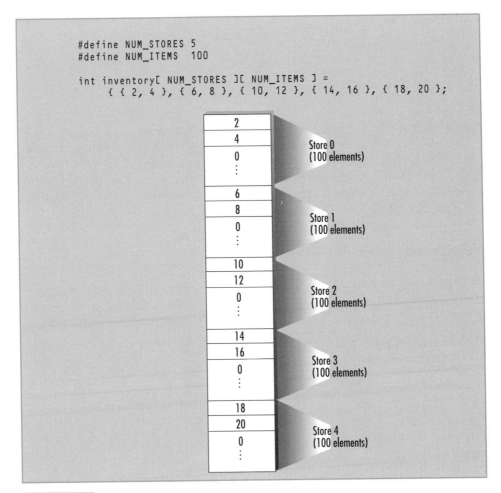

```
#define NUM_STORES 5
#define NUM_ITEMS  100

int inventory[ NUM_STORES ][ NUM_ITEMS ] =
    { { 2, 4 }, { 6, 8 }, { 10, 12 }, { 14, 16 }, { 18, 20 };
```

FIGURE 9-8   An initialized array

```
Price 1 = $7.77
Price 2 = $0.00
Price 3 = $58446449622150350700000000000000.00
Price 4 = $-0.00
Enter a price: 1.11
Price 0 = $3.33
Price 1 = $7.77
Price 2 = $1.11
Price 3 = $58446449622150350700000000000000.00
Price 4 = $-0.00
Enter a price: 9.99
Price 0 = $3.33
Price 1 = $7.77
Price 2 = $1.11
Price 3 = $9.99
Price 4 = $-0.00
Enter a price: 5.55
Price 0 = $3.33
Price 1 = $7.77
Price 2 = $1.11
Price 3 = $9.99
Price 4 = $5.55
```

✳ DISCUSSION: The program does not initialize the array, so each element will have an unpredictable value until you assign one of the input values. Because the initial values are random, your display will probably be different than the above RESULT except for the numbers that you enter. Curiously, Price 3 above is a very large number, but this can happen when a random floating-point number occurs.

Exercise 2A: Initialize an array.

✳ DO: In the array definition from Exercise 1, add initialization so that each element has a value equal to its index, that is, the first element is 0, the second element is 1, and so on. Run the program and repeat the input from Exercise 1.

✳ SOLUTION FILE: EX09-2A.C

✳ RESULT:

```
Enter a price: 3.33
Price 0 = $3.33
Price 1 = $1.00
Price 2 = $2.00
Price 3 = $3.00
Price 4 = $4.00
Enter a price: 7.77
Price 0 = $3.33
Price 1 = $7.77
```

```
Price 2 = $2.00
Price 3 = $3.00
Price 4 = $4.00
Enter a price: 1.11
Price 0 = $3.33
Price 1 = $7.77
Price 2 = $1.11
Price 3 = $3.00
Price 4 = $4.00
Enter a price: 9.99
Price 0 = $3.33
Price 1 = $7.77
Price 2 = $1.11
Price 3 = $9.99
Price 4 = $4.00
Enter a price: 5.55
Price 0 = $3.33
Price 1 = $7.77
Price 2 = $1.11
Price 3 = $9.99
Price 4 = $5.55
```

✳ **DISCUSSION:** The random numbers are gone because you have initialized the array.

Exercise 2B: Initialize with an assignment loop.

✳ **DO:** Remove the initialization from the array definition in Exercise 2A and set the same values into the array using assignments within a loop. Run the program and enter the same values as for Exercise 2A.

✳ **SOLUTION FILE:** EX09-2B.C

✳ **RESULT:** Same as Exercise 2A.

✳ **DISCUSSION:** When the values in an array don't change, it's better to initialize when you define it. If you initialize an array more than once or the values are locally significant, then it is better to use explicit assignments placed closer to where the array is used in the program.

Exercise 2C: Initialize with *memset()*.

✳ **DO:** Use the library function *memset()* to initialize the array to zero. Run the program and enter the same values as for Exercise 2.

✳ **SOLUTION FILE:** EX09-2C.C

✳ **RESULT:**

```
Enter a price: 3.33
Price 0 = $3.33
Price 1 = $0.00
Price 2 = $0.00
Price 3 = $0.00
Price 4 = $0.00
Enter a price: 7.77
Price 0 = $3.33
Price 1 = $7.77
Price 2 = $0.00
Price 3 = $0.00
Price 4 = $0.00
Enter a price: 1.11
Price 0 = $3.33
Price 1 = $7.77
Price 2 = $1.11
Price 3 = $0.00
Price 4 = $0.00
Enter a price: 9.99
Price 0 = $3.33
Price 1 = $7.77
Price 2 = $1.11
Price 3 = $9.99
Price 4 = $0.00
Enter a price: 5.55
Price 0 = $3.33
Price 1 = $7.77
Price 2 = $1.11
Price 3 = $9.99
Price 4 = $5.55
```

✳ **DISCUSSION:** The function *memset()* is especially useful for initializing large blocks of memory.

Exercise 2D:　　Initialize an array.

✳ **DO:** Remove the call to *memset()* from Exercise 2C. Find two other ways to accomplish the same task of initializing the array to zero. Hint: One of the ways uses the array define statement. Run each of the two programs and repeat the data entry of Exercise 2C.

✳ **SOLUTION FILE:** EX09-2D.C and EX09-2E.C

✳ **RESULT:** Same as Exercise 2C.

✳ **DISCUSSION:** Don't use the method in EX09-2E.C solely for the purpose of initializing an array to zero—it has the additional effect of extending the lifetime of the array, unnecessarily tying up memory.

Exercise 3:   Sort values in an array.

✳ **DO:** Instead of assigning values in the order that they are entered, sort input values so that they always appear in order from smallest to largest. Write a function that inserts values into the array in ascending numeric order. This is called an *insertion sort*. Call the function after accepting each new value from the keyboard, pass it the new value and a pointer to the array, and have it perform the following algorithm: Scan the array elements from top to bottom, looking for an empty element (0.00) or one that is greater than the new value. If you find an empty one first, assign the new value; otherwise move all array values down one position to make room for the new value before assigning it to that element. Run the program and enter the same values as for Exercise 2.

✳ **SOLUTION FILE:** EX09-3.C

✳ **RESULT:**

```
Enter a price: 3.33
Price 0 = $3.33
Price 1 = $0.00
Price 2 = $0.00
Price 3 = $0.00
Price 4 = $0.00
Enter a price: 7.77
Price 0 = $3.33
Price 1 = $7.77
Price 2 = $0.00
Price 3 = $0.00
Price 4 = $0.00
Enter a price: 1.11
Price 0 = $1.11
Price 1 = $3.33
Price 2 = $7.77
Price 3 = $0.00
Price 4 = $0.00
Enter a price: 9.99
Price 0 = $1.11
Price 1 = $3.33
Price 2 = $7.77
Price 3 = $9.99
Price 4 = $0.00
Enter a price: 5.55
Price 0 = $1.11
```

continued on next page

continued from previous page

```
Price 1 = $3.33
Price 2 = $5.55
Price 3 = $7.77
Price 4 = $9.99
```

✴ **DISCUSSION:** You can enter the prices in any order and the program will sort them into the correct sequence. This method of sorting (insertion sort) is conveniently straightforward, but it is not very fast and should not be used for more than a few data values.

Exercise 4:   Add a look-up table.

✴ **DO:** Add a look-up table to the program from Exercise 3. The purpose of the table is to allow you to determine price based on the number of items purchased. Make a table with 1000 entries and initialize it with indexes to the array of prices. You will enter a purchase volume, then use that volume to look up an index and subsequently a price. The schedule of volumes and associated prices is:

Volume	Price
1	$9.99
2	$7.77
3-5	$5.55
6-10	$3.33
>10	$1.11

At the end of the program from Exercise 3, add statements to accept a purchase volume from the keyboard, look up a price based on that volume, and display the resultant price. Put this in a loop so you can look up several prices; use a volume of 0 to end the loop. Run the program and enter the same prices as for Exercise 3, then request the prices for volumes of 1 through 11 and 500.

✴ **SOLUTION FILE:** EX09-4.C

✴ **RESULT:**

```
Enter a price: 3.33
Price 0 = $3.33
Price 1 = $0.00
Price 2 = $0.00
Price 3 = $0.00
Price 4 = $0.00
Enter a price: 7.77
```

```
Price 0 = $3.33
Price 1 = $7.77
Price 2 = $0.00
Price 3 = $0.00
Price 4 = $0.00
Enter a price: 1.11
Price 0 = $1.11
Price 1 = $3.33
Price 2 = $7.77
Price 3 = $0.00
Price 4 = $0.00
Enter a price: 9.99
Price 0 = $1.11
Price 1 = $3.33
Price 2 = $7.77
Price 3 = $9.99
Price 4 = $0.00
Enter a price: 5.55
Price 0 = $1.11
Price 1 = $3.33
Price 2 = $5.55
Price 3 = $7.77
Price 4 = $9.99

Purchase volume: 1
The price for 1 items is $9.99
Purchase volume: 2
The price for 2 items is $7.77
Purchase volume: 3
The price for 3 items is $5.55
Purchase volume: 4
The price for 4 items is $5.55
Purchase volume: 5
The price for 5 items is $5.55
Purchase volume: 6
The price for 6 items is $3.33
Purchase volume: 7
The price for 7 items is $3.33
Purchase volume: 8
The price for 8 items is $3.33
Purchase volume: 9
The price for 9 items is $3.33
Purchase volume: 10
The price for 10 items is $3.33
Purchase volume: 11
The price for 11 items is $1.11
Purchase volume: 500
The price for 500 items is $1.11
Purchase volume: 0
```

✳ **DISCUSSION:** As the solution file shows, you don't have to explicitly initialize all 1000 array elements to make this program work.

Exercise 5:   Determine the length of a string.

✳ **SOLUTION FILE:** EX09-5.C

✳ **DO:** Write a program to define a character array and initialize it to a string, then call a function to find the length of the string. Name the function *stringLength()*, pass it a pointer to the array, and have it return the integer length. Remember, the length of a string does not include the terminating null character.

✳ **RESULT:**

```
The length of string: "Yankee Doodle" is 13.
```

✳ **DISCUSSION:** The solution file uses "Yankee Doodle" for the string, but you can initialize the array to any character string. You might even want to enter a string from the keyboard with *gets()*. Notice the need for escape sequences to display double quotes in the output.

Exercise 6:   Reverse a string.

✳ **DO:** Add a function named *reverseString()* to your program from Exercise 5 to return a pointer to a string that is the reverse of one passed as a parameter. In other words, pass the original array pointer to the function, have the function reverse the string into a new array, and return a pointer to the new array as the value of the function. Hint: You can put the *stringLength()* function from Exercise 4 to good use here. Have the program display the reversed string when it runs.

✳ **SOLUTION FILE:** EX09-6.C

✳ **RESULT:**

```
The reverse of "Yankee Doodle" is "eldooD eeknaY"
```

✳ **DISCUSSION:** You need to declare the new array *static* in order to ensure that it remains valid after the function returns.

Exercise 7A: Define a three-dimensional array.

✳ **DO:** Write a program that defines a three-dimensional array to count how many ice cream sundaes you consume in a year. You like two sizes of sundaes that come in three flavors with four toppings, so you need a three-dimensional array to keep track of each combination. Initialize the array with a simple list of integers counting from 1 to 24. Also define a one-dimensional array of size 24, then use function *memcpy()* to copy the data from the three-dimensional array to the one-dimensional array. Display each element of the one-dimensional array along with its index. Also have the program display the number of sundaes that you ate of the second size, the second flavor, and the second topping (*sundae[1][1][1]*). Run the program to view the layout of the three-dimensional array in memory indirectly.

✳ **SOLUTION FILE:** EX09-7.A

✳ **RESULT:**

```
Index:  0 Value:  1
Index:  1 Value:  2
Index:  2 Value:  3
Index:  3 Value:  4
Index:  4 Value:  5
Index:  5 Value:  6
Index:  6 Value:  7
Index:  7 Value:  8
Index:  8 Value:  9
Index:  9 Value: 10
Index: 10 Value: 11
Index: 11 Value: 12
Index: 12 Value: 13
Index: 13 Value: 14
Index: 14 Value: 15
Index: 15 Value: 16
Index: 16 Value: 17
Index: 17 Value: 18
Index: 18 Value: 19
Index: 19 Value: 20
Index: 20 Value: 21
Index: 21 Value: 22
Index: 22 Value: 23
Index: 23 Value: 24

sundae[ 1 ][ 1 ][ 1 ] = 18
```

✳ **DISCUSSION:** There are six different ways that you could have defined the array:

```
sundae[ 2 ][ 3 ][ 4 ];
sundae[ 2 ][ 4 ][ 3 ];
```

```
sundae[ 3 ][ 2 ][ 4 ];
sundae[ 3 ][ 4 ][ 2 ];
sundae[ 4 ][ 2 ][ 3 ];
sundae[ 4 ][ 3 ][ 2 ];
```

For this exercise one is as good as another, but the choice will affect the value of *sundae[1][1][1]*. The display repeats initializer values in the exact order that they appear in the initializer list. This is to be expected because the program assigns the initializer values to array elements in order, regardless of how the dimensions are declared. The solution file uses integers 1 through 6, each repeated four times for the initializer list.

Exercise 7B: Initialize with braces.

✳ **DO:** Use two more levels of braces to partition the initializer values according to how the dimensions of the array are declared. Run the program again.

✳ **SOLUTION FILE:** EX09-7B.C

✳ **RESULT:** Same as Exercise 7A.

✳ **DISCUSSION:** If the number of initializers matches the number of array elements, and if you place the braces to match the size of each dimension, the values will still hold their positions. Not much action yet, but the next exercise will reveal some information.

Exercise 7C: Initialize partial array dimensions.

✳ **DO:** Delete the last initializer values for the flavor and toppings dimensions so that there are only two flavors out of three and three toppings out of four. That is, delete the values 4, 8, 9, 10, 11, 12, 16, 20, 21, 22, 23, and 24. Run the program and observe the positions of values that are zero.

✳ **SOLUTION FILE:** EX09-7C.C

✳ **RESULT:**

```
Index:  0 Value:  1
Index:  1 Value:  2
Index:  2 Value:  3
Index:  3 Value:  0
Index:  4 Value:  5
Index:  5 Value:  6
Index:  6 Value:  7
Index:  7 Value:  0
Index:  8 Value:  0
```

```
Index:  9 Value:  0
Index: 10 Value:  0
Index: 11 Value:  0
Index: 12 Value: 13
Index: 13 Value: 14
Index: 14 Value: 15
Index: 15 Value:  0
Index: 16 Value: 17
Index: 17 Value: 18
Index: 18 Value: 19
Index: 19 Value:  0
Index: 20 Value:  0
Index: 21 Value:  0
Index: 22 Value:  0
Index: 23 Value:  0

sundae[ 1 ][ 1 ][ 1 ] = 18
```

✳ **DISCUSSION:** This illustrates how you can control initialization of each dimension of a multidimensional array. It also shows that the dimension farthest from the array name is laid out first in memory; then the elements of that dimension are repeated a number of times equal to the second dimension; then the total elements of the first two dimensions are repeated a number of times equal to the third dimension. In this case the dimension sizes were in the order 4, 3, 2; if you had chosen another ordering, say 2, 3, 4, the positions of zeros in the display would be different.

Exercise 7D: Change the dimension ordering.

✳   **DO:** Change the ordering of the array dimensions. For example, if you had chosen a 2, 3, 4 ordering, change it to 4, 3, 2. You will also need to alter the initialization list to match the new dimension ordering—the placement of braces and values will be different.

✳ **SOLUTION FILE:** EX09-7D.C

✳ **RESULT:**

```
Index:  0 Value:  1
Index:  1 Value:  5
Index:  2 Value: 13
Index:  3 Value: 17
Index:  4 Value:  0
Index:  5 Value:  0
Index:  6 Value:  2
Index:  7 Value:  6
Index:  8 Value: 14
Index:  9 Value: 18
```

```
Index: 10 Value:  0
Index: 11 Value:  0
Index: 12 Value:  3
Index: 13 Value:  7
Index: 14 Value: 15
Index: 15 Value: 19
Index: 16 Value:  0
Index: 17 Value:  0
Index: 18 Value:  0
Index: 19 Value:  0
Index: 20 Value:  0
Index: 21 Value:  0
Index: 22 Value:  0
Index: 23 Value:  0

sundae[ 1 ][ 1 ][ 1 ] = 18
```

✳ **DISCUSSION:** The display clearly shows that the array layout in memory has changed; however it still follows the rule that the first dimension (farthest from the array name) is laid out first, then that dimension is repeated by the size of the second dimension, and so on.

SUMMARY

Arrays are important for organizing and holding large amounts of data. Arrays are connected groups of elements for data storage; the elements can be organized in one dimension or as a multidimensional matrix. In this chapter you picked up the skills necessary for defining, initializing, and accessing data in arrays. These operations are much the same as for single-valued variables, with the addition of indexes to reference individual elements of arrays. Accessing arrays between functions is different than for other variables—you must pass pointers that allow you access to the original data. Arrays can hold string data, and now that you have mastered the basics of arrays, you are ready to move on to Chapter 10 to learn how to manipulate strings.

STRINGS

haracter data is individual letters, numbers, and symbols; when you put characters together into words, phrases, and sentences, you have *strings* of text. This chapter is about text data and how to manipulate it in the C language. You will use strings in practically every program you write, for screen interaction, for showing error messages, for providing help information, for displaying and printing data values, and for storing data in files.

This chapter begins with an explanation of string data, including how to define and initialize strings and how to read strings from the keyboard and write strings to the display. Arrays and pointers are closely connected with strings, and the chapter explains how to use pointers to access string data in arrays. C provides for string manipulation with a rich assortment of standard library functions. The remainder of the chapter is devoted to an explanation of the most important of these functions.

LECTURE

You have had occasion to use some strings in previous chapters, so let's review the basics before progressing into more detail.

Review of String Basics

A string is a sequence of character codes ending with the null character. You write the null character as '\0'; it has a value of zero. Some programming languages (such as BASIC) use a separate byte or two to carry the length of the string; therefore strings are limited to the maximum integer that can be stored. In C, strings can be of any length because there is no explicit length value. There are two kinds of string data: variable strings and string constants.

String Constants

You use string constants as format specifiers for *printf()* and *scanf()*, as screen prompts for data entry, and to initialize arrays for a multitude of other purposes. A string constant is a series of characters enclosed by double quotes, as in this format specifier:

```
"A %s by any other name is still a %s."
```

The compiler stores this source code representation in memory, assigning each character to a contiguous byte, and it adds a null byte to the end of the string. Therefore the above string requires a total of 38 bytes of memory. You do not explicitly specify memory storage for string constants—the compiler handles this automatically. But string constants do take up memory (the size of your .EXE file will include any string constants you define), and for this reason you should not repeat string constants. If you need the same string more than once, put it in an array variable and copy the string data from there whenever needed. For example, strings of space characters (like "   ") are commonly used to blank out an area on the screen or to clear data fields. Instead of duplicating the string constant at every such occurrence, you should initialize an array with a blank string and reuse the data (or better yet, use library function *memset()*).

String Arrays

There is no such thing as a "string variable," but if you place string data in an array, it becomes variable. Whenever you manipulate or modify string data, you do it in arrays. Normally you will use data type *char* to declare an array for strings; you can use either *signed* or *unsigned char* because either specifies 1-byte elements to hold ASCII codes. Whenever possible, declare the size of an array with a symbolic constant to make your program more readable. Here is an example of defining an array for a string:

```
#define MAX_NAME_LENGTH 40
char flowerName[ MAX_NAME_LENGTH ];
```

C also allows you to use 2- or 4-byte integer arrays (type *int* or *long*) for strings, but this complicates string manipulation and should only be used in unusual circumstances.

Initializing String Arrays

There are several ways to initialize an array with string data. Perhaps the best is to assign a string constant in the definition of an array:

```
char flowerName[ MAX_NAME_LENGTH ] = "Orchid";
```

This statement initializes the first 7 elements of the 40-element array to the six letters of the flower name plus a null character; it sets the remaining elements to zero. Notice that the braces usually associated with an initializer list are not necessary here. An alternate form of assigning an initial string constant to an array definition is:

```
char flowerName[] = "Nasturtium";
```

By omitting the size of the array, you allow the compiler to determine the size from the length of the string constant. In this case the array has 11 elements.

You could use a list of individual character constants to initialize an array with a string:

```
char flowerName[] = { 'D', 'a', 'i', 's', 'y', '\0' };
```

This is inconvenient; not only do you have to list each character separately, but you also need to specify the null character explicitly. Use this method only in the rare instance when you need to initialize with special characters that cannot easily be included in a string constant (like the IBM graphic display codes in the range 129-255 of the ASCII table). Note that you can include escape sequences in a string constant (for example, "Line1\nLine2").

You can also set string data into an array outside of the definition statement. It is tempting to write a statement like this with the expectation that it will initialize an array:

```
flowerName = "Chrysanthemum";    /* NOT ALLOWED */
```

but C does not allow assignment of strings outside of array definitions, so don't make this mistake.

An excellent way to copy string data into an array is with the standard library function *strcpy()*:

```
strcpy( flowerName, "Violet" );
```

This statement copies the seven characters of the string constant "Violet" into the first seven elements of array *flowerName*, leaving the remaining elements untouched. You will learn more about *strcpy()* later in this chapter.

Finally, you could assign character constants to an array one by one:

```
flowerName[ 0 ] = 'R';
flowerName[ 1 ] = 'o';
flowerName[ 2 ] = 's';
flowerName[ 3 ] = 'e';
flowerName[ 4 ] = '\0';
```

This method is tedious and is not recommended except for unusual circumstances where you might need to assign special string values.

Reading and Writing Strings

The simplest I/O functions for reading and writing strings are *gets()* and *puts()*. You can also use *scanf()* and *printf()* with the *%s* conversion specifier. Here are two examples of how to read a string from the keyboard:

```
gets( flowerName );
scanf( "%s", flowerName );
```

Here are two examples of how to write a string to the screen:

```
puts( flowerName );
printf( "%s", flowerName );
```

Be aware that *scanf()* stops reading at the first whitespace character, so you cannot read through spaces with this function to get more than one word. Function *gets()* allows embedded spaces and stops only when you press (ENTER), so you can read multiple words with it. Figure 10-1 shows the result of reading the same phrase with both of these functions.

You can use an array variable instead of a string constant for the format specifier in a *scanf()* or *printf()* call. This is useful when you need to vary the format depending on the data. For instance, the following code fragment displays the correct English no matter how many flowers are involved:

```
char formatSpecifier1[] = "He gave me a single rose.";
char formatSpecifier2[] = "He gave me %d roses.";
if ( numFlowers == 1 )
    printf( formatSpecifier1 );
else
    printf( formatSpecifier2, numFlowers );
```

Pointers to Strings

You refer to strings with pointers. A pointer is the address of a memory location, so a character pointer is a way of addressing a particular element of a character array.

Character Pointers

You already know from Chapter 9 that the name of an array is a pointer to that array, and you also know that you can define a character pointer by preceding the name with the indirection operator (*). You can define a pointer and initialize it to the beginning of a string as follows:

```
char flowerName[] = "Fringed Gentian";
char *pFlower = flowerName;
```

This assigns the address of the first element in *flowerName* to pointer *pFlower*. Here the pointer name begins with a lowercase p to signify that it is a pointer. (This is just a chosen method of identifying pointer variables and is not a requirement of the C language.) Now you can use *pFlower* to access the string data. You can display the entire string:

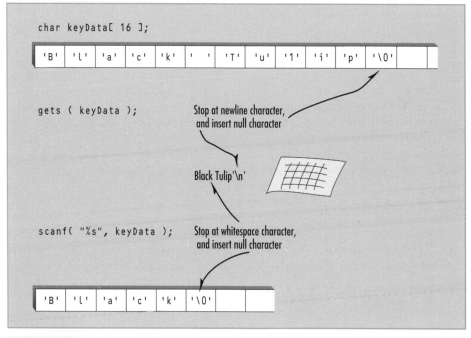

FIGURE 10-1 String input with *gets( )* and *scanf( )*

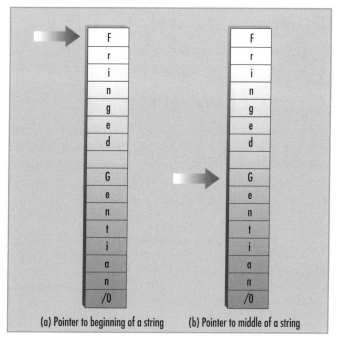

(a) Pointer to beginning of a string   (b) Pointer to middle of a string

FIGURE 10-2 Pointer to a string

```
    printf( "%s", pFlower );   /* Same as printf( "%s", flowerName ); */
```
Or you can display the second element of the string:

```
    printf( "%c", pFlower[ 1 ] );   /* Same as printf( "%c", flowerName[ 1 ] );
    */
```

Figure 10-2(a) illustrates a character array and a pointer to the beginning of the string data.

There is one very important difference between the name of an array and a pointer variable: You cannot change the value (address) of an array name, but you can assign any address to a pointer. The name of an array is a constant and a pointer variable is changeable! There, in a nutshell, is the reason for having pointer variables; you can use them to manipulate array data at any location.

Address Operator

The address operator (&) is a unary operator that returns the address of a variable. When you put it in front of a variable, you get the address of that variable. Another way of setting the pointer to the beginning of array *flowerName* is:

```
    pFlower = &flowerName[ 0 ];
```

another way of displaying the entire string is:

```
    printf( "%s", &flowerName[ 0 ] );
```

By changing the index you can refer to the address of any element in the array. So if you want to display only the word "Gentian" you would write:

```
printf( "%s", &flowerName[ 8 ] );
```

or

```
pFlower = &flowerName[ 8 ];
printf( "%s", pFlower );
```

Figure 10-2(b) illustrates the pointer to an element in the middle of the array.

The address operator is redundant if it is attached to the beginning of an array name without an index. So the following two addresses are the same:

```
flowerName
&flowerName
```

Arrays of Strings

You store data for a single string in a one-dimensional array. You can store more than one string in a two-dimensional array—this is called an *array of strings*. Here is an example of the array of strings that is illustrated in Figure 10-3:

```
char flowerParts[ 4 ][ 8 ] = { "Petal", "Pistil", "Stamen", "Stem" };
```

Each row of the array holds a different string. You could let the compiler determine the number of rows from the initializer list by leaving out the size of this dimension:

```
char flowerParts[][ 8 ] = { "Petal", "Pistil", "Stamen", "Stem" };
```

The pointer to the second string, "Pistil", is:

```
&flowerParts[ 1 ][ 0 ]
```

you can display all four strings with this loop:

```
for ( i=0; i<3; ++i )
{
    printf( "%s\n", &flowerParts[ i ][ 0 ] );
}
```

Another way to specify the pointer to the beginning of a particular string in a string array is to leave off the outer brackets (the brackets farthest from the identifier). Using this syntax, *flowerParts[1]* is the address of the second string. Here are five equivalent ways of getting the address of the first string:

```
flowerParts            /* Preferred form */
&flowerParts
flowerParts[ 0 ]       /* Preferred form */
```

continued on next page

continued from previous page

```
&flowerParts[ 0 ]
&flowerParts[ 0 ][ 0 ]
```

And here are three equivalent ways of addressing the second string:

```
flowerParts[ 1 ]          /* Preferred form */
&flowerParts[ 1 ]
&flowerParts[ 1 ][ 0 ]
```

You should not use the address operator when it is redundant, and you should use the shortest representation, so the recommended syntax for addressing a two-dimensional array is *flowerParts* or *flowerParts[0]* for the first string, and *flowerParts[1]* for the second. Therefore you could display all four strings this way:

```
for ( i=0; i<3; ++i )
{
    printf( "%s\n", flowerParts[ i ] );
}
```

typedef STRING

With *typedef* you can simplify your declarations of arrays for strings, especially arrays of strings (two-dimensional arrays). Experienced C programmers often declare a STRING data type like this:

```
typedef char STRING[ MAX_NAME_LENGTH ];
```

Subsequently they can use STRING to define arrays to hold string data.

Let's carefully analyze this statement. The *typedef* key word states that we are declaring a new data type. The remainder of the statement has the form of an array declaration with identifier STRING in place of the name of the array, so

```
char flowerParts[ 4 ][ 8 ] = { "Petal", "Pistil", "Stamen", "Stem" };
```

'P'	'e'	't'	'a'	'l'	'\0'		
'P'	'i'	's'	't'	'i'	'l'	'\0'	
'S'	't'	'a'	'm'	'e'	'n'	'\0'	
'S'	't'	'e'	'm'	'\0'			

FIGURE 10-3 An array of strings

STRING becomes the name of the new data type. STRING takes on the qualities of the array declaration: it is an array of type *char* and it has size MAX_NAME_LENGTH. We previously defined symbolic constant MAX_NAME_LENGTH to be 40, so STRING is a character array of size 40. You could use STRING to define an uninitialized array to hold the name of a flower:

```
STRING flowerName;
```

and you could define an initialized array of strings:

```
STRING flowerParts[] = { "Petal", "Pistil", "Stamen", "Stem" };
```

The result is a two-dimensional array of size 4 by 40 that is identical to the one in Figure 10-3. The data type STRING declares the first dimension of size 40, and the initializer list causes the second dimension to be of size 4.

Ragged Arrays

The two-dimensional arrays of strings that we have discussed so far are all *rectangular arrays*, that is, each row in the array has the same number of elements whether or not the strings are of the same length. There is another kind of array for strings, called a *ragged array,* in which the rows can have different amounts of storage. A ragged array is really an array of pointers that point to strings of different lengths. There are two ways to create a ragged array. One is to initialize an array of pointers with a list of string constants:

```
char *flowerParts[] = { "Petal", "Pistil", "Stamen", "Stem" };
```

The other is to define the array of pointers, then separately assign the addresses of strings:

```
char part1[] = "Petal";
char part2[] = "Pistil";
char part3[] = "Stamen";
char part4[] = "Stem";
char *flowerParts[4];
flowerParts[ 0 ] = part1;
flowerParts[ 1 ] = part2;
flowerParts[ 2 ] = part3;
flowerParts[ 3 ] = part4;
```

The second method is clearly more tedious, but both of these methods create the string shown in Figure 10-4.

The name *ragged array* stems from the fact that the right side of the array is not straight (as shown in the figure). Ragged arrays use less memory than rectangular arrays, but often the difference is not significant. Ragged arrays sometimes serve as look-up tables for string data, but perhaps the most important application is to hold command-line arguments for the main C program.

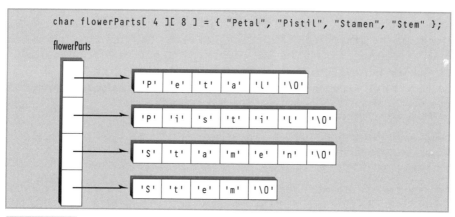

FIGURE 10-4 A ragged array

Command-Line Arguments

When you run a program, you can pass data on the command line in the form of character sequences separated by spaces. Each sequence is an argument that is a string constant. The main program has two parameters (remember, *main()* is really a function) to receive the strings. The first parameter is an integer that represents the number of command-line strings, and the second is a ragged array containing pointers to the strings. C does not require a prototype for the main program, but if you plan to accept command-line arguments, you must define the following parameters in the first line of the program:

```
void main( int argc, char *argv[] )
```

The first parameter is an integer that is a count of the number of arguments (argument count, or *argc*), and the second is an array of character pointers of indefinite size (argument vector, or *argv*). The operating system (DOS) determines the size of the associated array from the number of arguments that appear on the command line when you type the program request. Figure 10-5 depicts the process of passing the arguments from a command line to the main function of a program. The figure shows a program, VIEW.EXE, that displays a graphical image file. You specify the file name and a display size on the DOS command line following the name of the executable program.

Below is a program that accesses and displays each command-line argument:

```
#include <stdio.h>
void main( int argc, char *argv[] )
{
    int i;
    for ( i=0; i<argc; ++i )
```

```
    {
        printf( "%s\n", argv[ i ] );
    }
}
```

There is always at least one parameter. For DOS version 3.0 or later, the first parameter string is always the name of the program; earlier versions of DOS set the first parameter to the null string ('\0', which is a string with zero length). To enter command-line arguments in Turbo C++, select the *Arguments* item at the bottom of the *Run* menu and type the desired arguments in the dialog box.

Library String Functions

You will find most of the string operations that you'll ever need in the standard C library. You should use these functions freely because they have been optimized for efficiency and thoroughly tested to perform as advertised. Prototypes for most of the string functions are in header file STRING.H and others are in STDLIB.H (both in directory \TCLITE\INCLUDE). If you browse through STRING.H you will count 29 functions for manipulating strings; most are compatible with the ANSI standard. A few are not, but you may find them useful for programs where

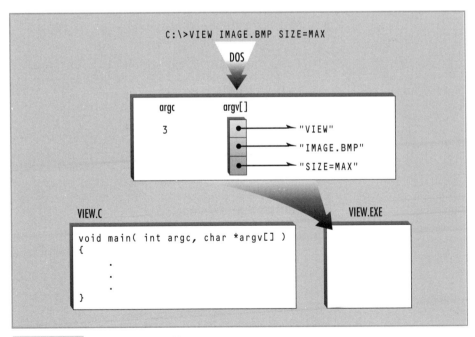

FIGURE 10-5 Passing command-line arguments

portability to other environments is not important. In the paragraphs below you will find examples of the most important string functions. You can find information about all of the functions described here under the Turbo C++ *Help* menu. We'll discuss string functions in five categories of operations: copying, comparing, searching, converting, and miscellaneous.

String Copy Functions

Several functions copy data from one string to another. Refer to Table 10-1 for information on the arguments and return values of string copy functions.

PROTOTYPE: char *strcpy(char *destination, char *source);

ARGUMENTS: destination is a pointer to an array to receive the string.
source is a pointer to the string to be copied.

RETURN VALUE: Pointer to the destination string.

OPERATION: Copies the source string to the destination, including the terminating null. Make sure the supplied destination array is large enough to hold the source string.

PROTOTYPE: char *strncpy(char *destination, char *source, size_t n);

(size_t is a defined type that equates to unsigned int)

ARGUMENTS: destination is a pointer to an array to receive the string.
source is a pointer to the string to be copied. n is the number of characters to copy.

RETURN VALUE: Pointer to the destination string.

OPERATION: Copies the first n characters from the source string to the destination. If the length of the source string is less than n characters, the function pads the destination with null characters to make up the difference; otherwise it does not add a null character. Make sure the supplied destination array is large enough to hold n+1 characters.

PROTOTYPE: char *strcat(char *destination, char *source);

ARGUMENTS: destination is a pointer to one string.
source is a pointer to another string.

RETURN VALUE: Pointer to the destination string.

OPERATION: Appends the source string to the destination string. The first character of source replaces the terminating null of destination, and the function adds a terminating null at the end of the result. Make sure the supplied destination array is large enough to hold both strings.

PROTOTYPE: char *strncat(char *destination, char *source, size_t n);

ARGUMENTS: destination is a pointer to one string.
source is a pointer to another string. n is the number of characters to use from source.

RETURN VALUE: Pointer to the destination string.

OPERATION: Appends the first n characters from the source string to the destination string. The first character of source replaces the terminating null of destination, and the function adds a terminating null at the end of the result. Make sure the supplied destination array is large enough to hold both strings.

PROTOTYPE: char *strset(char *destination, int c);

ARGUMENTS: destination is a pointer to a string.
c is a character value.

RETURN VALUE: Pointer to the destination string.

OPERATION: Sets each element in the destination string to the specified character value, not including the terminating null.

continued on next page

continued from previous page

PROTOTYPE: char *strnset(char *destination, int c, size_t n);

ARGUMENTS: destination is a pointer to a string.
                    c is a character value.
                    n is the number of elements of destination to set.

RETURN VALUE: Pointer to the destination string.

OPERATION: Sets the first n elements in the destination string to the specified character value, not including the terminating null.

Table 10-1   **String copy functions**

You can copy all of one string to another with *strcpy()*—perhaps the most frequently used copy function. Here is an example:

```
char poem1[ 80 ];
strcpy( poem1, "Roses are red; Violets are blue\n" );
```

The source string (second argument) can be either a string constant or a pointer to a string array. You can copy a specified number of characters from one string to another with *strncpy()*. In the following example, we take the first 26 characters from the second argument and insert them into *poem2* without a terminating null character:

```
char poem2[ 80 ];
strncpy( poem2, "Use strcpy and strncpy too for initializing strings", 26 );
```

You can add a string to the end of another (concatenate the strings) with function *strcat()*:

```
strcat( poem1, poem2 );
```

Figure 10-6 illustrates this operation. Notice that the first character of the second string replaces the ending null of the first string.

If you display the string in *poem1* you will see:

```
Roses are red; Violets are blue
Use strcpy and strncpy too
```

You could produce this result in one step with function *strncat()*. It concatenates a selected number of characters from the second string argument to the first string argument:

```
strncat( poem1, "Use strcpy and strncpy too for initializing strings", 26 );
```

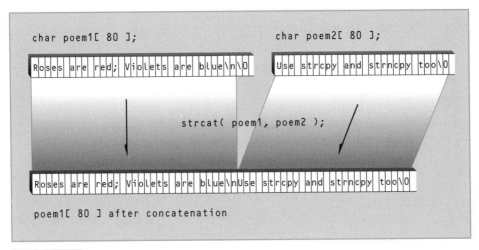

FIGURE 10-6 String concatenation

Functions *strset()* and *strnset()* load elements of an array with a character value. Function *strset()* loads all elements up to the terminating null and *strnset()* loads only a selected number of elements. This statement clears the entire *poem1* array (with space characters):

```
strset( poem1, ' ' );
```

This statement loads the first 10 elements of *poem2* with question marks:

```
strnset( poem2, '?', 10 );
```

The copy and concatenate functions are defined by the ANSI standard, but *strset()* and *strnset()* are not. For any of the copy functions you have the responsibility of making sure the destination array is large enough to hold the processed data. In the above examples, both *poem1* and *poem2* were defined to have 80 elements, more than enough room to hold the resulting strings. A program will complete copy operations regardless of array sizes, but if the destination is not large enough, the data will overlay other data or executable program code beyond the end of the array, potentially wreaking havoc.

String Compare Functions

C has one principal function for comparing strings, but there are several important variants—see Table 10-2.

PROTOTYPE: int strcmp(char *string1, char *string2);

ARGUMENTS: string1 is a pointer to a string.
                  string2 is a pointer to a second string.

RETURN VALUE: Negative if string1 is less than string2,
                  Zero if the strings are identical,
                  Positive if string1 is greater than string2.

OPERATION: Compares the two strings from the beginning, character-by-
                  character. If a difference occurs, returns difference between
                  the ASCII codes of the two mismatched characters.

PROTOTYPE: int strncmp(char *string1, char *string2, size_t n);
                  (size_t is a defined type that equates to unsigned int)

ARGUMENTS: string1 is a pointer to a string.
                  string2 is a pointer to a second string.
                  n is the number of characters to compare.

RETURN VALUE: Negative if string1 is less than string2,
                  Zero if the strings are identical,
                  Positive if string1 is greater than string2.

OPERATION: Compares the first n characters of two strings from the
                  beginning. If a difference occurs, returns difference between
                  the ASCII codes of the two mismatched characters.

PROTOTYPE: int strempi(char *string1, char *string2);
                  int stricmp(char *string1, char *string2);

OPERATION: Same as strcmp() except converts all characters to lowercase
                  before comparing so the comparison is case insensitive.

PROTOTYPE: int strncmpi(char *string1, char *string2, size_t n);

int strnicmp(char *string1, char *string2, size_t n);

OPERATION: Same as strncmp() except converts all characters to lowercase
               before comparing so the comparison is case insensitive.

Table 10-2   String compare functions

You can compare two entire strings with *strcmp()* or you can compare only a selected number of characters from the front of two strings with *strncmp()*. These two are the only string comparison functions that are ANSI compatible. You can also do comparisons in a case-insensitive manner with functions *strcmpi()* and *strncmpi()*. Each of these functions returns an integer that is zero when the strings are exactly the same, positive if string one (the first argument) is greater than string two (the second argument), and negative if string one is less than string two. How can strings be greater or less than each other? The functions compare string data one character at a time from the beginning. If all characters are the same to the terminating null, or to the selected number of characters, they are equal. When a comparison function encounters a difference, it calculates the return value by subtracting the ASCII code for the character in string one from the corresponding code in string two. Figure 10-7 illustrates the comparison algorithm. The return value signifies the *lexicographic* order of the differing characters.

In the following example, *strcmp()* returns a value of -4, which is the difference between 101 ('e') and 105 ('i'):

    strcmp("Violets", "Violins");

The comparison below returns a value of 0 because the first four characters in both strings are the same:

    strncmp("Violets", "Violins", 4);

The next comparison fails with a positive return value of 32 (the difference between 'v' and 'V'):

    strcmp("violets", "Violins");

However, a similar case-insensitive comparison of the first four characters returns zero:

    strncmpi("violets", "Violins", 4);

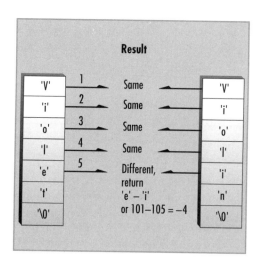

FIGURE 10-7 String compare algorithm

String Search Functions

C provides several functions to find substrings within other strings. Table 10-3 lists these functions, all of which are ANSI compatible.

PROTOTYPE: char *strstr(char *string1, char *string2);

ARGUMENTS: string1 is a pointer to a string.
string2 is a pointer to a second string.

RETURN VALUE: Pointer to the first occurrence of string2 in string1 or NULL (a zero pointer) if string1 does not contain string2.

OPERATION: Searches the first string for a character sequence identical to that in string two; the terminating null of string two is not a part of the search.

PROTOTYPE: char *strchr(char *string, int c);

ARGUMENTS: string is a pointer to a string.
c is a character value.

RETURN VALUE: Pointer to the first occurrence of c in string or NULL (a zero pointer) if string does not contain c.

OPERATION: Searches from the beginning of the string to find the first occurrence of c in the string.

PROTOTYPE: char *strrchr(char *string, int c);

OPERATION: Same as strchr() except searches from the end of the string to find the last occurrence of c.

Table 10-3   **String search functions**

Perhaps the most-used function is *strstr()*—it finds the first occurrence of the second string and returns a pointer to the beginning of the match in the first string. The following statement will return a pointer to the fifth element of *fileName:*

```
fileName[] = "DATA.DAT";
strstr( fileName, ".DAT" );
```

Similarly, you can search for the first occurrence of a single character in a string with *strchr()*. The second search argument for *strchr()* is a character instead of a string. The next call also returns a pointer to the fifth element of *fileName:*

```
strchr( fileName, '.' );
```

A companion function, *strrchr()*, searches for the last occurrence of a character in a string (notice the extra *r* in the function name). The following call returns a pointer to the seventh element of *fileName* (the last 'A'):

```
strrchr( fileName, 'A' );
```

String Conversion Functions

The conversion functions provide an easy way to convert string data to numbers or to force character data to uppercase or lowercase. None of the functions listed in Table 10-4 or discussed here is ANSI compatible, so you should not use them in programs that must be portable.

PROTOTYPE: char *strupr(char *string);

ARGUMENTS: string is a pointer to a string.

RETURN VALUE: Pointer to original string now containing uppercase data.

OPERATION: Converts any lowercase characters ('a' through 'z') in the string to uppercase.

PROTOTYPE: char *strlwr(char *string);

ARGUMENTS: string is a pointer to a string.

RETURN VALUE: Pointer to original string now containing lowercase data.

OPERATION: Converts any uppercase characters ('A' through 'Z') in the string to lowercase.

PROTOTYPE: int atoi(char *string);

ARGUMENTS: string is a pointer to a string containing numeric digits ('0' through '9'), optionally preceded by whitespace characters and a sign (+ or -).

RETURN VALUE: Integer value equivalent to the string.

OPERATION: Converts the number represented by the string to an equivalent integer value.

PROTOTYPE: long atol(char *string);

OPERATION: Same as atoi() except the return value is type long int.

PROTOTYPE: double atof(char *string);

OPERATION: Same as atoi() except the return value is type double and the numeric digits can also contain a decimal point ('.') and the string can end with an exponent ('d', 'D', 'e', or 'E' followed by a sign and numeric digits).

Table 10-4	String conversion functions

If you call *atoi()*, *atol()*, or *atof()*, you convert the string argument and return, respectively, an *int* value, a *long int* value, or a floating-point *double* value. Use these functions whenever you have internal string data that you have to use in calculations. For example, you might need to calculate the difference between years taken from date strings. You can find the year in a date string and convert it to an integer with one statement:

```
int year;
char date[] = "July 15, 1994";
year = atoi( strchr( strchr( date, ',' ), ' ' ) );
```

The two *strchr()* calls find the space after the comma between day and year, then *atoi()* converts the year. Function *atof()* can convert either a simple decimal number or a number in exponential form:

```
double d;
d = atof( "1.23" );
d = atof( "1.23e50 );
```

These calls are much like calling *sscanf()* with a conversion specifier of *%d*, *%ld*, or *%lf*, except that the string functions are specialized for the purpose and so are more efficient than *sscanf()*.

Functions *strupr()* and *strlwr()* alter the string argument so that it contains all uppercase or lowercase characters, respectively. This is done "in place" and modifies the original string data. These functions are handy for normalizing string data after keyboard input. The following code produces an uppercase string from either lowercase or uppercase input:

```
char keyInput[ 10 ];
scanf( "%s", keyInput );
strupr( keyInput );
```

Miscellaneous String Functions

Two important string functions do not fit the other categories. Table 10-5 describes these functions in detail.

PROTOTYPE:	size_t strlen(char *string);
ARGUMENTS:	string is a pointer to a string.
RETURN VALUE:	Length of the string.
OPERATION:	Counts the number of characters in the string up to, but not including, the terminating null.
PROTOTYPE:	char *strerror(int errno);
ARGUMENTS:	errno is a global variable defined in header file ERRNO.H.
RETURN VALUE:	Pointer to an error message string.
OPERATION:	Retrieves a message from the operating system that corresponds to the integer error number. The error number is determined by the last operation preceding the call to strerror() that is capable of generating a system-level error.

Table 10-5   Miscellaneous string functions

String Length

In Chapter 9 you developed a function to find the length of a string. While that was a useful exercise, a function already existed for that purpose: the standard ANSI library function *strlen()*. The following call returns a value of eight:

```
char fileName[ 20 ] = "DATA.DAT";
strlen( fileName );
```

The length of a string does not include the terminating null. There are many situations where you will need to know the length of strings. Because many string operations can exceed the size of an array, it is important to be able to test the length of strings. You may want to move string data into fixed-length fields for screen display or output to files—string lengths help determine when the data will fit the field lengths. You can also use string lengths to set the size of dynamically allocated memory for data storage (see Chapter 11).

Error Strings

You have access to DOS (or other operating system) error messages through the ANSI function *strerror()*. Some operations (especially file I/O, floating-point calculations, and memory allocation) involve operating system resources. DOS sets the value of a global variable, *errno*, to indicate the completion status of these operations. You can call function *strerror()* with *errno* as the argument and it will return a pointer to an error message string. Most of the DOS messages concern file errors. The following statement will display a message indicating "No such file or directory":

```
fopen(" ","s");
printf( "%s", strerror( errno ) );
```

You need to include header file ERRNO.H to define the global variable *errno* before calling this function; the file also defines constants reported to *errno* by DOS.

LAB

Exercise 1:   Experiment with string length and the terminating null.

✳ **DO:** Write a program that defines an uninitialized character array of size ten. Pretend that the array contains a string and display the string length and string data.

✳ **SOLUTION FILE:** EX10-1.C

✳ **RESULT:**

```
Length of the string is: 0
String data is:
```

✳ **DISCUSSION:** Because the string is uninitialized, it contains unknown data. You may get the same result as above—a null, zero-length string. On the other hand you may see a string with a lot of nonsense characters and the string may even be longer that the array size of ten. The output function (either *puts()* or *printf()*) will display characters until it encounters a null character, regardless of how far out in memory that might be. Our editor even locked up his computer with this exercise and had to reboot.

Exercise 2A: Display an array of strings.

✳ DO: Write a program that declares a STRING data type that is a character array with ten elements (use *typedef*). Use STRING to define an array of strings and initialize the two-dimensional array with these string constants: "Widget," "Freeble," "Thingy," "Gizmo," and "Dohickie." Display the contents of the string array.

✳ SOLUTION FILE: EX10-2A.C

✳ RESULT:

```
String 0 is Widget
String 1 is Freeble
String 2 is Thingy
String 3 is Gizmo
String 4 is Dohickie
```

✳ DISCUSSION: It is best to use symbolic constants to declare array sizes.

Exercise 2B: Sort strings alphabetically.

✳ DO: Modify the program from Exercise 2A to sort the strings into alphabetic order. Hint: You can do the job with an exchange sort—compare the first string with all others and exchange it with any that are higher in alphabetic order, then compare the second with the rest, and so on.

✳ SOLUTION FILE: EX10-2B.C

✳ RESULT:

```
String 0 is Dohickie
String 1 is Freeble
String 2 is Gizmo
String 3 is Thingy
String 4 is Widget
```

✳ DISCUSSION: You need a separate, working array in order to swap two strings. It temporarily holds a copy of one string so you can replace the original. An exchange sort is not the fastest technique for sorting, but it is simple to program and serves well when speed is not important.

Exercise 3:   Parse a string.

✳ **DO:** Write a program to read a full DOS file path name from the keyboard. Extract the directory, file name, and file extension and place them in three separate strings. Run the program and enter the path name C:\TCLITE\INCLUDE\STRING.H. Hint: It helps to use a character pointer. Remember that you can use indexes with a pointer. Also remember that you have to specify a backslash character as an escape sequence (\\).

✳ **SOLUTION FILE:** EX10-3.C

✳ **RESULT:**

```
Directory: C:\TCLITE\INCLUDE
File: STRING
Extension: .H
```

✳ **DISCUSSION:** The solution program did not include the last backslash in either the directory string or the file string, but it did include the dot with the extension—these are optional choices. Notice that the solution program explicitly inserts the ending null character for the directory and file name strings; it does so because the *strncpy()* function does not add a null when the number of copied characters is less than the length of the source string.

Exercise 4:   Report system error messages.

✳ **DO:** Make a copy of EX07-1.C (from the Chapter 7 lab). Add code to the new program that will display the DOS error status after every calculation. Run the program and enter the following two calculations:

$$1 + 1$$
$$1 * 1.e50$$

✳ **SOLUTION FILE:** EX10-4.C

✳ **RESULT:**

```
Enter a calculation: 1 + 1
Status: Error 0
 = 2.0

Enter a calculation: 1 + 1.e50
Status: Result too large
 = +INF

Enter a calculation: 0 Q 0
```

✳ **DISCUSSION:** You must trap the error number immediately after the operation of interest; otherwise it may change when the next statement executes. Notice that the system error message includes its own newline character at the end.

Exercise 5:   Program custom error messages.

✳ **DO:** Write a custom error-handling function called *processError()* that displays an error message and causes the program to quit. The function should include four predefined error messages that correspond to error codes 1 through 4—make up four simple messages. The prototype for this function is:

```
void processError( int errorCode, char *functionName );
```

The function should display the name of the calling function where the error occurred and the error message. Write a program to test the function with an error.

✳ **SOLUTION FILE:** EX10-5.C

✳ **RESULT:**

```
Main function: Input value out of range
```

✳ **DISCUSSION:** The solution program assumes that an error code of zero signals that no error occurred. The message array is declared *static* so that the program only initializes it once; if it were *automatic,* the program would initialize it every time the function is called. By returning a value of 1, function *exit()* signals the operating system that an error occurred.

Exercise 6:   Use command-line arguments.

✳ **DO:** Write a program that accepts up to two command-line arguments. If it receives no arguments, the program should display instructions on how to use the command-line arguments. The first argument (BANNER=ON or BANNER=OFF) controls whether or not the program displays a title. The second argument (QUIET=ON or QUIET=OFF) controls whether error messages sound the bell tone. Have the program display an error message if more than two command-line arguments are entered. Run the program with no command-line arguments, with one argument (BANNER=ON), and with three arguments (BANNER=OFF QUIET=OFF THIRDARG). Enter command-line arguments in the dialog box that appears after selecting *Arguments* from the *Run* menu.

✳ SOLUTION FILE: EX10-6.C

✳ RESULT:

```
Run 1: (NO COMMAND-LINE ARGUMENTS)
Program EX10-6 has two optional command-line arguments:

1. BANNER=ON  displays title information when the program starts.
   BANNER=OFF suppresses the title information (the default).

2. QUIET=ON   suppresses sound output (the default).
   QUIET=OFF   causes the bell sound to accompany error messages.

Examples:

EX10-6 BANNER=ON QUIET=OFF
EX10-6 BANNER=OFF QUIET=ON

Run 2: (BANNER=ON)
**********************************************
                  PROGRAM EX10-6
**********************************************


Run 3: (BANNER=OFF QUIET=OFF THIRDARG)
(beep)Too many command line arguments!
```

✳ DISCUSSION: The first parameter received by *main()* is always the program name, so you need to look at the second parameter to see the first command-line argument that you actually entered. In this program the arguments are position dependent; that is, the program cannot accept the QUIET switch for the first argument or the BANNER switch for the second. You can sound the bell by displaying the escape character '\7'.

Exercise 7A: Generate a text string.

✳ STARTER FILE: EX10-7A.C

✳ DO: The starter file contains a program that fills an array with a large text string. The string consists of random uppercase letters in random-length words that are separated by space characters. Examine the program to locate the array that holds the text string and run the program to see the data.

✳ RESULT:

```
HGUE LLD IC CGBKNDX NOV TJ EGXP VSM Y YQEI FMNMKS SEZY FTSYS DOEX CE VVB
GOYFBP VVPAY W QQMU LO O XHS BCKFK TD LJH XSNKFU ZZMM O ELHK UZ CDU IJA
ZVCPA FGBA VZLT DPST JHIC ZN L JVWXRB VYW UBBR LCMXHM KUDO GGPY FTUEZH JGGKD
JNEQ I JRZA JLHB MIWO W XUNS RREM CZ EHSQOI PIN DPZNV MABZS MV PS CA X ETL
RUKM P QGO RO DYXTBHWY PJXH HKQUR HBFVN LZP OVIX UORR V BZW OKIE AMI NUH P
JJ AXNN LQZDT OC NXG D ZNC FJ MO OKJ UWJR PY HRWB XGCCY UIWB R BCXFX BGC CC
Z UMRBZSHR FS XHUY ZWIU IIFDU OWC HE JA UZS IUUIWBE YAFVDE ODK JECZ FQPZ F
UDTXJK LLAAC OW DTCLF LY HCA NFNVZD HG DUM MCOROP GFZVQ WKFD GDA SOSD
GCMMRHYY AQC ZAXK YWY ZZPHTYZV YUF IGKRZX PA AY RSKT IESG ZZJM SNR WEJ VH
VJS JOGKFF GIO R WZQEO PPNJU LYM NVLSCW C MKID DJJ I UQIVV WVJFLK USAB KF MJ
NHS TDE D BRTE IX JL SEERTJJA OLHPVUH WIYT HCYSE MGNLJG HIR GF JMPHE Z UDCJ
DR VIUE FVRY RDEAU FURQ OCQKM SG C GNP QAHR RFCVR KDCL OOOXQ ZIRNW XADW XR
SW B V FKT NU DXDVCUD KAYZX OBQ VPGJGM GFP CQ BDWXZ RXOT XI GRCMNJGW QCHBJL
SSHCHL TLG NCZ UC NZ PUR NQD
```

✳ DISCUSSION: This program uses library function *rand()* which returns a random number in the range of 0 to 32767. The program limits random word sizes to less than ten by applying the modulus operator (%) to *rand()*; similarly, it limits the random letters to 26 (A to Z). Even though selected letters and words are truly random, successive runs will generate the same output. Your text data will be different than this because the random number function will produce different values.

Exercise 7B: Convert a string.

✳ DO: Add code to the program from Exercise 7A to convert the text to all lowercase characters. Run the program to see the text.

✳ SOLUTION FILE: EX10-7B.C

✳ RESULT:

```
hgue lld ic cgbkndx nov tj egxp vsm y yqei fmnmks sezy ftsys doex ce vvb
goyfbp vvpay w qqmu lo o xhs bckfk td ljh xsnkfu zzmm o elhk uz cdu ija
zvcpa fgba vzlt dpst jhic zn l jvwxrb vyw ubbr lcmxhm kudo ggpy ftuezh jggkd
jneq i jrza jlhb miwo w xuns rrem cz ehsqoi pin dpznv mabzs mv ps ca x etl
rukm p qgo ro dyxtbhwy pjxh hkqur hbfvn lzp ovix uorr v bzw okie ami nuh p
jj axnn lqzdt oc nxg d znc fj mo okj uwjr py hrwb xgccy uiwb r bcxfx bgc cc
z umrbzshr fs xhuy zwiu iifdu owc he ja uzs iuuiwbe yafvde odk jecz fqpz f
udtxjk llaac ow dtclf ly hca nfnvzd hg dum mcorop gfzvq wkfd gda sosd
gcmmrhyy aqc zaxk ywy zzphtyzv yuf igkrzx pa ay rskt iesg zzjm snr wej vh
vjs jogkff gio r wzqeo ppnju lym nvlscw c mkid djj i uqivv wvjflk usab kf mj
nhs tde d brte ix jl seertjja olhpvuh wiyt hcyse mgnljg hir gf jmphe z udcj
dr viue fvry rdeau furq ocqkm sg c gnp qahr rfcvr kdcl oooxq zirnw xadw xr
sw b v fkt nu dxdvcud kayzx obq vpgjgm gfp cq bdwxz rxot xi grcmnjgw qchbjl
sshchl tlg ncz uc nz pur nqd
```

✳ DISCUSSION: You should see the same data as in Exercise 7A except in all lowercase letters. It takes just one statement to accomplish this conversion.

Exercise 7C: Search a string.

✳ DO: Add statements to your program from Exercise 7B to search the text string for any occurrence of the article "a". If "a" exists, indicate the location by displaying the index. Be sure to include the leading and trailing spaces in the search. Run the program to see if and where the article exists.

✳ SOLUTION FILE: EX10-7C.C

✳ RESULT:

```
hgue lld ic cgbkndx nov tj egxp vsm y yqei fmnmks sezy ftsys doex ce vvb
goyfbp vvpay w qqmu lo o xhs bckfk td ljh xsnkfu zzmm o elhk uz cdu ija
zvcpa fgba vzlt dpst jhic zn l jvwxrb vyw ubbr lcmxhm kudo ggpy ftuezh jggkd
jneq i jrza jlhb miwo w xuns rrem cz ehsqoi pin dpznv mabzs mv ps ca x etl
rukm p qgo ro dyxtbhwy pjxh hkqur hbfvn lzp ovix uorr v bzw okie ami nuh p
jj axnn lqzdt oc nxg d znc fj mo okj uwjr py hrwb xgccy uiwb r bcxfx bgc cc
z umrbzshr fs xhuy zwiu iifdu owc he ja uzs iuuiwbe yafvde odk jecz fqpz f
udtxjk llaac ow dtclf ly hca nfnvzd hg dum mcorop gfzvq wkfd gda sosd
gcmmrhyy aqc zaxk ywy zzphtyzv yuf igkrzx pa ay rskt iesg zzjm snr wej vh
vjs jogkff gio r wzqeo ppnju lym nvlscw c mkid djj i uqivv wvjflk usab kf mj
nhs tde d brte ix jl seertjja olhpvuh wiyt hcyse mgnljg hir gf jmphe z udcj
dr viue fvry rdeau furq ocqkm sg c gnp qahr rfcvr kdcl oooxq zirnw xadw xr
sw b v fkt nu dxdvcud kayzx obq vpgjgm gfp cq bdwxz rxot xi grcmnjgw qchbjl
sshchl tlg ncz uc nz pur nqd

The first occurrence of pronoun 'i' is at index 226
```

✳ DISCUSSION: There were no occurrences of "a" in this text, so we switched to search for the pronoun "i". If you don't find "a" either, try another short word such as "i" or "if".

Exercise 7D: Search for characters.

✳ DO: Search the text string to find all occurrences of the letter "q". Display the index of each occurrence. You can either add to or replace the search statements for Exercise 7C.

✳ SOLUTION FILE: EX10-7D.C

✳ **RESULT:**

```
hgue lld ic cgbkndx nov tj egxp vsm y yqei fmnmks sezy ftsys doex ce vvb
goyfbp vvpay w qqmu lo o xhs bckfk td ljh xsnkfu zzmm o elhk uz cdu ija
zvcpa fgba vzlt dpst jhic zn l jvwxrb vyw ubbr lcmxhm kudo ggpy ftuezh jggkd
jneq i jrza jlhb miwo w xuns rrem cz ehsqoi pin dpznv mabzs mv ps ca x etl
rukm p qgo ro dyxtbhwy pjxh hkqur hbfvn lzp ovix uorr v bzw okie ami nuh p
jj axnn lqzdt oc nxg d znc fj mo okj uwjr py hrwb xgccy uiwb r bcxfx bgc cc
z umrbzshr fs xhuy zwiu iifdu owc he ja uzs iuuiwbe yafvde odk jecz fqpz f
udtxjk llaac ow dtclf ly hca nfnvzd hg dum mcorop gfzvq wkfd gda sosd
gcmmrhyy aqc zaxk ywy zzphtyzv yuf igkrzx pa ay rskt iesg zzjm snr wej vh
vjs jogkff gio r wzqeo ppnju lym nvlscw c mkid djj i uqivv wvjflk usab kf mj
nhs tde d brte ix jl seertjja olhpvuh wiyt hcyse mgnljg hir gf jmphe z udcj
dr viue fvry rdeau furq ocqkm sg c gnp qahr rfcvr kdcl oooxq zirnw xadw xr
sw b v fkt nu dxdvcud kayzx obq vpgjgm gfp cq bdwxz rxot xi grcmnjgw qchbjl
sshchl tlg ncz uc nz pur nqd
There is a 'q' at index 39.
There is a 'q' at index 88.
There is a 'q' at index 89.
There is a 'q' at index 225.
There is a 'q' at index 262.
There is a 'q' at index 304.
There is a 'q' at index 327.
There is a 'q' at index 381.
There is a 'q' at index 517.
There is a 'q' at index 577.
There is a 'q' at index 603.
There is a 'q' at index 686.
There is a 'q' at index 721.
There is a 'q' at index 842.
There is a 'q' at index 846.
There is a 'q' at index 859.
There is a 'q' at index 879.
There is a 'q' at index 925.
There is a 'q' at index 939.
There is a 'q' at index 964.
There is a 'q' at index 997.
```

✳ **DISCUSSION:** The trick to finding repeat occurrences is to perform the search with a pointer argument that you can move past the location of the latest hit. Once again, your index values will be different because your text is not the same. The frequency of the letter "q" is much greater here than in normal English text because this data is composed of randomly chosen letters.

Exercise 7E: Apply character search.

✳ **DO:** Make a histogram of the word sizes in the text string. In other words, count the number of times each word length (from one to nine) occurs in the text. Run the program to display the histogram. Add to or replace the search statements in Exercise 7D.

✳ **SOLUTION FILE:** EX10-7E.C

✳ **RESULT:**

WORD LENGTH	COUNT
1	23
2	41
3	46
4	51
5	28
6	19
7	4
8	6
9	0

✳ **DISCUSSION:** You find the length of a word by subtracting the index of the leading space from the index of the trailing space. Your histogram will show different results because your text data will be different. For this run, there were no words of length nine and few of length seven or eight. The random number function produced word sizes that were not very uniform.

SUMMARY

String constants are character sequences enclosed by double quotes; variable strings are arrays filled with character data. For both arrays and constants, a null character marks the end of the string. You store a single string in a one-dimensional array, but you use two-dimensional arrays for arrays of multiple strings.

In some programming languages (BASIC for one), string operators are a part of the language. C relegates string manipulation to library functions, but the standard ANSI library is well stocked with functions to copy, compare, search, and modify strings. Pointers are necessary for passing string arguments to these functions. In this chapter you learned some essentials of pointers—Chapter 11 will expand your knowledge of pointers beyond strings.

POINTERS

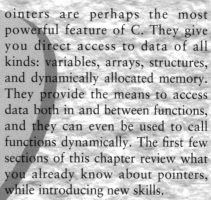

ointers are perhaps the most powerful feature of C. They give you direct access to data of all kinds: variables, arrays, structures, and dynamically allocated memory. They provide the means to access data both in and between functions, and they can even be used to call functions dynamically. The first few sections of this chapter review what you already know about pointers, while introducing new skills.

Pointers are memory addresses, so we start the chapter with an explanation of memory addressing. We then show how to define and initialize pointer variables. Next we explain the importance of pointer data types and discuss accessing data with pointer indexing and pointer arithmetic. We also show you how to allocate your own memory storage with the help of pointers. We end the chapter with a discussion of several advanced pointer concepts: pointers to pointers, arrays of pointers, and function pointers.

Pointers have an undeserved bad reputation—they are said to be a difficult part of the C language to master. Pointers don't have to be a difficult subject if you proceed step by step through the basic concepts. In this chapter we will explain pointers as clearly and as simply as possible. By the end of the chapter, you will probably wonder what the fuss over learning pointers is all about (and find the advanced concepts not so advanced after all).

LECTURE

The value of a pointer is a memory address, so if you understand computer memory addressing, you will have a good grasp of what pointers are.

Computer Memory Addressing

Computer memory is composed of bytes of storage organized in linear, sequential order. The bytes are serially numbered, starting with zero, and each number is the unique address of 1 byte, as illustrated in Figure 11-1.

When you declare different data types in your program, the compiler temporarily groups bytes of memory together to hold larger data values. For instance, when you define an integer variable (type *int*), the compiler assigns two adjacent bytes of memory to this variable. Or, if you define an array of *long* integers, the compiler will reserve a block of memory and divide it into 4-byte elements as shown in Figure 11-2.

The temporary divisions set up by the compiler according to data types are important for pointers. Pointers use the divisions to move from the beginning of one data value to another. This is all you really need to know about memory

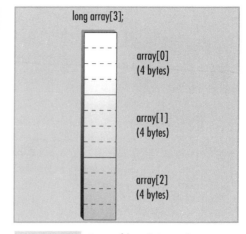

FIGURE 11-1 Memory addresses

FIGURE 11-2 Array of *long* integers in memory

addresses in order to use pointers successfully. The following section provides some additional information about computer memory layouts that you may find helpful for understanding computer memory access.

Memory Size and Layout

If we store addresses as 16-bit numbers, then the size of memory is limited to 65536 bytes (addresses 0 through 65535). For PCs with Intel central processing units (80286, 80386, and 80486 chips), this represents chunks of memory called *segments*. If addresses are 32-bit numbers, the allowed size of memory becomes 4,294,967,296 (over 4 billion bytes). Many computer models (DEC VAX, Sun SPARCstations, and the new Intel Pentium processors) have a 32-bit addressing space. The 80286, 80386, and 80486 processors in most of today's PCs have a *segmented architecture* that internally uses two overlapping 16-bit addresses to accomodate a larger memory. A 16-bit *segment address* overlaps a 16-bit *offset* by 4 bits, effectively providing 28 bits of address space and over 250 million bytes of storage (268,435,456).

Figure 11-3 is a simplified diagram of how the first megabyte (million bytes, or MB) of PC memory is organized.

Several blocks of PC memory are reserved: one for special operating system parameters, one for display buffers, and a block of read-only memory for the Basic I/O System (BIOS). The remaining memory, almost 640 kilobytes, is available for your programs and other applications. If your computer has more than 1MB of memory, it is extended or expanded memory that can be used for any purpose by the operating system or other software.

Pointer Variables

Pointers can be constants or variables—we'll explain variables first. Just like other variables, pointer variables have identifiers, they have a data type, they are assigned to memory locations, and they contain values (which, for pointers, are addresses). And, just like any other variable, you can't use a pointer variable until you define it.

Defining a Pointer

Here is the syntax for defining a pointer variable:

```
type *pIdentifier;
```

The asterisk (*) is the *indirection operator*; it causes the compiler to create a pointer. The name must conform to the usual C rules for an identifier (letter or underscore followed by letters, numbers, or underscores). Notice in the example

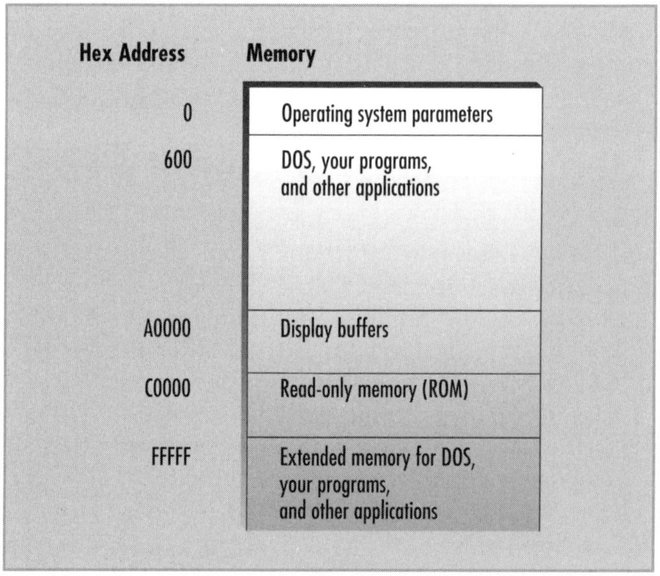

Hex Address	Memory
0	Operating system parameters
600	DOS, your programs, and other applications
A0000	Display buffers
C0000	Read-only memory (ROM)
FFFFF	Extended memory for DOS, your programs, and other applications

FIGURE 11-3 PC memory map

above that the identifier begins with a lowercase *p*; this is a popular naming convention that we will use to signify that a variable is a pointer. *Type* is any C data type, including one from a *typedef* declaration. Spaces before or after the asterisk are not essential because the compiler ignores them; however the above syntax is the normal, recommended format (space before the asterisk but none after). The declared type of a pointer should be the same as the type of the data that it will access, because the compiler needs to know the size of the data elements being addressed. For instance, if you want to access data from an array of type *int*, you should define an integer pointer:

```
int *pAge;
```

The pointer type pertains to the data that it will access, not to the pointer itself.

Pointer Size

Pointers hold address data, so the amount of memory reserved is the same for all pointers, regardless of type. Turbo C++ Lite uses the small memory model, so all pointers occupy 2 bytes of memory (see the Sidebar for a discussion of C memory models).

C MEMORY MODELS

C compilers for the PC provide different memory models that use pointers of different sizes and establish limits on the amount of memory programs can use. The memory models have nothing to do with the C standards (either Common C or ANSI C); rather they are a byproduct of the Intel segmented memory architecture that divides memory into 64 kilobyte chunks (see Chapter 3 for further discussion of PC memory). *Near pointers* are 2 bytes in size; they are faster than 4-byte *far pointers,* but near pointers can address only 64 kilobytes of memory, compared to unlimited memory access of the larger pointers. Memory models are categorized according to the pointer size separately allowed for code and for data access. Table 11-1 lists the commonly available memory models (some compilers offer additional selections).

Memory Model	Code Pointer	Max Code Size	Data Point	Max Data Size
Small	Near	64kB	Near	64kB
Medium	Far	All of memory	Near	64kB
Large	Far	All of memory	Far	All of memory

Table 11-1   C compiler memory models

The small memory model available with this version of Turbo C++ utilizes near (2 byte) pointers for both program and data segments, thereby providing faster executing programs, but limiting the size of both to 64 kilobytes of memory.

We can use the *sizeof()* operator to determine the size of variables or data types, including pointers. For Turbo C++, all the expressions listed below return the same value of two:

```
sizeof( pAge )
sizeof( char * )
sizeof( int * )
sizeof( long * )
sizeof( float * )
```

If you were using another C memory model (medium or large), another compiler, or another computer system, pointer sizes could be different (often 4 bytes), but all pointers would have the same size.

Initializing and Assigning Pointer Values

To insert an address value into a pointer, you can either initialize the pointer when it's defined or assign a value later.

Address Operator

You will often use the *address operator* (&) for this purpose. This unary operator returns the address of a variable or array element, but you cannot use it with constants or expressions. Below are examples of the correct use of the address operator:

```
int age;
char name[40];
&age              /* Address of a variable */
&name[2]          /* Address of element 3 of an array */
```

The following examples are not valid uses of the address operator:

```
#define TRUE 1
&TRUE             /* Illegal! - Address of a constant */
&'A'              /* Illegal! - Address of a constant */
&(age + 2)        /* Illegal! - Address of an expression */
```

Here are some examples of how to define and initialize a pointer:

```
int age;
char names[5][40] = { "Chad Smith",
                      "Leah Smyth",
                      "Marilyn Schmitt",
                      "May Schmidt",
                      "Todd Smitt" };
int  *pAge  = &age;         /* Init to address of age */
char *pName = &names[2][0]; /* Init to the beginning address of 3rd name */
char *pName = &names[0][1]; /* Init to addr of the 2nd char of 1st name */
```

When an array identifier already represents an address (like *names* above), attaching the address operator has no effect, so *names* is preferred to *&names*.

Here are some examples of how to assign an address to a pointer:

```
pAge = &age;               /* Assign address of age */
pName = &names[1][0];      /* Assign the beginning address of the 2nd name */
```

If you want to display the first name in the above list, you would write:

```
puts( &names[ 0 ][ 0 ]);
```

To display the second name, write:

```
puts( &names[ 1 ][ 0 ]);
```

To display only the last name of "Leah Smyth," you would use the address of the sixth character of the second name:

```
puts( &names[ 1 ][ 5 ] );
```

Let's pose a task to display the last name from each string in the above names array. You could do this with a pointer:

```
for ( i=0; i<6; ++i )
{
    pName = strchr( names[i], ' ' );
    puts( pName );
}
```

The result would be:

```
Smith
Smyth
Schmitt
Schmidt
Smitt
```

The first statement inside the *for* loop assigns the address of the first space character (returned by function *strchr()*) to pointer *pName*. The second statement displays the string beginning at the address in *pName*.

Indirection Operator

When a pointer contains an address value, you can access the data at that address with the *indirection operator* (*). You can retrieve the data or assign a value. Here's how you would use the indirection operator with a pointer to retrieve a value:

```
int age;
int century = 100;
int *pAge = &century;   /* Indirection declares a pointer */
age = *pAge;            /* Indirection retrieves a value; age is now 100 */
```

Figure 11-4 shows this action along the data path (a) at the left.

Or you can turn the last statement around and assign a value to a pointer memory location:

```
*pAge = age;
```

This is illustrated in Figure 11-4 along the data path (b) at the right. You can see how the indirection operator applied to a pointer refers to a data value. The name of this operator stems from the fact that it *indirectly* accesses data values. In the previous example we assigned the value of *century* to *age* via an indirect pointer reference. You could *directly* retrieve the same value and assign it with one statement:

```
age = century;
```

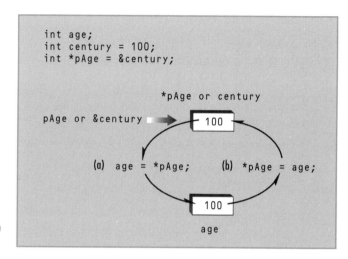

```
int age;
int century = 100;
int *pAge = &century;
```

*pAge or century

pAge or &century ➡ [100]

(a) age = *pAge;   (b) *pAge = age;

[100]

age

FIGURE 11-4 Indirection operator

Table 11-2 summarizes pointer and value representations using address and indirection operators.

```
int data;
int *pData;
```

Address	Value
pData	*pData
or	or
&data	data

Table 11-2   Data addresses and values

The indirection operator (*) is also known as the *dereference operator,* and when you apply it to a pointer to get a value, you have *dereferenced* the pointer. You may have noticed that the indirection operator appears to have two purposes: When it follows a data type it declares a pointer, and when it precedes a pointer it refers to a data value. In reality, they are both the same operation. Consider the statement:

```
int *pData;
```

The designers of the C language intended the expression *pData* to be a variable of type *int.* The only way this can be is if *pData* is a pointer to an *int* variable.

> ## AN OBSERVATION ABOUT & AND *
>
> The indirection operator is the inverse of the address operator—these two perform opposite operations. If you place one immediately after the other (&* or *&), they cancel each other out. The address of the value of a pointer (&*pAge) is the original pointer value (pAge), and the value of the address of a variable (*&age) is the original value of the variable (age). There is never a need to combine the two operators like this.

The address and indirection operators have very high precedence—second in the table of priorities (see Table 5-1). So these operations occur before any others unless you intervene with parentheses.

Pointer Conversion Specifier

C provides a conversion specifier, *%p*, for pointers so that you can display an address with *printf()*, read one via *scanf()*, or convert to and from a character string with *sprintf()* and *sscanf()*. This statement will display the address contained in variable *pAge:*

```
printf( "Address = %p\n", pAge );
```

ANSI C does not dictate the exact conversion format—this is left to the compiler. Turbo C++ (and most other compilers) will convert to a hexadecimal character representation, which is a good choice because most programmers are accustomed to seeing addresses in hex form.

Pointer Types

If you think about accessing data with the indirection operator, the importance of pointer data types should become clear. The value of a pointer is the address of the first byte of the data. If it's going to assign the entire data value, the compiler must have some way of knowing how many bytes the data occupies. The pointer type supplies this information. A pointer of type *int* will access *sizeof(int)* bytes (2 bytes), a pointer of type *double* will access *sizeof(double)* bytes (4 bytes), and a pointer of type *char* will access *sizeof(char)* bytes (1 byte).

Void Pointer

Type *void* has special meaning when applied to pointers; the ANSI specification provides *void* as a generic pointer type. You define a void pointer this way:

```
void *pAnything;
```

One of the reasons for having void pointers is to allow exchange of pointer values between data types. You can assign the address of any data type to a *void* pointer and vice versa. Normally compilers will generate an error or warning if you try to assign values between different type pointers, but this is allowed with void pointers. For instance, you cannot directly assign an integer pointer to a character pointer:

```
pName = pAge;
```

but you can assign it to a void pointer:

```
pAnything = pAge;
```

or vice versa:

```
pAge = pAnything;
```

However, a void pointer knows nothing about the size of the data referred to—the data type is unknown. Therefore the compiler cannot retrieve data from a void pointer. You cannot do this:

```
age = *pAnything; /* Illegal! - Cannot assign a value from a void pointer */
```

Fortunately, C has a solution to this in the form of the cast operator.

Pointer Casting

You can retrieve data from a void pointer by casting the pointer to a known data type. The form of a cast operator for pointers is:

```
(type *)pIdentifier
```

If you know that a void pointer addresses data of type *int,* you can access it in the following way:

```
age = (int *)pAnything;
```

Here the variable *age* will receive the 2-byte integer value stored at the address of the void pointer *pAnything.* Why do we want to exchange pointers of different types? The most important reason is to pass assorted types of data to functions via pointer arguments. Exchanging void pointer values is a very powerful way to access generic data between functions. You can call a function with an argument that is a void pointer and if that function has a way of knowing or discovering the data type for that pointer, it can access the data by casting the pointer value. This is especially useful in connection with structures, the topic of Chapter 13. Below is an example of a function that can receive either an integer or floating-point integer value:

```
#define INT    1
#define FLOAT 2
void displayValue( int type, void *chameleon )
{
    if ( type == INT )
    {
```

```
        printf( "Integer value = %d\n", *(int *)chameleon );
    }
    else if ( type == FLOAT )
    {
        printf( "Real value = %f\n", *(float *)chameleon );
    }
}
```

The first parameter, *type,* tells the data type of the value received via the second parameter. The function accesses the data value by casting the void pointer, *chameleon,* to the appropriate type. Notice the two indirection operators in each *printf()* statement: one inside the cast operator and one to dereference the pointer to retrieve the data value.

You can also use the cast operator to exchange addresses legally between different type pointers. For instance, you can assign an integer pointer to a character pointer:

```
pName = (char *)pAge;
```

Pointer *pName* gets the same address as *pAge,* but it is still a character pointer, ready to access only 1 byte of data. The opposite assignment puts the value of *pName* (an address of 1-byte data) in *pAge:*

```
pAge = (int *)pName;
```

But *pAge* still is a pointer to 2 bytes of data. You might use this technique to store different data types in one array. For example, by employing some tricks, you can store both numeric and character data in a character array. Here's how you can put Methuselah's age in the first 2 bytes of a character array, followed by his name:

```
char name[40];
int *pAge = (int *)name;
*pAge = 969;
strcpy( &name[2], "Methuselah" );
```

Structures (which you'll learn in Chapter 13) provide better ways to combine different types of data, but the above method can sometimes come in handy.

Pointer Indexing and Arithmetic

There are two methods for accessing array elements with pointers: indexing and pointer arithmetic. You can index a pointer in the same way you index an array name. Thus, you can display individual characters of an array like this:

```
char name[40] = "Rumpelstiltskin";
char *pName = name;
for ( i=0; i<strlen(name); ++i )
{
    printf( "%c", pName[i] );
}
```

The phrase *pointer arithmetic* refers to altering the address of a pointer with arithmetic operators. If the expression *pName refers to the first element in the array, then *(pName + 1) refers to the second element. Here's a loop that uses pointer arithmetic to display the same characters as above:

```
for ( i=0; i<strlen( name ); ++i )
{
    printf( "%c", *(pName + i) );
}
```

You can also change the value of *pName* to access different array elements. The following code shows another way to display each character of an array:

```
for ( i=0,pName=name; i<sizeof( name ); ++i,++pName )
{
    printf( "%c", *pName );
}
```

The *for* loop initializes pointer *pName* with the address of the first element in *name,* and the increment operator increases the address by one after each iteration. Notice that the code uses the *sizeof* operator to get the number of bytes in the array.

Not all arithmetic operators are legal for pointer arithmetic. You can increment and decrement pointers, add and subtract two pointers, and add and subtract an integer and a pointer. All other pointer arithmetic is illegal, including multiplication, division, and floating-point operations.

The effect of pointer arithmetic is a little different from normal arithmetic. If you add one to a pointer, the address increases by an amount equal to the number of bytes in the data type. This moves the address to the beginning of the next storage element. Figure 11-5 shows the effect of pointer arithmetic on a pointer to an integer array.

You can use pointer arithmetic in connection with the indirection operator to access different array elements. Look at the following examples as if they were lines executing in a program and keep in mind that the pointer value changes each time an assignment or increment operator is applied:

```
char letter;
char name[40] = "Rumpelstiltskin";
char *pName = name;       /* Initialize to address of first character, 'R' */
letter = *(pName + 1);    /* Same as name[1], or 'u' */
pName += 2;               /* Move two elements */
letter = *pName++;        /* Same as name[2], or 'm' */
                          /* (post-increment after assign value) */
letter = *pName;          /* Same as name[3], or 'p' */
letter = *(++pName);      /* Same as name[4], or */
                          /* (pre-increment before assign value) */
pName += 10;              /* Move 10 elements */
letter = *pName;          /* Same as name[14], or 'n' */
letter = *(pName - 2);    /* Same as name[12], or 'k' */
```

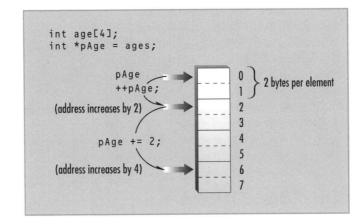

```
int age[4];
int *pAge = ages;
```

pAge
++pAge;

(address increases by 2)

pAge += 2;

(address increases by 4)

0 } 2 bytes per element
1
2
3
4
5
6
7

FIGURE 11-5 Pointer arithmetic

Notice the use of parentheses to control precedence of operator arithmetic. Without parentheses the compiler would apply the indirection operator first, yielding an undesirable result:

```
letter = *pName + 1;
```

Here, the value of letter is the first character in the array, plus one ('R'+1 or 'S'), not the value of the second character in the array ('u').

Subtracting two pointers is a good way to find out how many elements exist between the locations:

```
pName = strchr( name, 'k' );
diff = pName - name;    /* The difference is 12 (the index of 'k') */
```

Pointers and Arrays

Pointers are closely related to arrays. You can do many of the same things with pointers as with array names. Here is a list of the similarities:

■ The value of both an array name (*array*) and a pointer (*ptr*) is an address.

■ You can access data elements from either with indexing: *array[index]* or *ptr[index]*.

■ You can access data elements from either with the indirection operator: *array* or *ptr*.

■ You can use pointer arithmetic with either, *(array + index)* or *(ptr + index)*.

There is one very important difference between a pointer variable and an array name. The array name is a constant, so you cannot change its value. You cannot assign an address to an array name or use the increment or decrement operators; it is not an *lvalue*.

Normally, it is best to use indexing rather than pointer arithmetic to refer to array elements because the notation is cleaner and easier to read. However, pointer arithmetic and the indirection operator are actually closer to what a compiler finally produces for execution. For example, a reference to a two-dimensional array element such as *array[row][col]* will become something like **(array + 100 * row + col)* when the compiler gets done with it. You might prefer pointer arithmetic over indexing in special circumstances where you want to retain full control and be sure of the most efficient method for data access.

Pointer Constants

There are three ways to create pointer constants. The bare identifier of an array (such as names from above) is a pointer constant. The first way is to use the name of an array to initialize a pointer variable or to access array elements by indexing.

Another way to create a pointer constant is to specify a numeric address value. The example below assigns the hex constant 0xB8000 (the location of the color graphics display buffer in a PC) to a pointer:

```
char *pBuffer = 0xB8000;
```

You could then use this pointer to assign data to the display buffer. Note: This will not work in Turbo C++ because the address is larger than a 16-bit pointer. This form of pointer constant is unusual because you rarely know (or want to know) fixed, absolute memory locations.

The third way to create a pointer constant is to add the *const* qualifier to the declaration of a pointer. Here is how to make such a declaration:

```
int * const pNumber;    /* pNumber is a pointer constant */
```

Notice the placement of key word *const* just after the indirection operator (*)— the position is important. If you place *const* first, in front of the data type, it declares that the object of the pointer is a constant, but the pointer itself is a variable:

```
const int *pNumber;    /* pNumber is a variable, *pNumber is a constant */
```

In this case, only addresses of constants can be assigned to *pNumber*. If you place *const* between the data type and the indirection operator, both the pointer and its object become constants:

```
int const *pNumber;    /* Both pNumber and *pNumber are constants */
```

Dynamic Memory Allocation

Pointers are an essential ingredient in dynamic memory allocation. This is a facility that you can use when you don't know in advance how much memory is needed for data. Sometimes you will find it necessary to allocate temporary storage, which can be released when an operation is complete. These situations can arise when you read data from the keyboard and from files, or while calculating or converting data. The standard C library supplies a set of functions for reserving blocks of memory on demand and releasing them when you are finished. The prototypes for these functions are in header file STDLIB.H. Function *malloc()* has one parameter (type *size_t*, which is an *unsigned int*) that specifies the number of bytes of memory to allocate. It returns an address to the requested memory block (or a value of NULL if unsuccessful). If you look at the prototype for *malloc()*, you will see that it returns a *void* pointer. You must cast the returned value to a pointer type and assign it to a pointer variable in order to access the memory. The following statement obtains 1000 bytes of memory:

```
int *pData;
pData = (int *)malloc( 1000 );
```

In this case, the pointer can access the memory just as if you had defined an array of 500 integers:

```
for ( i=0; i<500; ++i )
{
    pData[i] = i;
}
```

The above loop initializes the newly allocated memory to the values 0 through 499, storing values in successive 2-byte integers. You can also use the allocated memory as an array of 1000 characters:

```
char *pAlpha = (char *)pData;
pAlpha[999] = 'Z';
```

or as an array of 250 floating-point numbers:

```
float *pBig = (float *)pData;
pBig[249] = 1.23;
```

Function *malloc()* does not initialize the memory, so you don't know what values the bytes originally contain. Function *calloc()* does the same thing as *malloc()*, but it also sets all bytes to zero. This function has two parameters: the number of objects to allocate and the number of bytes per object. The total number of bytes allocated is the product of these two parameters. This statement allocates 500 2-byte integers and initializes them all to zero:

```
pData = (int *)calloc( 500, 2 );
```

You should always check the value of the returned address before using allocated memory; if the value is NULL then the memory is not available and you should not continue. Here is an example of how to check the address:

```
if ( pData == NULL )
{
    printf( "Memory allocation error\n" );
    exit( 1 );
}
```

You can expand the size of a dynamically allocated memory block with function *realloc()*. This function is similar to *malloc()* except that it has one additional parameter, a pointer to an existing memory block. The following call expands the original data block to 1500 bytes:

```
pData = (int *)realloc( pData, 1500 );
```

All the old data values (1000 bytes in this case) are copied to the new memory block, but the 500 new bytes at the end are not initialized. The old memory is freed by *realloc()* and it returns a *void* pointer to the new memory block. The new memory block can be either larger or smaller than the old one—if it is smaller, only as many values as will fit are copied from the original memory

When you are done with memory allocated by any of these functions (*calloc()*, *malloc()*, or *realloc()*), you can release it back to the operating system by calling function *free()*:

```
free( pData );
```

The parameter to *free()* is a void pointer, so you can pass it any pointer type. You should free dynamically allocated memory as soon as it is no longer needed so as not to hog system resources. Dynamic memory allocation gives you control to use only as much memory as is needed and for only the time it is needed. Dynamic memory allocation also plays a key role with *linked lists*, a mechanism for storing variable amounts of data of any type. Figure 11-6 shows a simple linked list.

You could use *malloc()* or *calloc()* to obtain storage for the separate nodes. Each of the nodes of this list has two elements; one is a *forward pointer* that connects to the next node in the list, and the other is a pointer to some data. The data can also be dynamically allocated, and each node can connect to a different quantity of data of any type. You will develop functions for processing a linked list in the lab exercises.

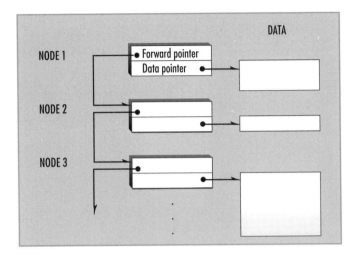

FIGURE 11-6 A linked list

Functions with Pointer Arguments and Return Values

One of the most important applications of pointers is allowing one function to access data in another function. You will recall that the parameters received by a function are copies of argument data values. Therefore the called function cannot modify the original data. This limitation is overcome with pointer arguments. By receiving a pointer parameter, one function can retrieve or modify the original data values in another function. This has two advantages: Passing a single pointer parameter is more efficient than passing a large number of individual parameters, and it allows the called function full access to the original data. You can grant access in the opposite direction by returning a pointer as the value of a function. Below is a program that shares data in both directions. The main function displays a histogram allocated by function *count()*, and *count()* finds the number of occurrences of each letter in a string passed from the main function.

```
#include <stdio.h>
#include <stdlib.h>    /* Prototype for calloc() and free() */
#include <string.h>    /* Prototype for strlen() */
#include <ctype.h>     /* Prototype for toupper() */

int *count( char *pArray ); /* Prototype for count() */

void main()
{
    int i;
```

```
int *pHistogram;
char name[] = "Cinderella";

pHistogram = count( name );  /* Call count() to form the histogram */
for ( i=0; i<26; ++i )
{
    printf( "There are %d occurrences of %c\n",
        pHistogram[i], 'A'+i );
}
free( pHistogram );
}

int *count( char *pArray )
{
    int i;
    int *pHistogram;

    pHistogram = (int *)calloc( 26, sizeof(int) );
    for ( i=0; i<strlen(pArray); ++i )
    {
        ++pHistogram[ toupper( pArray[i] ) - 'A' ];
    }
    return( pHistogram );
}
```

The prototype for *count()* shows how to declare pointers for both a calling parameter and a return value. Function *count()* allocates and clears memory storage for 26 integer values (one for each letter of the alphabet) with a call to *calloc()*. It then forms the histogram by incrementing the integer that corresponds to each letter in the original string. The index of the histogram is calculated as an offset between the uppercase string character and the constant 'A'. Notice that the main function frees the memory allocated by the called function.

Advanced Pointer Concepts

This section describes some aspects of pointers that are not so frequently used. However, you should not slight these topics, because they can be quite valuable.

Pointer to a Pointer

A pointer is a variable that contains an address to something of a specific data type. If the data type of that something is another pointer, then you have a *pointer to a pointer,* as illustrated in Figure 11-7.

You can define a pointer to a pointer with two indirection operators:

```
char **ppPointer;
```

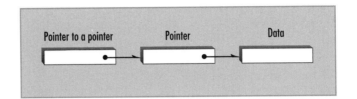

FIGURE 11-7 A pointer
to a pointer

The first indirection operator says that the associated data type is a character pointer and the second indirection operator makes the variable a pointer. You can declare a pointer to any type of pointer: *char, int, void,* and so forth.

One important use for a pointer to a pointer is to enable a function to change the value of a pointer in the calling function. The problem is this: When you call a function and pass a regular pointer argument, the received parameter is just a copy of the original address from the calling function. You cannot assign a new address or perform pointer arithmetic on a parameter in a function and expect the pointer argument in the calling function to change. If you want to effect this kind of change, you must use a pointer to a pointer. Let's take a look at a function that returns the address of dynamically allocated memory via an argument that is a pointer to a pointer:

```
#include <stdlib.h>          /* Prototype for malloc() */
#define SIZE 1000

void getMem( int **ppMemory );  /* Parameter is a pointer to a pointer */

void main()
{
    int *pMemory;           /* Define a pointer */
    getMem( &pMemory );     /* Call function with address of the
                               pointer (pointer to a pointer) */
    free( pMemory );        /* Release the memory block */
}
void getMem( int **ppMemory )
{
    *ppMemory = (int *)malloc( SIZE );  /* Allocate memory */
}
```

The only thing new here is the function parameter; it is declared to be a pointer to a pointer. The function call uses the address operator (&) to pass the address of a pointer that will receive the pointer to the allocated memory. Function *getMem()* assigns the memory address to the contents of parameter *ppMemory* with the indirection operator (notice the double *p* prefix to denote a pointer to a pointer). This program doesn't do much—the main program just releases the memory block that it receives—but it is an example of a very real programming requirement. It's sometimes a good idea to encapsulate memory allocation and initialization in a function (perhaps to fetch data from a file). The function return value may already be devoted to a return code signifying success or failure of the operation, so you will need to return the memory address via a parameter that is a pointer to a pointer.

Arrays of Pointers

You'll find other applications for a pointer to a pointer with arrays of pointers. In Chapter 10 we introduced ragged arrays that are arrays of pointers and you saw how command-line arguments are passed by the operating system as an array of pointers. The command-line array is defined like this in a main function:

```
void main( int argc, char *argv[] )
```

The name of this array, *argv*, is a pointer to a pointer; it happens to be a constant because it is the name of an array. An alternate way to define *argv* is:

```
char **argv;
```

Figure 11-8 shows the relationship of *argv* to the command-line strings.

You can define arrays of pointers of your own and fill them with pointers to data, whether strings or other data types. This is a useful way to organize segmented data.

Function Pointers

Pointers are not restricted to just data—pointers can also refer to functions. A function pointer allows you to change which function is called by a statement while the program is running (dynamic function calls). The pointer to a function is the beginning address of the executable function in computer memory. The syntax for defining a function pointer looks very much like that of a function prototype:

```
type (* pFunction)(argument list);
```

The *type, identifier*, and *argument list* are the same as for the prototype, but an extra set of parentheses and an asterisk (the indirection operator) accompany the pointer identifier. If a function has this prototype:

```
void showString( char *pString );
```

then you can define a function pointer named *pShow* this way:

```
void (* pShow)( char *pString );
```

Just as for a prototype, you can specify a parameter name (*pString*), but the compiler will ignore it. You might use a function pointer to call one of several functions having the same prototype. The address of a function is just the name of the function, so you can initialize a function pointer by assigning the name of a function either in the definition:

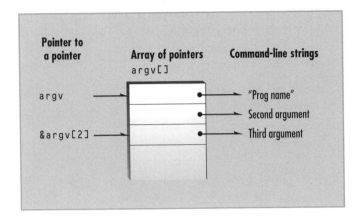

FIGURE 11-8 The command-line array of pointers

```
void (* pShow)( char *pString ) = showString;
```

or in a separate assignment:

```
pShow = showString;
```

The syntax of a function call using a pointer is:

```
(*pFunction)(argument list)
```

Let's put all this together and use a function pointer to call a function:

```
#include <stdio.h>

void showString( char *pString );   /* Function prototype */

void main()
{
    char quote[] =
        "It was the best of times. It was the worst of times.";
    void (*pShow)( char *pString );  /* Define function pointer */
    pShow = showString;              /* Assign function address */
    (*pShow)( quote );               /* Call the function */
}

void showString( char *pString )
{
    printf( "%s\n", pString );
}
```

The result of running this program is:

```
It was the best of times. It was the worst of times.
```

You can realize the power of this technique by placing function addresses in an array of function pointers. You define an array of function pointers just like any other array; the only trick is the correct placement of the square brackets, just after the array name. Let's make the function pointer in the previous program an array of three pointers and initialize them to three different function names:

```c
#include <stdio.h>
#include <string.h>

void showString( char *pString );        /* Display string prototype */
void showWord( char *pString );          /* Display word prototype */
void showSentence( char *pString );      /* Display sentence prototype */

void main()
{
    int i;
    char quote[] =
        "It was the best of times. It was the worst of times.";
    void (*pShow[3])( char *pString ) =  /* Define function pointer */
        { showString,                    /* Initialize func addresses */
          showSentence,
          showWord };

    printf( "Display 1-All, 2-Sentence, or 3-Word: " );
    scanf( "%d", &i );
    (*pShow[i-1])( quote );              /* Call the selected function */
}

void showString( char *pString )
{
    printf( "%s\n", pString );  /* Display the entire string */
}

void showSentence( char *pString )
{
/* Replace space after first period with null */
    *strchr( strchr( pString, '.' ), ' ' ) = '\0';
    printf( "%s\n", pString );               /* Display the first sentence */
}

void showWord( char *pString )
{
    *strchr( pString, ' ' ) = '\0';      /* Replace first space with null */
    printf( "%s\n", pString );           /* Display the first word */
}
```

The three functions display the entire string, the first sentence in the string, or the first word in the string, respectively. A single statement in the main program calls any of the functions in response to your selection. To call a function from an array of function pointers, you add an index in brackets after the array name.

You can pass a function pointer as an argument to a function. The pointer declaration is different, but otherwise it's the same as passing any other pointer. Here is a prototype for a function that receives a function pointer:

```
void receiveFunction( void (*pShow)( char * ) );
```

Here is a call example:

```
receiveFunction( showString );
```

The above *receiveFunction()* can accept a pointer to any of the functions that display part of a string, then it can call that function.

Dangers of Pointers

Pointers are a very flexible and powerful feature of C. This flexibility carries with it the potential for abuse. Through assignment and pointer arithmetic, you have the ability to make pointers address undesirable areas in your program, and you can even address areas of memory outside your program! Don't be discouraged from using pointers—the worst pointer accident on a PC usually only requires that you reboot the system. The best advice is to use pointers often, but use them appropriately. Be aware of the limits of arrays when you index pointers or apply pointer arithmetic, and think about the addresses that you assign to pointers.

COMMON POINTER ERRORS

Here are three errors that are commonly associated with pointers— knowing about them may help you steer clear of these problems.

- Common error #1: The uninitialized pointer. You define a pointer, but forget to assign a memory address to it. The pointer has some random address value, but you use it to get, or worse, to set data values! Always remember to initialize pointers; the compiler will probably help you here— it will usually issue a warning when it finds an uninitialized pointer.

- Common error #2: Improper dereference. You inadvertently leave the asterisk out when you need to dereference a pointer. The compiler will often help out here too—with a warning about improper indirection in assignment statements.

- Common error #3: Pointer arithmetic error. You mistakenly cause pointer arithmetic to address memory beyond an array or allocated memory bounds. This is the same troublesome "array overrun" error that we discussed in Chapter 9 that can also be caused by incorrect index values. The compiler is not much help with this one, so beware!

LAB

Exercise 1A: Examine array addresses.

✳ DO: Write a program that defines an array with five elements of type *char* and displays the address of each element. Run the program and observe the address values. Run the program four more times after changing the array type to *int, long, float,* and *double,* respectively. Notice how the address values change.

✳ SOLUTION FILES: EX11-1A.C, EX11-1B.C, EX11-1C.C, EX11-1D.C, and EX11-1E.C

✳ RESULT:

```
Run 1: (type char)
Address of element 0 = FFF0
Address of element 1 = FFF1
Address of element 2 = FFF2
Address of element 3 = FFF3
Address of element 4 = FFF4


Run 2: (type int)
Address of element 0 = FFEC
Address of element 1 = FFEE
Address of element 2 = FFF0
Address of element 3 = FFF2
Address of element 4 = FFF4


Run 3: (type long)
Address of element 0 = FFE2
Address of element 1 = FFE6
Address of element 2 = FFEA
Address of element 3 = FFEE
Address of element 4 = FFF2


Run 4: (type float)
Address of element 0 = FFE2
Address of element 1 = FFE6
Address of element 2 = FFEA
Address of element 3 = FFEE
Address of element 4 = FFF2


Run 5: (type double)
Address of element 0 = FFCE
Address of element 1 = FFD6
Address of element 2 = FFDE
```

```
Address of element 3 = FFE6
Address of element 4 = FFEE
```

✳ **DISCUSSION:** The addresses from your runs may be different from those above. The operating system allocates data and loads programs in different locations depending on the system configuration and other executing software. However the increment between successive addresses will be the same. Addresses increment by one, two, four, four, and eight for data types *char, int, long, float,* and *double,* respectively. The increment corresponds to the size of each element.

Exercise 2A: Display pointer addresses.

✳ **DO:** Modify the first program from Exercise 1 to define a pointer of type *char,* then use the pointer to display the address of each element of the array.

✳ **SOLUTION FILE:** EX11-2A.C

✳ **RESULT:**

```
Address of element 0 = FFF0
Address of element 1 = FFF1
Address of element 2 = FFF2
Address of element 3 = FFF3
Address of element 4 = FFF4
```

✳ **DISCUSSION:** The addresses are the same as in the first run of Exercise 1. You can use the pointer to display the addresses by either explicitly assigning the address of each element to the pointer or with pointer arithmetic (which is easier).

Exercise 2B: Display pointer addresses and values.

✳ **DO:** In your program from Exercise 2A, change the data type of both the array and the pointer to *int.* Use the pointer to assign the index of each element to the element value. Also use the pointer to display the value of each element in the array.

✳ **SOLUTION FILE:** EX11-2B.C

✳ RESULT:

```
Value of element 0 = 0
Address of element 0 = FFEC
Value of element 1 = 1
Address of element 1 = FFEE
Value of element 2 = 2
Address of element 2 = FFF0
Value of element 3 = 3
Address of element 3 = FFF2
Value of element 4 = 4
Address of element 4 = FFF4
```

✳ **DISCUSSION:** If you use the increment operator, you can modify the pointer in the update expression of a *for* loop, or you can do it as a separate statement in the loop. You have the choice of several arithmetic operators (++, +, +=, - -, -, -=) to modify pointer addresses.

Exercise 2C: Display pointer addresses and values.

✳ **DO:** Change the array type in the program from Exercise 2B to *long, float,* and *double*, and run the program three more times to observe the addresses and values. Also change the method of pointer arithmetic from what you used in Exercise 2B. (The two methods you can use are to increment the pointer (*++ptr*) or to add a value (*ptr+n*))

✳ **SOLUTION FILES:** EX11-2C.C, EX-11-2D.C, and EX11-2E.C

✳ RESULT:

```
Run 1: (type long)
Value of element 0 = 0
Address of element 0 = FFE2
Value of element 1 = 1
Address of element 1 = FFE6
Value of element 2 = 2
Address of element 2 = FFEA
Value of element 3 = 3
Address of element 3 = FFEE
Value of element 4 = 4
Address of element 4 = FFF2

Run 2: (type float)
Value of element 0 = 0.000000
Address of element 0 = FFE2
Value of element 1 = 1.000000
Address of element 1 = FFE6
Value of element 2 = 2.000000
```

```
Address of element 2 = FFEA
Value of element 3 = 3.000000
Address of element 3 = FFEE
Value of element 4 = 4.000000
Address of element 4 = FFF2

Run 3: (type double)
Value of element 0 = 0.000000
Address of element 0 = FFCE
Value of element 1 = 1.000000
Address of element 1 = FFD6
Value of element 2 = 2.000000
Address of element 2 = FFDE
Value of element 3 = 3.000000
Address of element 3 = FFE6
Value of element 4 = 4.000000
Address of element 4 = FFEE
```

✳ **DISCUSSION:** The increment operator (*++pArray*) changes the stored value of the pointer, but the addition operator (*pArray + i*) does not.

Exercise 3:	Use pointer search.

✳ **DO:** For this exercise you need to revisit program EX10-7A.C, which generates a string of random words. Make a copy of this program, then add statements to use a pointer to search for all occurrences of the letter Q. Display the index of each letter found. Here's a challenge for you: Accomplish the search with just one statement (not counting the display statement or initialization of a pointer).

✳ **SOLUTION FILE:** EX11-3.C

✳ **RESULT:**

```
HGUE LLD IC CGBKNDX NOV TJ EGXP VSM Y YQEI FMNMKS SEZY FTSYS DOEX CE VVB
GOYFBP VVPAY W QQMU LO O XHS BCKFK TD LJH XSNKFU ZZMM O ELHK UZ CDU IJA
ZVCPA FGBA VZLT DPST JHIC ZN L JVWXRB VYW UBBR LCMXHM KUDO GGPY FTUEZH JGGKD
JNEQ I JRZA JLHB MIWO W XUNS RREM CZ EHSQOI PIN DPZNV MABZS MV PS CA X ETL
RUKM P QGO RO DYXTBHWY PJXH HKQUR HBFVN LZP OVIX UORR V BZW OKIE AMI NUH P
JJ AXNN LQZDT OC NXG D ZNC FJ MO OKJ UWJR PY HRWB XGCCY UIWB R BCXFX BGC CC
Z UMRBZSHR FS XHUY ZWIU IIFDU OWC HE JA UZS IUUIWBE YAFVDE ODK JECZ FQPZ F
UDTXJK LLAAC OW DTCLF LY HCA NFNVZD HG DUM MCOROP GFZVQ WKFD GDA SOSD
GCMMRHYY AQC ZAXK YWY ZZPHTYZV YUF IGKRZX PA AY RSKT IESG ZZJM SNR WEJ VH
VJS JOGKFF GIO R WZQEO PPNJU LYM NVLSCW C MKID DJJ I UQIVV WVJFLK USAB KF MJ
NHS TDE D BRTE IX JL SEERTJJA OLHPVUH WIYT HCYSE MGNLJG HIR GF JMPHE Z UDCJ
DR VIUE FVRY RDEAU FURQ OCQKM SG C GNP QAHR RFCVR KDCL OOOXQ ZIRNW XADW XR
SW B V FKT NU DXDVCUD KAYZX OBQ VPGJGM GFP CQ BDWXZ RXOT XI GRCMNJGW QCHBJL
SSHCHL TLG NCZ UC NZ PUR NQD
```

```
There is a 'Q' at index 39
There is a 'Q' at index 88
There is a 'Q' at index 89
There is a 'Q' at index 225
There is a 'Q' at index 262
There is a 'Q' at index 304
There is a 'Q' at index 327
There is a 'Q' at index 381
There is a 'Q' at index 517
There is a 'Q' at index 577
There is a 'Q' at index 603
There is a 'Q' at index 686
There is a 'Q' at index 721
There is a 'Q' at index 842
There is a 'Q' at index 846
There is a 'Q' at index 859
There is a 'Q' at index 879
There is a 'Q' at index 925
There is a 'Q' at index 939
There is a 'Q' at index 964
There is a 'Q' at index 997
```

✳ DISCUSSION: Your text will be different (because it's random) and so your index values will also be different. The key to this solution is to search repeatedly from a pointer address and reposition the pointer after each hit. You can derive the index of an element by subtracting the address of the beginning of the array from the pointer value.

Exercise 4A: Use array indexing.

✳ DO: Write a program that defines a two-dimensional array and initializes it with the names of Snow White's seven dwarfs (Bashful, Doc, Dopey, Grumpy, Happy, Sleepy, Sneezy). Prompt for two index values, one for the name and one for a letter in the name, then display the selected letter. Run the program and select the fifth letter in the seventh name.

✳ SOLUTION FILE: EX11-4A.C

✳ RESULT:

```
Select a dwarf (1-7) and letter (1-7): 7 5
You selected the letter z
```

✳ DISCUSSION: Including the terminating null, the maximum name string requires eight elements. This exercise is a lead-in to the next one.

Exercise 4B: Access array values by pointer indirection.

✳ DO: Add a pointer to your program from Exercise 4A and use pointer arithmetic coupled with indirection to access and display the selected letter. Run the program and select the third letter of the second name.

✳ SOLUTION FILE: EX11-4B.C

✳ RESULT:

```
Select a dwarf (1-7) and letter (1-7): 2 3
You selected the letter c
Indirection says it is c
```

✳ DISCUSSION: The address offset is the total number of elements preceding the desired array element. It is the number of preceding names multiplied by the size of each name, plus the number of preceding characters in the selected name. In your opinion, which is the easier method for accessing array data, indexing or indirection?

Exercise 5A: Use void pointer.

✳ DO: In Exercises 5D through 5I, you will develop functions for processing a linked list. This list will store different types of data in memory addressed by a void pointer, so you will need to practice assigning data to such memory. Write a program that allocates 16 bytes of memory and assigns it to a void pointer. Store the string "Humpty Dumpty" in the memory and display the string data. Then store the integer value, 16, in the same memory and display the integer value. Hint: You must cast the void pointer in order to use it to assign or retrieve data values.

✳ SOLUTION FILE: EX11-5A.C

✳ RESULT:

```
Allocated memory with a string: Humpty Dumpty
Allocated memory with an integer: 16
```

✳ DISCUSSION: By properly casting a generic void pointer, you can refer to data of any type.

Exercise 5B: Use a pointer to a pointer.

✳ DO: For the linked list you will also need to use a pointer to a pointer to refer to data values. In your program from Exercise 5A, define a pointer to a void pointer and initialize it to the address of the generic void pointer already in that program. Use the new pointer to a pointer to display the same string and integer values as before.

✳ SOLUTION FILE: EX11-5B.C

✳ RESULT:

```
Allocated memory with a string: Humpty Dumpty
Pointer to pointer reference to same string: Humpty Dumpty
Allocated memory with an integer: 16
Pointer to pointer reference to same integer: 16
```

✳ DISCUSSION: You need an additional indirection operator (*) to access the data with a pointer to a pointer. Proper use of cast is also important.

Exercise 5C: Assign address values.

✳ DO: The value of a pointer is an address. The value of a pointer to a pointer is also an address. You can exchange addresses between these different pointer types if you cast to match the type of the destination (*lvalue*). This will be an important technique for developing the linked list. In your program from Exercise 5B, *pMem* is a pointer and *ppMem* is a pointer to a pointer. Add statements to assign the value of *pMem* to *ppMem* and vice versa.

✳ SOLUTION FILE: EX11-5C.C

✳ RESULT: Same as Exercise 5B.

✳ DISCUSSION: The compiler will make the requested assignments without error messages if you correctly cast the values.

Exercise 5D: Make a linked list.

✳ DO: Implement the linked list illustrated in Figure 11-6. The list is made of nodes; allocate memory for each node as it is needed. A node has space for two void pointers: The first pointer (a forward link) holds the address of the next node in the list and the second pointer holds the address of some data. Write a main program that allocates a root node for the list and initializes both pointers to zero. Write a function named *appendNode()* that allocates a new node and attaches it to the list via the forward link. This function needs to find the end of the list, allocate memory for a new node, and assign its address to the forward link of the last node. Also write a function named *listSize()* that counts and displays the number of nodes in the list. Call *listSize()* immediately after allocating the root node and again after a single call to *appendNode()*.

✳ SOLUTION FILE: EX11-5D.C

✳ RESULT:

```
List has 0 nodes
List has 1 nodes
```

✳ DISCUSSION: Both functions, *appendNode()* and *listSize()* use a similar loop that steps through the list by following the forward links. The nodes are composed of two pointers, so when *appendNode()* allocates memory it assigns the address to a variable that is a pointer to a pointer (*pNewNode*).

Exercise 5E: Add data to a linked list.

✳ DO: Expand the duties of function *appendNode()* to include adding data to a new node; have the function accept a second address parameter and assign it to the data pointer (second pointer) of the new node. Instead of appending just one node without any data, have the main program add seven nodes with the names of the seven dwarfs. The main program is responsible for defining and initializing strings for the seven names. In order to see the data, add a *printf()* statement to function *listSize()* to display the string data attached to each node.

✳ SOLUTION FILE: EX11-5E.C

✳ RESULT:

```
List has 0 nodes
Bashful
Doc
Dopey
Grumpy
Happy
Sleepy
Sneezy
List has 7 nodes
```

✳ **DISCUSSION:** The node data pointer is a void pointer, so the new *appendNode()* parameter should also be a void pointer. The calling function (*main()*) must cast the data argument to a void pointer.

Exercise 5F: Add mixed data types to a linked list.

✳ **DO:** In addition to the seven names, add seven more nodes to the list and attach integer data to these new nodes (the ages of the seven dwarfs). You will need to define (or allocate) an array of integers and pass addresses of elements in the array to *appendNode()*.

✳ **SOLUTION FILE:** EX11-5F.C

✳ **RESULT:**

```
List has 0 nodes
Bashful
Doc
Dopey
Grumpy
Happy
Sleepy
Sneezy
!
"
#
$
%
&
'
List has 14 nodes
```

✳ **DISCUSSION:** The solution file initializes the integers to age values of 33 through 39. The solution file actually allocates new memory for each integer so that the list values are separate from the original defined arrays. Because the *printf()* statement in *listSize()* displays with the %s conversion specifier, these integers show up as characters (!, etc). What we really need is some way to adjust the display format to the type of data. Let's do this in the next exercise.

Exercise 5G: Use function pointers.

✳ **DO:** You could correctly display the data if each node could store not only data, but a reference as to how to handle the data. Expand the size of the nodes from two pointers to three so that you can store a function pointer in the third element. This will be a pointer to a function appropriate for displaying the data attached to the node. Write two new functions, named *displayString()* and *displayInt()*, to display string and integer data respectively. The parameter to each function is a void pointer to some data. Once again expand the task of *appendNode()* so that it inserts a function pointer into the new node—it receives the function pointer as a parameter. Thus, when the main program adds a node, it now passes a pointer for the data and a pointer to the appropriate display function to *appendNode()*. Replace the *printf()* statement in *listSize()* with a function call using the function pointer from the node.

✳ **SOLUTION FILE:** EX11-5G.C

✳ **RESULT:**

```
List has 0 nodes
Bashful
Doc
Dopey
Grumpy
Happy
Sleepy
Sneezy
33
34
35
36
37
38
39
List has 14 nodes
```

✳ **DISCUSSION:** This is a rather difficult exercise, so don't be too discouraged by the task. This exercise illustrates the *encapsulation* of data and functions together (a basic feature of object-oriented programming languages like C++). A symbolic constant for the size of nodes makes it a trivial matter to increase the size to three. The easiest way to deal with function pointers is to declare a *typedef*:

```
typedef void DISPFUNC( void * );
```

You can use this new type in the declarations of pointer variables and function prototypes, and for casting data types.

Exercise 5H: Free allocated memory.

✳ **DO:** Write a function called *emptyList()* that will free memory blocks that were allocated for the list data. The function should find the data pointer in each node and free memory referenced by that pointer. Call the function just before the last call to *listSize()* at the end of the main program.

✳ **SOLUTION FILE:** EX11-5H.C

✳ **RESULT:**

```
List has 0 nodes
Bashful
Doc
Dopey
Grumpy
Happy
Sleepy
Sneezy
33
34
35
36
37
38
39
List has 14 nodes
(null)
(null)
(null)
(null)
(null)
(null)
(null)
0
0
0
0
0
0
0
List has 14 nodes
```

✳ **DISCUSSION:** Because there is no longer any data, the display functions show (null) and zero for string and integer output respectively. Function *printf()* indicates (null) for a zero-length string and zero for the value returned from a null pointer.

Exercise 5I: Free node memory.

✳ **DO:** Complete the clean-up process by freeing memory devoted to the nodes themselves. Add statements to *emptyList()* that will free the memory originally allocated for the nodes. Hint: You need to get the pointer to the next node before freeing the current node.

✳ **SOLUTION FILE:** EX11-5I.C

✳ **RESULT:**

```
List has 0 nodes
Bashful
Doc
Dopey
Grumpy
Happy
Sleepy
Sneezy
33
34
35
36
37
38
39
List has 14 nodes
List has 0 nodes
```

✳ **DISCUSSION:** Function *emptyList()* does not free the root node—the root node exists until the program ends, at which time the operating system frees all allocated memory. To separate it from the list, you need to set the forward link of the previous node to NULL. The library function *free()* does not alter values in freed memory blocks; it leaves the memory alone and makes it available for the operating system to reuse.

SUMMARY

Computer memory consists of bytes with sequential addresses. Pointer values are addresses of memory. Preceded by a data type, the indirection operator (*) defines a pointer variable. The indirection operator also assigns data to, or retrieves values from, a pointer. You can assign an address to a pointer with the address operator (&) which returns the address of a variable. Pointer arithmetic is the modification of pointer values with increment, decrement, addition, and subtraction operators. You can access different array elements by indexing or applying arithmetic to pointers. The type of a pointer corresponds to the type of data it accesses; the type determines the number of bytes transferred during an assignment and how much the value of an address changes during increment of a pointer.

The primary skills you need to remember from this chapter are:

■ How to define pointers for particular types of data

■ How to initialize and assign addresses to pointers

■ How to use pointers to access array elements

■ How to access data between functions with pointers

■ How to allocate memory dynamically

FILE I/O

iles provide the means for permanent storage of programs and data; they can accommodate massive amounts of data efficiently and inexpensively. Through library functions, C gives you the capability to read and write file information in a variety of ways. In this chapter you will learn how data is stored in files and about the different kinds of files (text and binary) and data (unformatted and formatted). We'll explain the two main categories of I/O functions in C (Level 1 and Level 2) and how to choose the best functions for different I/O tasks. In the lab section you will gain experience reading and writing files with Level 2 I/O functions.

If you write many C programs, you will have occasion to use all kinds of data in files. You may want to format character data such as names, addresses, and telephone numbers to text files; you may need to store numeric data (financial or engineering) in unformatted files; or you may need to combine text and numeric data together in a file with labelling. You may be transferring so much data that you need to maximize the speed of file I/O. As you can see, there are a lot of choices to make with file I/O; the following sections will give you the information you need to make these choices.

LECTURE

Files hold all kinds of information; they are the only place where you can keep programs and data when you turn off the computer. Files can reside on hard disk, on removable disk media (magnetic or optical), on shared disks in a network, on magnetic tape, or even in random access memory (RAM). The C functions do not care where files reside—this is determined by your computer configuration and the name argument that you supply to the C statements that open files.

File Basics

Your programs have to go through the operating system (such as DOS) to read or write files. Figure 12-1 shows the relationship of files to your program.

The Basic Input/Output System (BIOS) is the lowest-level component of DOS that deals with file input and output (I/O). Because the operating system ultimately handles file I/O, it is not surprising that some characteristics of files vary for different operating systems.

Under DOS, files have names that are restricted to eight characters or less, and they can have an extension which is optional of up to three characters attached to the base name with a period (FILENAME.EXT). Many UNIX operating systems allow file names to be much longer.

DOS has a limit on the number of files that can be open at any one time. This limit exists because an open file consumes system resources. You can set the limit by inserting or modifying a parameter (FILES =) in the CONFIG.SYS file found in your boot directory (usually C:\). For instance, FILES = 10 allows a maximum of ten files to be open at one time. Settings from 10 to 30 are typical and the maximum allowed is 255.

End-of-Line and End-of-File

C stores files as streams of bytes that can be segmented into *lines* by control characters. In general, lines in a file are variable length, that is, all lines don't have

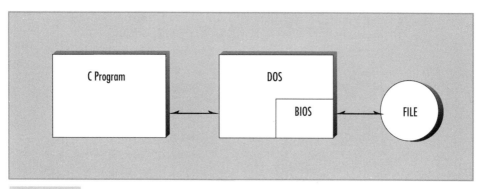

FIGURE 12-1 File I/O with DOS

the same number of characters. Not all operating systems use the same control characters at the end of lines. UNIX places a newline character (\n) at the end of each line. DOS has two kinds of files: *binary* and *text*. Figure 12-2 shows some data in both file types.

A DOS *binary* file is the same as a UNIX file, but a DOS *text* file has a carriage return character (\r) that precedes the newline character at the end of each line. A DOS text file also sometimes places a (CTRL-Z) character (ASCII code 26) at the end of a file.

The default file type for C is text, but you can request binary I/O via a parameter in the file open function. Don't be misled into thinking that only character data can be stored in a text file and only binary data can be stored in a binary file. In fact, either data type can be stored in either file type. The real distinction is whether the operating system alters certain characters during I/O operations. A file opened for binary I/O allows you to transfer all 256 possible values of a byte of data without alteration, whereas a file opened for text I/O requires the operating system to translate certain character codes, as shown in Figure 12-3.

During output to a text file, DOS expands each newline character (\n) to a pair of characters—a carriage return (\r) and newline (\n). It may also (depending on the compiler and system) write a (CTRL-Z) character at the end of the file. During input from a text file, DOS strips the carriage return from the end of each line and it also discards the end-of-file character (CTRL-Z) if it exists.

Certain kinds of data must be transferred without any translation at all—graphics images and binary numbers to name two. For this kind of data you will have to specify binary mode in the file open statement. For character and other forms of formatted data, the default text files will work just fine.

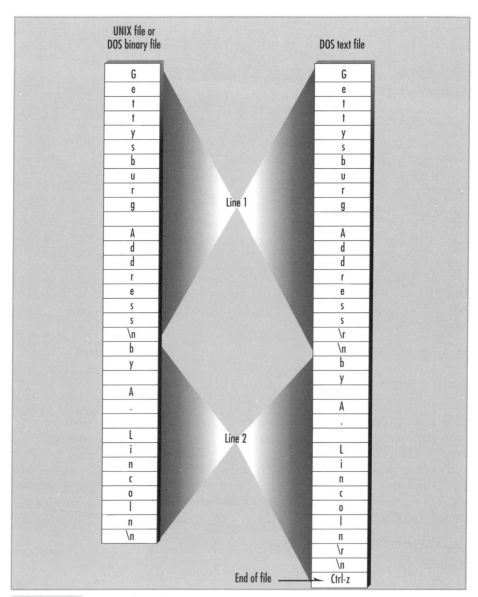

FIGURE 12-2 Binary and text files

File I/O

The designers of C did not include file I/O as a part of the core language. Instead, I/O is handled through functions supplied as a part of the standard library that accompanies a C compiler. There are two classes of I/O functions in C. *Level 1* is also known as *low-level I/O* because it interacts directly with the operating system. *Level 2* I/O functions are built on top of the Level 1 functions and are independent of the operating system. The ANSI standard defines only the Level 2 functions, so only these will be truly portable between operating systems and compilers. You can write programs with Level 1 functions, but be aware that they may not work on another system. Use Level 1 functions if speed is an overriding concern; otherwise stick with Level 2 I/O. We'll first describe Level 1 functions, then devote the bulk of the chapter to Level 2 I/O functions.

Level 1 I/O

Figure 12-4 illustrates Level 1 file I/O, which is unformatted and unbuffered. This means that the data flows directly between the file and RAM storage defined by your program—DOS does not alter the data (format it) or temporarily store it (buffer it). Level 1 I/O can be faster than Level 2 because a program does not have to format the data. However, if you transfer data in small chunks, you can request too many disk operations and end up with a less efficient program.

File Handles

Level 1 functions refer to a file through an assigned *handle*. A handle is an integer variable with a value that is unique for a given file. You must define a handle for

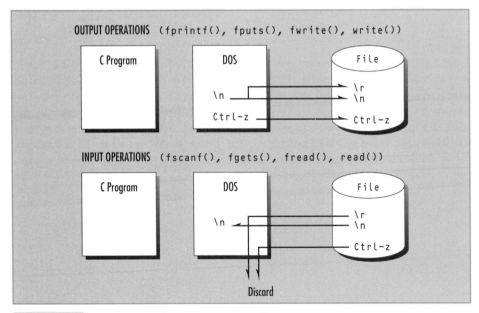

FIGURE 12-3 Character translations for DOS text files

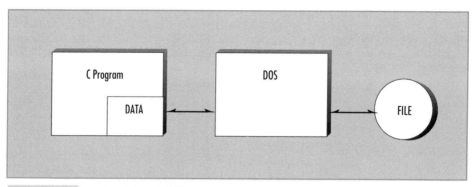

FIGURE 12-4 Low-Level (Level 1) file I/O

each file that you open, but you never need to know the value of a handle—it is significant only to the I/O functions.

Opening and Closing Level 1 Files

Before reading or writing a file, you must first obtain the value of a handle by calling the *open()* function. When you are finished with the file, you should release it with a call to the *close()* function. The prototypes for these functions are in header file IO.H:

```
int open( char *fileName, int access, ... );
int close( int handle );
```

The *close()* function releases the handle value and frees up any operating system resources associated with the file; it returns zero if successful and nonzero otherwise. Function *open()* returns a file handle that is -1 if the open was not successful. The first parameter for *open()* is a pointer to a name string and the second parameter is an access code. The access code determines whether the file is available for reading, for writing, or for both; it also determines whether a requested nonexistent file is to be created and whether the file will be treated as a binary or text file. The access code is an integer value that is the logical OR of any combination of the symbolic constants from Table 12-1 (defined in header FCNTL.H).

This list contains the most commonly used constants for opening Level 1 files; they are defined in FCNTL.H and, unless otherwise noted, they can be combined with a logical OR (II).

Constant	Meaning
O_RDONLY	Read only
O_WRONLY	Write only
O_RDWR	Read or write

The above three constants cannot be combined with each other

O_CREATE	Create the file if it doesn't exist
O_APPEND	Write from the end of the file
O_BINARY	Binary mode
O_TEXT	Text mode

The above two constants cannot be combined with each other

Table 12-1   Level 1 file access constants

Below are several examples of opening a file for Level 1 I/O:

```
int fileHandle;
char fileName[] = "MYFILE.DAT";

fileHandle = open( fileName, O_RDWR );        /* Read or write */
fileHandle = open( "YOURFILE", O_RDONLY );  /* Read only */
fileHandle = open( fileName, O_WRONLY | O_CREATE, S_IWRITE );
                                       /* Create a write-only file */
```

You should always check the value of a file handle immediately after the *open()* call:

```
if ( fileHandle == 0 )
{
    printf( "Error attempting to open file: %s\n", fileName );
    /* return or exit, but don't proceed */
}
```

The *open()* function has a third parameter that specifies the mode of I/O as S_IREAD, S_IWRITE, or both. These symbolic constants are defined in header SYS\STAT.H. The ellipsis (...) in the prototype makes this parameter optional; it is required only with a file access of O_CREAT.

Level 1 Reading and Writing

Prototypes for the Level 1 functions to read and write files are in header IO.H:

```
int read( int fileHandle, char *dataBuffer, int numBytes );
int write( int fileHandle, char *dataBuffer, int numBytes );
```

These functions have the same parameters: The first is the file handle, the second is a pointer to the data to be transferred, and the third is the number of bytes to transfer. Function *read()* returns the number of bytes read: 0 if the end of file is reached without reading any data or -1 if an error occurred. Function *write()* returns the number of bytes written, or -1 if an error occurred. You should always check the return value of a file I/O function. Here is a complete example of how to write some data to a file then read it back:

```c
#include <stdio.h>
#include <stdlib.h>    /* Prototype for exit() function */
#include <string.h>    /* Prototypes for string functions */
#include <io.h>        /* Prototypes for I/O functions */
#include <sys\stat.h>  /* Symbolic constants for I/O arguments */
#include <fcntl.h>     /* Symbolic constants for mode arguments */
int main()
{
    int fileHandle;
    int numBytes;
    char fileName[] = "LINCOLN.TXT";
    char someData[] = "This is what Mr. Lincoln said:";

/*-- Open the file (write only) --*/
    fileHandle = open( fileName, O_WRONLY | O_CREAT, S_IWRITE );
    if ( fileHandle == 0 )
    {
        printf( "Error attempting to open: %s\n", fileName );
        exit( 1 );
    }

/*-- Write some data --*/
    numBytes = write( fileHandle, someData, strlen( someData ) );
    if ( numBytes != strlen( someData ) )
    {
        printf( "Write error code: %d\n", numBytes );
        close( fileHandle );
        exit( 1 );
    }

/*-- Close the file --*/
    close( fileHandle );

/*-- Reopen the file --*/
    fileHandle = open( fileName, O_RDONLY );
    if ( fileHandle == 0 )
    {
        printf( "Error attempting to open: %s\n", fileName );
        exit( 1 );
```

```
    }

/*-- Read the data --*/
    numBytes = read( fileHandle, someData, 1000 );
    if ( numBytes <= 0 )
    {
        printf( "Read error code: %d\n", numBytes );
        close( fileHandle );
        exit( 1 );
    }

/*-- Close the file --*/
    close( fileHandle );
    printf( "%d bytes read from file %s\n", numBytes, fileName );
}
```

The *printf()* at the end of this program will report that 30 bytes were read. Notice that the *read()* statement requests 1000 bytes and that the program reports an error only if it reads 0 bytes. In contrast, after the *write()* statement, the program tests for exactly the number of bytes requested because it should write no more and no less. By closing the file after writing to it the first time, then reopening, the program reads data from the beginning. Otherwise the file remains positioned at the end after the write statement where there is no data to be read. Notice that the program closes the file before the *exit()* statement if an error occurs. You should always be sure that your read buffer is big enough to accept the number of bytes requested—here we know the number of bytes is the same as were written. A read function does not know the size of a buffer; it will transfer requested data to the given address, overflowing other data if the buffer is too small.

Changing Location in a Level 1 File

Function *lseek()* provides a way to reposition to any byte within a file so that you can read or write selected data. The prototype is:

```
long lseek( int fileHandle, long bytePosition, int anchor );
```

This function sets the file position a number of bytes (given by the second parameter) relative to the position specified by the third parameter (*anchor*). The anchor position is one of the following from header STDIO.H:

- SEEK_SET — beginning of the file
- SEEK_CUR — current location in the file
- SEEK_END — end of the file

Function *lseek()* returns the new file position as the number of bytes from the beginning of the file, or -1 if an error occurs. In the previous example program, if

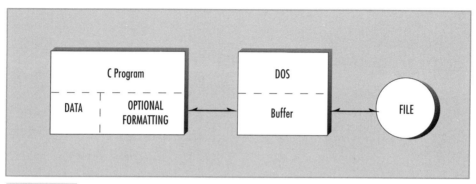

FIGURE 12-5 Stream (Level 2) file I/O

you had originally opened the file for reading and writing (O_RDWR), then you could have called *lseek()* to position at the beginning instead of closing and reopening it after the write operation.

```
lseek( fileHandle, OL, SEEK_SET );
```

Notice the long integer constant specifying 0 bytes from the beginning of the file.

Now that you have the essential elements of Level 1 I/O, let's take a look at the more useful, portable, and standard, Level 2 functions.

Level 2 I/O

Level 2, also known as *stream I/O,* is buffered and it can be either formatted or unformatted. Figure 12-5 shows the flow of data for Level 2 I/O.

Buffering is a process that the operating system (DOS) carries out on its own—it is invisible to you. In order to smooth out the flow of data, the operating system temporarily stores it in a buffer in RAM so that it can transfer the data in larger amounts. This makes I/O more efficient. When you close a file, DOS flushes any remaining data to or from the buffer. (Remaining output data is written to files and remaining input data is discarded.)

By choosing the appropriate Level 2 functions, you can transfer raw, unformatted data or you can format it. Formatting is the process of converting ASCII codes into binary numbers (integers or floating-point numbers) or vice versa. Whenever you call *printf()* or *scanf(),* you perform formatting.

File Pointers

Level 2 I/O functions refer to files through *file pointers*. A file pointer serves the same purpose for Level 2 functions that a handle serves for Level 1 functions. For each file that you open, you will need to define a pointer variable of type *FILE*:

```
FILE *filePointer;
```

FILE is a predefined data type from header STDIO.H that declares a structure for controlling a file. You'll learn more about structures in the next chapter, but suffice it for now to say that the *FILE* structure contains all the variables associated with file handling. One of these variables is a pointer that keeps track of the current position in the file where I/O is to occur. Keep a clear distinction between two important pointers for files: the *FILE* pointer that represents an open file and the file *location* pointer (an item within *FILE*) that tracks I/O position. Figure 12-6 illustrates these two pointers.

Opening and Closing Level 2 Files

Before you transfer data to or from a file, you must open it and obtain a pointer value. You do this with a call to *fopen()*:

```
filePointer = fopen( fileName, accessMode );
```

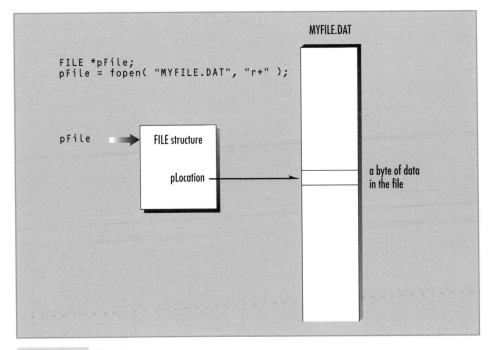

FIGURE 12-6 File pointers

This function returns a pointer value (an address to a *FILE* structure), or NULL if it cannot open the file. NULL is a symbolic constant defined in STDIO.H that signifies a zero address. The first argument is a null-terminated string containing the file name, and the second argument is a string that specifies whether reading, writing, or both will be allowed. Table 12-2 lists the possible access mode strings. Study this table to become familiar with the options.

Mode string	Meaning
"r"	Read only from beginning of file
"r+"	Read or write from beginning of file

"r" modes will not create a new file.

"w"	Write from beginning of file
"w+"	Write or read from beginning of file
"a"	Write from end of file (append)
"a+"	Write or read from end of file

All "w" and "a" modes create a file if it doesn't exist.
For an existing file, modes "w" and "w+" discard the
current contents of the file.

"rb"	b at the end of any mode string
"r+b"	means binary mode with no
"wb"	translation of control characters
"w+b"	
"ab"	
"a+b"	

Table 12-2   Level 2 file open modes

Here are examples of how to open a file in different modes:

```
FILE *filePointer;
char fileName[] = "MYFILE.DAT";

filePointer = fopen( fileName, "r" );  /* Read only */
filePointer = fopen( fileName, "w" );  /* Write only */
filePointer = fopen( fileName, "r+" ); /* Read or write */
filePointer = fopen( fileName, "w+" ); /* Read or write */
filePointer = fopen( fileName, "a" );  /* Write only at end */
filePointer = fopen( fileName, "a+" ); /* Read or write at end */
```

Always check the returned value from *fopen()* and don't continue normal processing if a NULL results:

```
if ( filePointer == NULL )
{
    printf( "Failed to open file %s\n", fileName );
    /* exit or return */
}
```

When your program ends, the operating system will automatically close all files left open, but you shouldn't wait for DOS to do this. As soon as you are finished with a file you should explicitly close it:

```
fclose( filePointer );
```

This call transfers any data remaining in the file buffer, frees memory associated with the buffer and *FILE* structure, and disassociates the file from the file pointer. Open files consume system resources, so your program becomes more efficient if you release these resources as soon as possible.

Unformatted Level 2 Reading and Writing

Unformatted I/O is faster than formatted I/O because the computer does not have to convert any data—it goes straight to the DOS buffer. Unformatted data is also smaller than formatted data. With a large amount of data, especially floating-point numbers, unformatted files can be significantly smaller than the equivalent formatted files. For instance, at least 16 ASCII characters would be required to represent the full 15-digit precision of an 8-byte floating-point number (type *double)* as a formatted number. Thus a formatted file of such numbers would be twice as large as an unformatted file. Prototypes for the unformatted Level 2 I/O functions are:

```
size_t fwrite( void *dataBuffer, size_t numBytes,
            size_t numItems, FILE *filePointer );
size_t  fread( void *dataBuffer, size_t numBytes,
            size_t numItems, FILE *filePointer );
```

Type *size_t* is a standard declared type that is an *unsigned int*. Both functions return the total number of items transferred, and both have the same parameters. The first parameter is a pointer to your data, the second parameter is the number of bytes in each item to transfer (usually the size of each element), the third parameter is the number of items (or elements) to transfer, and the fourth parameter is the file pointer. Any number less than *numItems* returned from *fwrite()* indicates an error, and from *fread()* it indicates either an error or end of file.

Unformatted Level 2 I/O is very similar to the same Level 1 operations. Here is a program that writes a file with unformatted Level 2 functions, then reads the data back again:

```c
#include <stdio.h>
#include <stdlib.h>
#include <string.h>
int main()
{
    FILE *filePointer;
    int numBytes;
    char fileName[] = "LINCOLN.TXT";
    char someData[] = "This is what Mr. Lincoln said:";

/*-- Open the file (write only) --*/
    filePointer = fopen( fileName, "w" );
    if ( filePointer == NULL )
    {
        printf( "Error attempting to open: %s\n", fileName );
        exit( 1 );
    }

/*-- Write some data --*/
    numBytes = fwrite( someData, 1,
                       strlen( someData ), filePointer );
    if ( numBytes != strlen( someData ) )
    {
        printf( "Write error code: %d\n", numBytes );
        fclose( filePointer );
        exit( 1 );
    }

/*-- Close the file --*/
    fclose( filePointer );

/*-- Reopen the file --*/
    filePointer = fopen( fileName, "r" );
    if ( filePointer == NULL )
    {
        printf( "Error attempting to open: %s\n", fileName );
        exit( 1 );
    }

/*-- Read the data --*/
    numBytes = fread( someData, 1, 1000, filePointer );
    if ( numBytes <= 0 )
    {
        printf( "Read error code: %d\n", numBytes );
        fclose( filePointer );
        exit( 1 );
    }
```

```
/*-- Close the file --*/
    fclose( filePointer );
    printf( "%d bytes read from file %s\n", numBytes, fileName );
}
```

You don't have to format character data. As this example illustrates, if the data is in character form, an unformatted file I/O will transfer the ASCII codes unaltered.

Formatted Level 2 Reading and Writing

Figure 12-7 illustrates the difference between formatted and unformatted data I/O.

This illustration shows the binary values for three different data types being transferred directly from memory (RAM) to an unformatted file at the bottom. At the top, it shows the same three values converted and written to a formatted file as a sequence of ASCII codes. Notice that the value of a character byte ('A') is the same in both cases, but the numeric data changes during the formatting process.

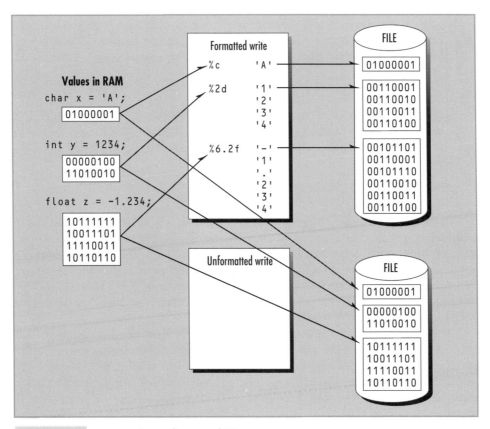

FIGURE 12-7   Formatted vs unformatted I/O

Notice also that the number of bytes of data is larger in the formatted file than in the unformatted file.

Unformatted data transfers faster and generally takes less disk space, but formatting can make data readable and more accessible. Formatted file I/O is a variation of the familiar old keyboard and screen I/O functions. File I/O functions *fprintf()* and *fscanf()* are just like *printf()* and *scanf()* except that they have an added first parameter, the file pointer. All the format specifiers and modifiers from Figures 4-1 through 4-4 in Chapter 4 apply to *fprintf()* and *fscanf()* as well as *printf()* and *scanf()*. For example, after opening a file you can convert and write a numeric value like this:

```
fprintf( filePointer, "Left margin = %.2f\n", leftMargin );
```

Notice the newline control character in the format specifier. It causes the file to start a separate line of data—with a carriage return (\r) and line feed (\n) for a DOS text file, or just a newline under UNIX. Formatting can create extra text information (such as "Left margin =" above) or it can determine how the data values themselves appear ("%.2f").

If you write a string to a file with *fprintf()* then read it back with *fscanf()*, you may not get the same data because the input operation stops at a whitespace character. In other words, these two operations are not always complementary:

```
fprintf( filePointer, "%s", string );
fscanf( filePointer, "%s", string );
```

For instance, if you write "Fourscore and seven years ago" to a file and read it back with the above *fscanf()*, you would get just "Fourscore." It is often better to use the file functions *fgets()* and *fputs()* which are specialized for string I/O. The prototypes are in STDIO.H:

```
char *fgets( char *stringData, int numChar, FILE *filePointer );
int fputs( char *stringData, FILE *filePointer );
```

Function *fgets()* transfers data into *stringData* until it either reads *numChar-1* characters or encounters a newline character (\n), which it transfers. Thus it can read multiple words separated by spaces. The second parameter, *numChar*, is the total size of the buffer, *stringData*. When *fgets()* finishes, it adds a null character (\0) to the end of the data—this is why it quits after *numChar-1* characters. This function returns a pointer to the resulting string, or NULL if the input operation failed for any reason.

The first parameter for *fputs()* is a pointer to null-terminated string data, and the second parameter is the output file pointer. Function *fputs()* does not write the terminating null to the file, and, unlike console function *puts()*, nor does it automatically write a newline character, so the total number of characters that are written is *strlen(stringData)*. This function returns an integer value of zero if successful and EOF (-1) otherwise.

You can conveniently accomplish formatted I/O with *fgets()* and *fputs()* in conjunction with the buffered string functions *sscanf()* and *sprintf()* described in Chapter 4. The following two statements format some data into a string (*stringData*) then write the string to a file:

```
sprintf( stringData, "Left margin = %.2f\n", leftMargin );
fputs( stringData, filePointer );
```

You can read the entire string back with a call to *fgets()*:

```
fgets( stringData, numBytes, filePointer );
```

Then you can process the string as required. The following statement extracts the margin value and converts it to a floating-point number:

```
fscanf( strchr( stringData, '=' ) + 1, "%f", &leftMargin );
```

The first argument expression calls *strchr()* to find the address of the character following the equal sign. This causes *fscanf()* to convert the numeric part of the string to a floating-point number.

Changing Location in a Level 2 File

ANSI defines a function, *fseek()*, that allows you to jump directly to any desired location in a file—the prototype from STDIO.H is:

```
int fseek( FILE *filePointer, long offset, int anchor );
```

The first parameter is the file pointer and the second is a byte offset from the file position specified by the third argument. The anchor position options are:

■ SEEK_SET — beginning of the file
■ SEEK_CUR — current file position
■ SEEK_END — end of the file

Function *fseek()* repositions the file location pointer (see Figure 12-6) according to the parameters, then returns zero if successful and nonzero if unsuccessful. This function is very useful when you need to "rewind" to the beginning of a file or when you want to read backwards from the end of a file. It is also important for direct access to fixed-length records—you can easily calculate the position of a given record, directly seek that location, and read the data.

A companion function to *fseek()* is *ftell()*, which returns the current location of the file pointer as the number of bytes from the beginning of the file. For example, you can display the location of the last byte in a file with these two calls:

```
fseek( filePointer, 0L, SEEK_END );
printf( "Last character is at byte %ld", ftell( filePointer ) );
```

Another informational function that has only one parameter (the file pointer) is *feof()*; it returns TRUE (nonzero) if the current pointer position is at the end of the file, or FALSE if not. You might use this function to terminate a loop while searching through a file, or to know after the fact whether an operation has reached the end of file.

Predefined Pointers

C provides three standard file pointers, one for input from the keyboard (*stdin*) and two for output to the screen (*stdout* and *stderr*). These are all pointer constants of type *FILE* that your program automatically opens; you can use them as arguments to functions but you cannot change their values. The console I/O functions (*getchar()*, *gets()*, *puts()*, *printf()*, and *scanf()*) automatically perform I/O through the *stdin* and *stdout* pointers. The following two statements are equivalent:

```
printf( "Screen output\n" );
fprintf( stdout, "Screen output\n" );
```

You can use DOS commands to redirect the console input and output streams (perhaps to files). Thus you can write error messages to *stderr* that can go to a separate destination from *stdout*.

I/O to the Printer and Communications Ports

With DOS, if you want to send output to the parallel printer port, you can open the printer as if it were a file named PRN. And to handle I/O with the serial communications ports, you can open files COM1 or COM2.

LAB

Exercise 1:   Open a file.

* DO: Write a program that prompts for a file name and access mode string, then opens the file for Level 2 I/O and displays the value of the file pointer. Run the program to open an existing file for read access, then try to open a nonexistent file for read access. Run the program two more times to open an existing and nonexistent file for write access. Warning! The contents of the existing file will be destroyed during this exercise, so don't use a file that you need to keep. We suggest you copy the contents of LINCOLN.TXT (the Gettysburg Address) to a new file, SCRATCH.DAT, for this purpose.

* SOLUTION FILE: EX12-1.C

✳ RESULT:

```
Enter a file name: NOFILE
Enter an access mode string: r
File pointer = 0000

Enter a file name: SCRATCH.DAT
Enter an access mode string: r
File pointer = 024C

Enter a file name: NOFILE
Enter an access mode string: w
File pointer = 024C

Enter a file name: SCRATCH.DAT
Enter an access mode string: w
File pointer = 024C
```

✳ DISCUSSION: Opening a nonexistent file in read mode is an error resulting in a NULL pointer (0000). Opening an existing file yields a valid pointer address—the address that you see will probably be different than the value above. Opening a nonexistent file in write mode creates a new file—the pointer value can be reused between runs because the program closes the file. Opening an existing file in write mode prepares the file to receive new data at the beginning and all the previous data is discarded! File SCRATCH.DAT will be empty at the end of the last run.

Exercise 2A: Develop file dump utility.

✳ DO: Write a file "dump" utility. This is a program that reads all the bytes in a file (including control characters) and displays them. A dump utility often comes in handy during program development when you need to examine the contents of a file directly. A convenient display format is 8 bytes of data per line in both character and hexadecimal format. Hint: You will need to specify binary access in order to prevent character translation. Run the program to dump the contents of EX12-1.C.

✳ SOLUTION FILE: EX12-2A.C

✳ RESULT:

```
Enter a file name: EX12-1.C
23 69 6E 63 6C 75 64 65 | # i n c l u d e
20 3C 73 74 64 69 6F 2E |   < s t d i o .
68 3E  D  A  D  A 76 6F | h >
```

```
              v o
69 64 20 6D 61 69 6E 28   | i d   m a i n (
29  D  A 7B  D  A 20 20   | )

              {

20 20 63 68 61 72 20 66   |     c h a r   f
69 6C 65 4E 61 6D 65 5B   | i l e N a m e [
31 36 5D 3B  D  A 20 20   | 1 6 ] ;

20 20 63 68 61 72 20 6D   |     c h a r   m
6F 64 65 5B 34 5D 3B  D   | o d e [ 4 ] ;

 A 20 20 20 20 46 49 4C   |
              F I L
45 20 2A 66 69 6C 65 50   | E   * f i l e P
6F 69 6E 74 65 72 3B  D   | o i n t e r ;

 A  D  A 20 20 20 20 70   |


              p
72 69 6E 74 66 28 20 22   | r i n t f (   "
45 6E 74 65 72 20 61 20   | E n t e r   a
66 69 6C 65 20 6E 61 6D   | f i l e   n a m
65 3A 20 22 20 29 3B  D   | e :   "   ) ;

 A 20 20 20 20 73 63 61   |
              s c a
6E 66 28 20 22 25 73 22   | n f (   " % s "
2C 20 66 69 6C 65 4E 61   | ,   f i l e N a
6D 65 20 29 3B  D  A 20   | m e   ) ;

20 20 20 70 72 69 6E 74   |       p r i n t
66 28 20 22 45 6E 74 65   | f (   " E n t e
72 20 61 6E 20 61 63 63   | r   a n   a c c
65 73 73 20 6D 6F 64 65   | e s s   m o d e
20 73 74 72 69 6E 67 3A   |   s t r i n g :
20 22 20 29 3B  D  A 20   |   "   ) ;

20 20 20 73 63 61 6E 66   |       s c a n f
28 20 22 25 73 22 2C 20   | (   " % s " ,
6D 6F 64 65 20 29 3B  D   | m o d e   ) ;

 A  D  A 20 20 20 20 66   |
```

```
                    f
69 6C 65 50 6F 69 6E 74   | i l e P o i n t
65 72 20 3D 20 66 6F 70   | e r   =   f o p
65 6E 28 20 66 69 6C 65   | e n (   f i l e
4E 61 6D 65 2C 20 6D 6F   | N a m e ,   m o
64 65 20 29 3B  D  A 20   | d e   )  ;

20 20 20 70 72 69 6E 74   |       p r i n t
66 28 20 22 46 69 6C 65   | f (   " F i l e
20 70 6F 69 6E 74 65 72   |   p o i n t e r
20 3D 20 25 70 5C 6E 22   |   =   % p \ n "
2C 20 66 69 6C 65 50 6F   | ,   f i l e P o
69 6E 74 65 72 20 29 3B   | i n t e r   )  ;
 D  A 7D  D  A  D  A  0   |

}
```

✳ DISCUSSION: The solution program uses a vertical character (|) to separate the hexadecimal output on the left from the character display on the right. The character display is easier to read, but some values are not displayable as characters, so the hex format is needed to show all the data. You have to be very observant when you look at the output of a file dump. When displayed as a character, the newline control character (hex A) causes the cursor to move to the next line, and the carriage return (hex D) moves the cursor to column one, so the character output is sporadically interrupted.

Exercise 2B: Direct output to this printer.

✳ DO: If you have a printer attached to the parallel printer port of your PC, add statements to duplicate the dump output on the printer. Repeat the run from the previous exercise.

✳ SOLUTION FILE: EX12-2B.C

✳ RESULT: Same as Exercise 2A, but with printed output.

✳ DISCUSSION: The printer has the special file name of PRN. All of the output formats for the printer can be the same as for the screen display.

Exercise 3:   Report file size.

✳ DO: Write a program that reports the total number of bytes in a file. Run the program to find the size of file LINCOLN.TXT.

✳ SOLUTION FILE: EX12-3.C

✳ RESULT:

Enter a file name: LINCOLN.TXT

File size = 1517 bytes

✳ DISCUSSION: There are several ways to find the size of a file; the solution file shows one of the simplest. Alternatively you could read the file one byte at a time and count the bytes, or you could read blocks of data and accumulate the counts returned from the read function. You can verify the file size with the DOS directory command (C:\> DIR LINCOLN.TXT).

Exercise 4A: Determine the number of lines in a file.

✳ DO: Write a program that finds the number of lines in a file and reports the number of bytes in the longest line. Run the program and select file LINCOLN.TXT.

✳ SOLUTION FILE: EX12-4A.C or EX12-4B.C

✳ RESULT:

```
Enter a file name: LINCOLN.TXT
There are 25 lines in LINCOLN.TXT--the longest is 77 bytes.
```

✳ DISCUSSION: The fact that you don't know the length of any lines in the file poses a problem because you don't know how big a buffer to define for the read statement. One answer to this dilemma is to read the data one byte at a time (as does EX12-4A.C). However, accessing a file is one of the slowest operations that a computer performs, so it behooves you to transfer as much data as possible with each I/O access. EX12-4B.C contains a faster program that reads a larger amount of data into a buffer of arbitrary size. The program then scans the buffer to find newline characters.

Exercise 5A: Search a file.

✳ DO: Write a program that searches the contents of a file to match a phrase of one or more words. Display the line data and line number where the first match occurs. Run the program and search file LINCOLN.TXT for the first occurrence of the word "nation."

✳ SOLUTION FILE: EX12-5A.C

✳ RESULT:

```
Enter a file name: LINCOLN.TXT
Enter a search string (max 20 characters): nation
"nation" found on line 5:
a new nation, conceived in Liberty, and dedicated to the proposition that
all
```

✳ DISCUSSION: With the prior knowledge that lines are less than 100 characters long, you can read each line into a 100-byte buffer and use a string search function to look for a match.

Exercise 5B: Search a file.

✳ DO: Enhance your program from Exercise 5A to find all occurrences of the search string, not just the first one. Search LINCOLN.TXT for all lines that contain "nation."

✳ SOLUTION FILE: EX12-5B.C

✳ RESULT:

```
Enter a file name: LINCOLN.TXT
Enter a search string (max 20 characters): nation
"nation" found on line 5:
a new nation, conceived in Liberty, and dedicated to the proposition that
all

"nation" found on line 8:
Now we are engaged in a great civil war, testing whether that nation or any

"nation" found on line 9:
nation so conceived and so dedicated, can long endure. We are met on a great

"nation" found on line 11:
a final resting place for those who here gave their lives that that nation

"nation" found on line 23:
resolve that these dead shall not have died in vain--that this nation, under
```

✳ DISCUSSION: The change to EX12-5A.C to allow more than one match is trivial—in fact the modified program is simpler.

Exercise 6:   Search and replace file data.

✳ **DO:** Modify the program from Exercise 5B to replace each matched string with a new phrase. Enter the new phrase from the keyboard and display each altered line. The new phrase can be shorter, longer, or the same size as the search phrase. Run the program and replace every occurrence of the word "nation" in LINCOLN.TXT with "country." Hint: Write a second file.

✳ **SOLUTION FILE:** EX12-6.C

✳ **RESULT:**

```
Enter a file name: LINCOLN.TXT
Enter a search string (max 20 characters): nation
Enter a replacement string (max 20 characters): country
"nation" replaced on line 5:
a new country, conceived in Liberty, and dedicated to the proposition that
all

"nation" replaced on line 8:
Now we are engaged in a great civil war, testing whether that country or any

"nation" replaced on line 9:
country so conceived and so dedicated, can long endure. We are met on a
great

"nation" replaced on line 11:
a final resting place for those who here gave their lives that that country

"nation" found on line 23:
resolve that these dead shall not have died in vain--that this country,
under
```

✳ **DISCUSSION:** It's fairly easy to reconstruct a line in a temporary buffer. Use pointer variables in connection with string functions. Copy the section of original line data that precedes the matched phrase, then append the replacement phrase, and finally append the remainder of the original line.

Exercise 7A: Accomplish direct access to fixed-length records.

✳ **STARTER FILE:** EX12-7A.C

```
#include <stdio.h>
#include <stdlib.h>

int main()
```

```
{
    int i;
    char line[20];
    FILE *filePointer;

    filePointer = fopen( "FIXED.DAT", "w" );
    if ( filePointer == NULL )
    {
        printf( "Could not open file: FIXED.DAT\n" );
        exit( 1 );
    }

    for ( i=1; i<100; ++i )
    {
        sprintf( line, "Record number %02d\n", i );
        fputs( line, filePointer );
    }

    fclose( filePointer );
}
```

✳ DO: The starter file contains the above program which creates a data file containing 99 fixed-length records. Study the source code for this program to become familiar with how it writes the data, then run the program to create file FIXED.DAT.

Write a new program that can directly read any selected line from FIXED.DAT. Have the program accept a line number from the keyboard, then read the line and display it. To write this program, you will have to decide exactly how many bytes are in each line of FIXED.DAT, which is a text file. Run the program and select line 17.

✳ SOLUTION FILE: EX12-7B.C

✳ RESULT:

```
Select a line number (1-99): 17
Record number 17
```

✳ DISCUSSION: You can use EX12-2A.C (the dump utility) to examine all the data in each line, including control characters.

SUMMARY

DOS *text* files separate lines with two control characters: \r and \n, and text file I/O performs translation on these characters and the end-of-file character (CTRL-Z). DOS *binary* files are like UNIX files that end each line with one newline character; there is no data translation during I/O with binary files.

Level 1 (low-level) I/O functions are not standardized in C and are therefore not portable. Level 2 (stream) I/O functions are defined by the ANSI standard. You should use the Level 2 functions because they are portable and have more complete functionality. Level 2 functions are buffered and can be used for either formatted or unformatted data transfer. Table 12-3 summarizes common standard file I/O functions.

Operation	Level 1 function	Level 2 functon
Open an existing file for reading	handle= open(fileName,O_RDONLY);	pFile=fopen (fileName,"r");
Open an existing file for writing	handle= open(fileName,O_WRONLY);	pFile = fopen (fileName,"w");
Open an existing file for reading and writing discarding existing data	handle = open(fileName, O_RDWR);	pFile = fopen (fileName,"w+");
Open an existing file for reading and writing in binary mode	handle= open(fileName,O_RDWR I O_BINARY);	pFile=fopen(fileName, "w+b");
Open an existing file for writing at the end	handle= open(fileName, O_WRONLY I O_APPEND);	pFile=fopen(fileName,"a");
Open a new file for reading and writing	handle= open(fileName, O_RDWR I O_CREATE,S_IREAD I S_IWRITE);	pFile=fopen(fileName, "w+");
Close a file	close (handle);	fclose (pFile);
Read data unformatted	read (handle, data, count);	fread (data,size count, pFile);

Write data unformatted	write (handle, data, count);	fwrite (data,size count, pFile);
Read data formatted		fscanf (pFile); formatString. variable list);
Write data formatted		fprintf (pFile, formatString, variable list);
Change location relative to beginning of file	lseek (handle, offset, SEEK_SET);	fseek (pFile, offset, SEEK_SET);
Change location relative to current file position	lseek (handle, offset, SEEK_CUR);	fseek(pFile, offset, SEEK_CUR);
Change location relative to end of file	lseek (handle,offset,SEEK_END);	fseek(pFile, offset SEEK_END);

Table 12-3   Common file I/O functions

Before using a file you must specify the read/write access mode and obtain a pointer value by calling an open function. You should always check the return value from an open statement to know that a file is ready for I/O. You can then read and write data to the file either with unformatted I/O statements (*fread()* or *fwrite()*) or with formatted I/O calls (*fprintf()*, *fscanf()*, *fgets()*, *fputs()*). Other functions allow you to find or change the current position in a file (*fseek()*, *ftell()*, *feof()*). It is good programming practice to close files as soon as you are finished with them.

13

*Average time to
complete this chapter
(including lab and
quiz) is 8 hours.*

STRUCTURES AND UNIONS

structure is a data type that can combine a variety of other data types. This is an extremely practical feature of the C language and it is widely used by experienced programmers. On the other hand, *unions* find only specialized application and are rarely seen. A union provides the ability to share the same memory among several different data types.

This chapter will show you how to take advantage of structures to organize data, to access data between functions, and to perform file I/O. At the end, the chapter has a short section that explains the unique applications for unions.

LECTURE

Structures offer several advantages for your programs:

- They allow you to organize related data items under a common group name and in a common memory location. This simplifies data access and makes your programs more readable.

- They make function calls more efficient by minimizing the number of arguments required.

- They simplify file I/O operations when items are defined in the same order as file records.

Declaring and Defining Structures

The syntax for declaring a structure is:

```
struct TAG
{
    member_list
} name_list;
```

The key word *struct* signifies that this is a structure declaration. The TAG is a C identifier that refers to the structure; it is common practice to use uppercase letters in the tag name. Braces enclose the optional *member_list,* which is a group of separately declared variables of any data type. You can declare a structure having as many members as desired, even none, but there would be no point in declaring a structure without any members. The *name_list* is also optional; it allows you to define variables that are structures of this type.

Only two parts of the declaration are always necessary: key word *struct* and the ending semicolon. Therefore, a structure declaration can exhibit many combinations. We like to limit the combinations to just two, which can serve all necessary purposes. One form of declaration establishes a template for the structure and does not include the name list. Here is a declaration for a structure containing members for a person's name and year of birth:

```
#define MAX_NAME_LENGTH 20

struct PERSON
{
    char firstName[MAX_NAME_LENGTH];
    char lastName[MAX_NAME_LENGTH];
    int  birthYear;
};
```

This is a declaration as opposed to a definition—it establishes the characteristics of a structure but does not allocate memory. The template is known by the identifier *PERSON* (the tag). It has three members: a character array for the first name, a character array for the last name, and an integer for the year. To use an actual object with these characteristics, you must define a structure variable by combining the template tag with a variable name in a second form of the structure statement:

```
struct PERSON president;
```

This statement allocates memory for the variable named *president*, and it attaches all the properties of the *PERSON* structure to that variable. That is, *president* has an array for the first name, an array for the last name, and an integer for the year of birth, as shown in Figure 13-1.

The above definition statement for a structure is similar to that for any other data type—only it is prefixed with the key word *struct*. The size of a structure is the accumulated total of the member sizes. You can use the *sizeof* operator with structure tags and variables. For this example, either *sizeof(PERSON)* or *sizeof(president)* returns 42, which is the size of two 20-byte character arrays plus 2 bytes for the integer.

PORTABILITY OF STRUCTURES

The size of a structure is not always the simple sum of the member sizes. Some computer systems, compilers, or compiler options impose a requirement that all variables be aligned on a certain memory boundary. Some systems restrict memory allocation so that entities can begin only every 4 bytes. This means that all 1 or 2 byte quantities will be separated by 4 bytes, making the total memory span of two such variables 8 bytes. Even though the actual variables occupy only their allotted space, the total memory consumed is larger; therefore the total structure size is larger, as shown in Figure 13-2.

The *sizeof* operator will return the total memory size of a structure, including dead space. This can be a trap if you move the program to another system because the size of the structure may change. This can be especially tricky if you have written unformatted structure data containing dead space to a file. You can minimize the dead space (perhaps eliminating it altogether) by placing larger members first in the structure. For instance, start a structure with all floating-point members (types *float* and *double*) and *long* integers (size 4 or 8), then list 2-byte members (such as *int*), and put character data (type *char*) last. Thus, any dead space will likely be at the end of the structure.

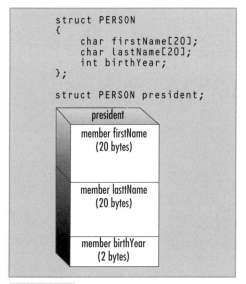

```
struct PERSON
{
    char firstName[20];
    char lastName[20];
    int birthYear;
};

struct PERSON president;
```

president

member firstName
(20 bytes)

member lasttName
(20 bytes)

member birthYear
(2 bytes)

FIGURE 13-1 A structure variable

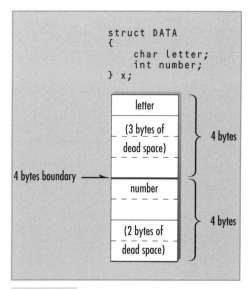

```
struct DATA
{
    char letter;
    int number;
} x;
```

letter

(3 bytes of
dead space)

4 bytes

4 bytes boundary

number

(2 bytes of
dead space)

4 bytes

FIGURE 13-2 Allocated structure with dead space

Programmers often find it expedient to create *typedef* identifiers for structures; you can do this by substituting a *typedef* identifier for the variable name:

```
typedef struct PERSON HUMAN;
```

Now you can define a structure variable more simply:

```
HUMAN president;
```

In summary, you will find it convenient to use a two-step approach to declaring and defining structures: First declare a structure template with one statement that establishes a template tag:

```
struct TAG
{
    members
};
```

then define any number of structure variables with additional statements that include the tag identifier:

```
struct TAG variable;
```

If you place the first declaration in a header file, you can conveniently reuse the tag to define structure variables in other source files.

In this book we left-justify and line up both braces under key word *struct* to enhance readability:

```
struct NAME
{
    member_list
};
```

Many programmers prefer an alternate placement that requires one less line:

```
struct NAME {
    member_list
};
```

Both forms are perfectly acceptable; you can choose either one, but be consistent throughout a programming project.

ALTERNATE STRUCTURE DECLARATIONS

You may see other forms of the structure declaration in C programs—let's take a quick look at a couple of them. Here are two structure variables, king and queen, defined without a tag

```
struct
{
    char firstName[MAX_NAME_LENGTH];
    char lastName[MAX_NAME_LENGTH];
    int birthYear;
} king, queen;
```

This is a compact way of defining structure variables, but you cannot refer to this structure template without completely redeclaring it, because it has no tag identifier. Therefore this form is good only for defining local variables. Here is another way to declare a structure *typedef:*

```
typedef struct
{
    char firstName[MAX_NAME_LENGTH];
    char lastName[MAX_NAME_LENGTH];
    int birthYear;
} HUMAN;
```

This combines the structure declaration with *typedef,* so you can define variables of type HUMAN without the *struct* key word. These variations of structure declaration are all legal and you may encounter them as you continue to work with the C language.

Structure Members

Each variable in a structure is called a *member* of the structure. The name of a structure (such as *president*) refers to the entire structure. You refer to an individual member by combining the structure name and the member name with the structure member operator.

Structure Member Operator

The *structure member operator (.)* connects a member name to its structure identifier:

```
structure_name.member_name
```

You cannot refer to a member without the structure name attached; otherwise you use structure members the same way as any separate variable. For example, you can assign a value to member *birthYear* in structure *president*:

```
president.birthYear = 1809;
```

Or you can use it as an argument to a function:

```
printf( "The president was born in %d\n", president.birthYear );
```

You can reuse a member identifier outside of the structure without conflict; therefore you can have two variables, *president.birthYear* and just plain *birthYear* in the same function (however it's best not to have two variables with such similar names).

Structure Assignment

The ANSI standard provides for assignment between structures of the same type. This means that you can do this:

```
struct PERSON president;
struct PERSON lincoln;
president = lincoln;
```

And the program will copy the values for each member of *lincoln* to the similar member of *president*. Some older, non-ANSI compilers may not allow structure assignment, so you would have to assign each member individually:

```
strcpy( president.firstName, lincoln.firstName );
strcpy( president.lastName, lincoln.lastName );
president.birthYear = lincoln.birthYear;
```

The structure assignment does all this in one statement.

Arrays in Structures

Arrays can also be structure members, as the above example illustrates with members *firstName* and *lastName*. Arrays require no special treatment beyond attaching the structure name to the structure member operator. You can use them as arguments to string functions:

```
strcpy( president.firstName, "Abraham" );
```

And you can refer to different array elements:

```
president.lastName[0] = lincoln.lastName[0];
```

Structures Within Structures

You can see how simple it is to have an array member of a structure. It is also easy to declare a structure to be a member of another structure. The only prerequisite is that you declare the member structure first so that the compiler knows what to insert in the other structure. Let's replace the *birthYear* member of the *PERSON* structure with a *DATE* structure:

```
struct DATE
{
    int day;
    int month;
    int year;
};

struct PERSON
{
    char firstName[MAX_NAME_LENGTH];
    char lastName[MAX_NAME_LENGTH];
    struct DATE birthDate;
};
```

The declaration of *DATE* precedes the appearance of that tag inside the declaration of *PERSON*. This way, the compiler has all the information it needs to complete the *PERSON* structure. The new member of structure *PERSON* is the variable *birthDate*, a *DATE* structure containing three values. Notice that we have not defined any variables yet. You can define a *PERSON* variable that will include all of the members of both structures:

```
struct PERSON grandfather;
```

Figure 13-3 illustrates the composition of this structure, which contains another structure.

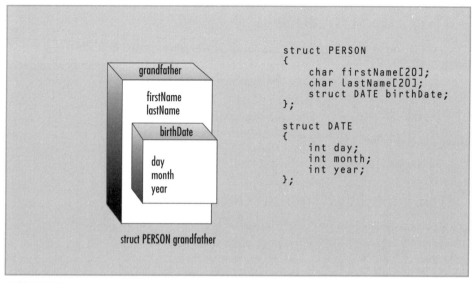

```
struct PERSON
{
    char firstName[20];
    char lastName[20];
    struct DATE birthDate;
};

struct DATE
{
    int day;
    int month;
    int year;
};
```

FIGURE 13-3 A structure within a structure

Here are all the direct members of *grandfather*:

```
grandfather.firstName
grandfather.lastName
grandfather.birthDate
```

And here are the additional submembers of *birthDate*:

```
grandfather.birthDate.day
grandfather.birthDate.month
grandfather.birthDate.year
```

To access members of the inner structure, you attach both structure names with structure member operators. You then access these submembers just as you would any other separate variable:

```
grandfather.birthDate.year = 1940;          /* Assign a value */
scanf( "%d", &grandfather.birthDate.day );   /* Read a value */
```

Structure Bit-Fields

C provides for a special type of structure member called a *bit-field* or just *field* that can refer to a storage quantity as small as 1 bit. You can use fields to slice up integer variables into smaller chunks of data. The syntax for declaring fields looks like this:

```
struct TAG
{
    type name1 : size1;
    type name2 : size2;
        .
        .
        .
};
```

The data type of members can only be *int (signed)* or *unsigned int—unsigned* is the usual choice. Each field has a name that is associated with the number of bits specified following the colon. The compiler assigns fields to an integer in the order given by the list of members. It starts at one end of the integer and partitions the bits according to the specified sizes. For example, the following structure declares fields for 2 nibbles and a byte in an integer:

```
struct FIELDS
{
    unsigned nibble1 : 4;
    unsigned nibble2 : 4;
    unsigned byte : 8;
};
```

You can define a structure variable based on this template and assign values to the members independently.

```
struct FIELDS word;

word.nibble1 = 0x5;
word.nibble2 = 0xA;
word.byte = 'A';
```

Figure 13-4 shows the result of these operations.

The first 4 bits contain the value 5, the second 4 contain the value 10, and the last 8 contain 65, the ASCII code for A. C does not specify which end of the integer to begin assigning values, so it can be different for each compiler; in the lab section we'll find out which end Turbo C++ starts at.

You can choose fields of any size; you don't have to fill up the word; and you can accumulate fields larger than one word—the compiler assigns fields to as many integer words as necessary.

You access field members just as you do other members, with the structure member operator (.) or structure pointer operator (->). However, you cannot use the addess operator; bit-field members don't have addresses because they can be smaller than the smallest addressable memory element, the byte.

A bit-field member returns the value as a right-justified integer. In the above example, *word.nibble2* has a value of 10 rather than 2560, which is the value of 10 left-shifted 8 bits to the original bit-field position.

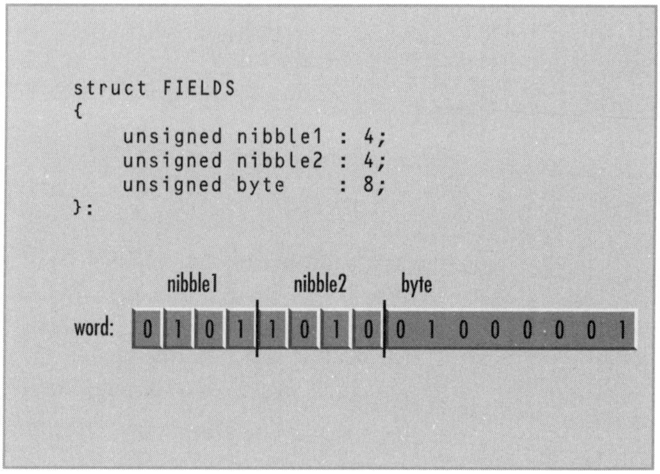

```
struct FIELDS
{
    unsigned nibble1 : 4;
    unsigned nibble2 : 4;
    unsigned byte    : 8;
}:
```

nibble1   nibble2   byte

word: `0 1 0 1 1 0 1 0 0 1 0 0 0 0 0 1`

FIGURE 13-4 Structure
bit-fields

Bit-fields are convenient for data that must be packed tightly to save space. However, packing data makes a program run slower. You can accomplish bit packing by explicitly using masks and shifting (see Chapter 5), but bit-fields are easier because the compiler does the work of shifting and masking for you.

Initializing Structures

You can initialize the members of a structure in the statement that defines the structure. You do this by inserting an initializer list just before the semicolon:

```
struct TAGNAME variable_name = { initializer_list };
```

The braces are necessary and items in the initializer list must match the data types of the structure members. The compiler assigns values from the initializer list to members in strict sequence from the beginning. If the data types do not match, the compiler will attempt to convert values by promotion or demotion to make them fit the member data type. However this may not yield the result that you desire, so you should explicitly make the values match. Here is how you can initialize a *PERSON* structure:

```
struct PERSON president = { "Abraham", "Lincoln", 12, 2, 1809 };
```

This statement defines a structure named *president* occupying 46 bytes of memory and assigns values to the members as listed below:

```
Member                      Value
president.firstName         string "Abraham" plus 12 more nulls
president.lastName          string "Lincoln" plus 12 more nulls
president.birthDate.day     12
president.birthDate.month   2
president.birthDate.year    1809
```

The compiler sets elements of arrays beyond the initialization string to zero, and it does the same for any remaining structure members beyond the end of the initializer list. Notice how the initializer list includes members of the DATE structure in the sequence of values.

Arrays of Structures

A structure bundles different types of information into one package. By defining a single PERSON variable, you allocate storage for all the data describing one individual. But what if you need to process information on all the employees of a company or all the members of a club? The answer is to use arrays of structures. You can define an array of *PERSON* structures in which each element is a structure with a complete set of member variables for holding information about an individual. For example, suppose you are interested in U.S. history and want to have information on all the presidents; here's how you can define an array with space for up to 50 presidents:

```
struct PERSON presidents[50];
```

Figure 13-5 diagrams this array.

The first element in this array is *presidents[0]*, and the last element is *presidents[49]*. You can assign a name and birthday to the third element in the array like this:

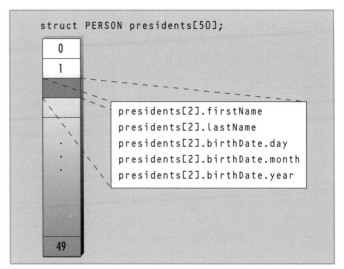

```
struct PERSON presidents[50];

  0
  1



  .
  .
  .


 49
```

```
presidents[2].firstName
presidents[2].lastName
presidents[2].birthDate.day
presidents[2].birthDate.month
presidents[2].birthDate.year
```

FIGURE 13-5 An array of structures

311

```
strcpy( presidents[2].firstName, "Thomas" );
strcpy( presidents[2].lastName, "Jefferson" );
presidents[2].birthDate.day = 13;
presidents[2].birthDate.month = 4;
presidents[2].birthDate.year = 1743;
```

Notice the placement of the index brackets for a structure array, at the end of the structure name. Also, notice how a reference to an array within the structure (*presidents[2].firstName*) represents the address of the array member—this is no different than for a separate array. You can access a single element of a member array within a structure array by adding a second index: *presidents[2].firstName[0]* is the first character in array *firstName* from the third element of the *presidents* array (the value is 'T'), and *presidents[2].lastName[1]* is the second character of array *lastName* (value 'e'). The following statement uses the address of this element to display only the last eight characters of the last name ("efferson"):

```
printf( "%s", &presidents[2].lastName[1] );
```

You initialize an array of structures simply by extending the initializer list to include values for as many structure elements as needed. The statement below initializes all members of the first four elements of the *presidents* array:

```
struct PERSON presidents[50] = {
    "George", "Washington", 11, 2, 1732,
    "John", "Adams", 30, 10, 1735,
    "Thomas", "Jefferson", 13, 4, 1743,
    "Alexander", "Hamilton", 11, 1, 1755 };
```

All members of the remaining 46 elements are initialized to zero.

Pointers to Structures

A structure pointer is a pointer variable declared with a structure data type. Such pointers work in exactly the same way as they do for simple variables. Here is a pointer to a *PERSON* structure:

```
struct PERSON *pPerson;
```

You can find the address of a structure with the address operator (&) and assign it to this pointer:

```
struct PERSON president;
pPerson = &president;
```

You could also initialize the pointer during definition in the usual manner:

```
struct PERSON *pPerson = &president;
```

Given a structure pointer holding a valid address, you can use the indirection operator to refer to the structure itself and its members. After the above pointer is initialized, *pPerson* is the same as *president* and *pPerson.firstName* is the same as *president.firstName*.

With structure pointers you can easily exchange structure data between functions and you can easily transfer structure data to and from files—we'll cover these topics a little later in this chapter. You can also access members of a structure via a pointer to the structure.

Structure Pointer Operator

The *structure pointer operator* is a two-character symbol (->), a hyphen (-) followed by a greater-than character (>). You access a structure member by linking the member name to the structure pointer through this operator. Here are several examples:

```
struct PERSON president;
struct PERSON *pPerson = &president;
pPerson->firstName          /* Same as president.firstName */
pPerson->lastName[0]        /* Same as president.lastName[0] */
pPerson->birthDate.day      /* Same as president.birthDate.day */
```

Structure Pointer Arithmetic

If you define an array of structures, you can initialize a pointer to one of the array elements:

```
struct PERSON presidents[50];
pPerson = &presidents[2];
```

Now you can use the pointer to access any of the members of the third array element:

```
pPerson->birthDate.year = 1743;
```

This is the same as:

```
presidents[2].birthDate.year = 1743;
```

Pointer arithmetic is particularly great for structure arrays because you can readily get to different elements of the array. When you increment a structure pointer, the address increases an amount equal to the size of the structure—in other words the address skips to the beginning of the next element. Above, the pointer addresses the third element; you can move to the fourth element and assign a value like this:

```
++pPerson;
pPerson->birthDate.year = 1755;
```

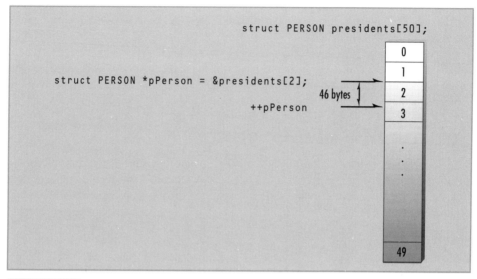

FIGURE 13-6 Pointer to an array of structures

Figure 13-6 illustrates this pointer movement.

You can use the addition operator without changing the value of the pointer:

```
(pPerson + 1)->birthDate.year = 1755;
```

Here we have used parentheses to force the pointer arithmetic to calculate the address of the next array element before accessing the structure member, *birthDate.year*.

Pointers to structures are sometimes used to construct a linked list. If you declare a pointer to a structure to be a member of that structure, then it serves as a link to another similar structure. Figure 13-7 shows how this works.

As the code in the figure shows, each node in the list is a dynamically allocated structure variable. Pointer variables within each node structure (*forwardPointer*) serve as links to hold the addresses of other nodes. You allocate the nodes as you need them and attach them to the list by assigning values to the pointers. This is very similar to the linked list that you developed in the Chapter 11 lab, without the benefit of structures.

Structures and Functions

Used as function parameters, structure pointers are very powerful. By passing a single address, you give a function complete access to all members of a structure.

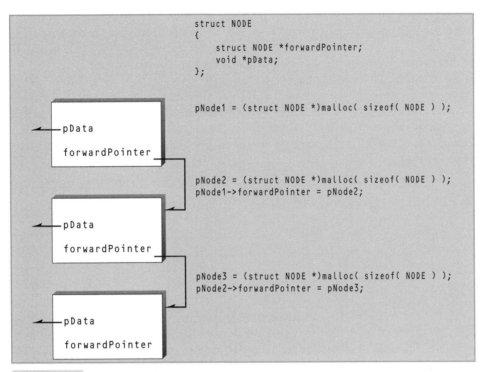

FIGURE 13-7 A linked list of structures

In the following example, a *main()* program defines a structure, then calls a function to fill the members with values from the keyboard:

```c
#include <stdio.h>
/* Declaration of structures DATE and PERSON goes here */
void fill( struct PERSON * );    /* Function prototype */

void main()
{
    struct PERSON me;  /* Define a structure */
    fill( &me );       /* Call function with structure pointer */
}

void fill( struct PERSON *pPerson )
{
    printf( "Enter firstname and lastname: " );
    scanf( "%s %s", pPerson->firstName,
                    pPerson->lastName );
    printf( "Enter birthday (mm<Enter> dd<Enter> yyyy<Enter>): " );
    scanf( "%d %d %d", &pPerson->birthDate.month,
                       &pPerson->birthDate.day,
                       &pPerson->birthDate.year );
}
```

Let's look at the use of the address operator in this program. In the *fill()* function call, the *main()* program passes the address of structure *me* to the function. In the *scanf()* arguments, it specifies the addresses of different members of the structure (*birthDate.month*, *birthDate.day*, and *birthDate.year*).

In Chapter 11 we discussed the technique of passing a void pointer to a function for different types of data. This technique applies particularly to structure data. After receiving a void pointer parameter, a function can adjust to the appropriate structure type by casting the pointer. Let's illustrate this by modifying the above example. If you change the parameter in *fill()* to a void pointer, the function call becomes:

```
fill( (void *)&me );
```

and the first few lines of the *fill()* function become:

```
void fill( void *pParam )
{
    struct PERSON *pPerson = (PERSON *)pParam;
    .
    .
    .
```

Otherwise the program needs no modification. The first statement in *fill()* initializes pointer *pPerson* by casting and assigning the void parameter pointer, *pParam*. What is the advantage of using a void pointer parameter? It's an advanced technique that allows a function to accept many types of structure data dynamically.

It is possible to return a structure as the value of a function; this is another very powerful mechanism for passing structure data. You could accomplish the same result as the above example with a return value to the function instead of a pointer argument. In this new approach the function will define its own automatic structure and fill it with values, then return the structure. The automatic structure will disappear (be out of scope) at the end of the function, but not before the values are copied by the assignment statement that calls the function.

```
#include <stdio.h>
/* Declaration of structures DATE and PERSON goes here */
struct PERSON fill( void );    /* Function prototype */

void main()
{
    struct PERSON me;  /* Define a structure */
    me = fill();       /* Call function and assign result */
}

struct PERSON fill( void )
{
    struct PERSON temp;
```

```
    printf( "Enter firstname and lastname: " );
    scanf( "%s %s", temp.firstName,
                    temp.lastName );
    printf( "Enter birthday (mm<Enter> dd<Enter> yyyy<Enter>): " );
    scanf( "%d %d %d", &temp.birthDate.month,
                       &temp.birthDate.day,
                       &temp.birthDate.year );
    return( temp );
}
```

In this version, *temp* is the automatic structure variable that exists only during execution of the function *fill()*. This form of passing data protects data in the calling program from any possible corruption by the called function because the function has no direct access.

Compilers that are ANSI compliant can pass structures themselves as arguments to functions (in addition to structure pointers). Many previous Common C compilers did not allow this. As with any other argument, when you pass a structure you pass a copy of the values in the original structure, and the called function cannot change the original values. Let's add a function to display the structure in the above example after the values are assigned:

```
#include <stdio.h>
/* Declaration of structures DATE and PERSON goes here */
struct PERSON fill( void );    /* Input function prototype */
void show( struct PERSON );    /* Display function prototype */

void main()
{
    struct PERSON me;   /* Define a structure */
    me = fill();        /* Call function and assign result */
    show( me );         /* Display the values */
}

/* Function fill() goes here... */

void show( struct PERSON anonymous )
{
    printf( "Name: %s %s\n", anonymous.firstName,
                             anonymous.lastName );
    printf( "Birthday: %d/%d/%d\n", anonymous.birthDate.month,
                                    anonymous.birthDate.day,
                                    anonymous.birthDate.year );
}
```

Function *show()* accepts copies of values from the original structure *me* in the parameter *anonymous*. It can display or alter these values in *anonymous*, but it cannot change the original values in *me*.

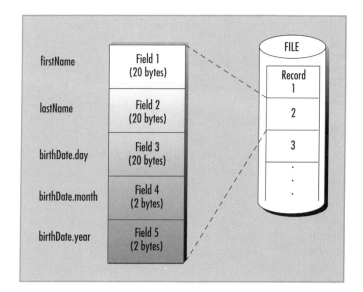

FIGURE 13-8 Structure data in a file

Structures and File Data

Structures offer a particularly convenient way to accomplish file I/O. You can write the entire contents of a structure to a file in one statement by passing function *fwrite()* a pointer to, and the size of, the structure:

```
fwrite( pPerson, sizeof( struct PERSON ), 1, filePointer );
```

This is an unformatted write operation and so the file should be opened for binary I/O. If you think of each structure of data as corresponding to a *record* in the file, then the member values correspond to record *fields*. It is common practice for programmers to design structures and files with this relationship in mind. Figure 13-8 relates structure members to file record fields.

You would input the data from the file with an *fread()* statement of similar construction:

```
fread( pPerson, sizeof( struct PERSON ), 1, filePointer );
```

Of course, you can also read and write structure data with formatted statements; this is slower, it produces larger files, and you must format the structure members individually, but if you need the file records to contain ASCII information in a particular form, then formatted I/O is the choice.

Unions

A *union* is a data declaration that is like a structure except that all members overlay each other in the same memory space. The syntax for a union is the same as that for a structure, but you substitute the key word *union* in place of *struct*:

```
union TAG
{
    member_list;
} name_list;
```

The member list is usually variables of different types. The chief purpose of a union is to allow a memory location to represent different data types at different times. Here is the declaration of a union template that can hold either an integer value or a floating-point value:

```
union EITHER
{
    int   digits;
    float real;
};
```

Here is a union variable based on the above template:

```
union EITHER number = 12;
```

With this example, you begin to see some of the similarities between unions and structures; they have these characteristics in common:

- They have the same syntax.
- They have the same operators for member access—member operator (.) and pointer operator (->).
- They have the same array capabilities.
- They share the same treatment for pointer arithmetic.

However there are three important differences:

- You can initialize a union only with the data type of the first member declared.
- The size of a union is the size of the largest member.
- A union takes the value of the member that was most recently assigned a value.

In the example above, *number* was initialized with an integer, so you can only access the value from member *number.digits*. The other member, *number.real*, will not yield a correct value until you assign a floating-point number:

```
number.real = 1.23;
```

FIGURE 13-9 A masquerading union variable

at which time the value of member *number.digits* becomes invalid. A union is like the masquerade in Figure 13-9, taking on different appearances at different times.

There are not many useful applications for unions, but they provide a means to save space if large amounts of data can be time shared in common memory. If you have two compatible data types of the same size, such as integers and characters, you can translate between them with a union. For example, you can extract the values of the upper and lower bytes of a 16-bit integer as follows:

```
#include <stdio.h>
void main()
{
    union DATA
    {
        int digits;
        char bytes[2];
    };

    union DATA x = { 258 };
```

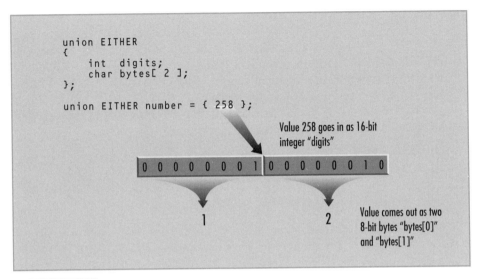

```
union EITHER
{
    int digits;
    char bytes[ 2 ];
};

union EITHER number = { 258 };
```

Value 258 goes in as 16-bit integer "digits"

`0 0 0 0 0 0 0 1 0 0 0 0 0 0 1 0`

1

2

Value comes out as two 8-bit bytes "bytes[0]" and "bytes[1]"

FIGURE 13-10   Data representation in a union

```
    printf( "Value of the first byte is %d\n"
            "Value of the second byte is %d\n",
            x.bytes[0], x.bytes[1] );
}
```

The output of the program is:

```
Value of the first byte is 2
Value of the second byte is 1
```

This program initializes the union to the 16-bit integer value of 258, then accesses the data as two separate 8-bit values. Figure 13-10 shows this action.

LAB

This lab will guide you through the process of developing a program for entering, storing, and displaying family information. The program demonstrates certain features that could be of assistance to someone interested in geneaology.

Exercise 1:   Declare a structure.

✳ **DO:** Declare the template for a structure (with tag identifier *KIN*) that will hold information about an individual family member. The structure should include members for an individual's name, date of birth, and place of birth. Place the declaration in a header file named FAMILY.H so you can include it in several source files. Write a program that displays the size of the structure and run it.

✳ **SOLUTION FILES:** EX13-1.C and FAMILY.H

✳ **RESULT:**

```
Number of bytes in structure KIN is 117
```

✳ **DISCUSSION:** The size of your structure might be different than the size of this one. There are any number of ways to compose a structure to satisfy the stated requirements. We declared three substructures, *DATE, NAME,* and *PLACE*, because they represent natural entities that might well be needed again. We also included member *spouseIndex* in anticipation of linking husbands and wives in a family tree later on.

Exercise 2:   Use a structure pointer.

✳ **DO:** Write a function called *getNewRelative()* that dynamically allocates memory for a *KIN* structure and returns a pointer to the new variable after filling it with data from the keyboard. Write another function called *showRelative()* that accepts the structure parameter and displays member values. Finally, write a program to call both of these functions so that you enter information for one person and echo the data back to the screen. Put each function in a separate file. Hint: You will need to create a project file to compile and link these modules. The supplied project file FAMILY.PRJ will serve for Exercises 2 through 7 if you use the solution file names and copy the main program to FAMILY.C in each case.

✳ **SOLUTION FILES:** EX13-2A.C, EX13-2B.C, EX13-2C.C

✳ **RESULT:**

```
Enter name (first<Enter> middle<Enter> last<Enter>):
John
Quincy
Adams
Enter birth place (city<Enter> state<Enter> zip<Enter>):
Braintree
```

```
Massachusetts

Enter birth date (mm<Enter> dd<Enter> yyyy<Enter>):
7
11
1767

Name: John Quincy Adams
Birthday: 7/11/1767
Birthplace: Braintree, Massachusetts
```

✳ **DISCUSSION:** The call to function *showRelative()* causes a compiler warning because of the structure argument. (You can see warnings if you use the *Compile* menu selection instead of *Run*.) Turbo C++ wants to be sure we are aware that the parameter received is not a pointer to the original structure in the calling program. We need *gets()* for the keyboard input in order to accept blank names and multiple-word names. It is preferable not to mix *scanf()* input statements with *gets()* because *scanf()* leaves a newline character in the input buffer; therefore we use *gets()* throughout, followed by *sscanf()* to convert numeric values. When *getNewRelative()* allocates memory, it casts the pointer value so it is a pointer to type *struct KIN*. Notice how the main program frees this memory before ending. We've added prototypes for the new functions to header FAMILY.H. We're ignoring structure member *spouseIndex* for now.

Exercise 3:   Use a structure variable.

✳ **DO:** Write a new function *getRelative()* to replace *getNewRelative()*. Instead of returning a pointer to dynamically allocated memory, have the new function return a structure variable (type *struct KIN* instead of *struct KIN **). Make appropriate changes to the main program to accommodate this difference. Run the program and enter the same data as for Exercise 2. (If you are using project file FAMILY.PRJ, remember to put the main program in FAMILY.C.)

✳ **SOLUTION FILES:** EX13-3A.C and EX13-3B.C

✳ **RESULT:** Same as Exercise 2.

✳ **DISCUSSION:** Function *getRelative()* uses the structure member operator (.) instead of the structure pointer operator (->) to access members. It is no longer necessary to free memory in the main program because there is no dynamically allocated memory. We added a prototype for the new function (*getRelative()*) to header FAMILY.H.

Exercise 4:   Use an array of structures.

✻ DO: Define an array of structures big enough to hold information for 100 family members; initialize all values in the array to zero. Modify your main program from Exercise 3 to accept data from the keyboard into any element of the array. When keyboard input is finished, display the first four elements of the array. Run the program and enter information for two family members. (To use project file FAMILY.PRJ, develop the program in file FAMILY.C.)

✻ SOLUTION FILE: EX13-4.C

✻ RESULT:

```
Select a family array index (-1 to quit): 1
Enter name (first<Enter> middle<Enter> last<Enter>):
John
Quincy
Adams
Enter birth place (city<Enter> state<Enter> zip<Enter>):
Braintree
Massachusetts

Enter birth date (mm<Enter> dd<Enter> yyyy<Enter>):
7
11
1767

Select a family array index (-1 to quit): 2
Enter name (first<Enter> middle<Enter> last<Enter>):
Abigail
Smith
Adams

Enter birth place (city<Enter> state<Enter> zip<Enter>):
Weymouth
Massachusetts

Enter birth date (mm<Enter> dd<Enter> yyyy<Enter>):
0
0
1744

Select a family array index (-1 to quit): -1

Name:
Birthday: 0/0/0
Birthplace:

Name: John Quincy Adams
Birthday: 7/11/1767
```

```
Birthplace: Braintree, Massachusetts

Name: Abigail Smith Adams
Birthday: 0/0/1744
Birthplace: Weymouth, Massachusetts

Name:
Birthday: 0/0/0
Birthplace:
```

✳ **DISCUSSION:** Notice the zero entries for Abigail's unknown birth month and day. In the solution program, the initialization list for the array contains a single zero—this causes all the remaining values to be zero too. Four sets of braces are necessary to keep the compiler from issuing a warning because the variable is an array (*family*) of structures (*KIN*) containing another structure (*NAME*) with an array (*first*). You can ignore the warnings and get by with just one set of braces if you wish.

Exercise 5:   Write structures to a file.

✳ **DO:** Write a function, *writeRelatives()* called from the main program, that will write the *family* array of structures to a file. Develop source code for the new function in a separate file. Run the program and enter information for two relatives. Hint: Unformatted write usually requires opening a file in binary mode.

✳ **SOLUTION FILES:** EX13-5A.C and EX13-5B.C

✳ **RESULT:** Same display as Exercise 4; creates file FAMILY.TRE.

✳ **DISCUSSION:** Function *writeRelatives()* receives a pointer to the *family* array and performs an unformatted write of FAMILY_SIZE items to the file (total bytes written is FAMILY_SIZE * sizeof(KIN)). If the open statement fails, the function forces a program *exit()*; if successful, it closes the file. Now the entered information is retained in FAMILY.TRE; you can read it back from this file instead of retyping it.

Exercise 6:   Read structures from a file.

✳ **DO:** Write a function, named *readRelatives()*, that reads the family tree from the file that Exercise 5 created; put the new function in a file of its own. Call the function at the beginning of the main program to get current data before modifying the family tree. Add one more family member to the tree.

✳ **SOLUTION FILES:** EX13-6A.C and EX13-6B.C

✳ **RESULT:**

```
Name:
Birthday: 0/0/0
Birthplace:

Name: John Quincy Adams
Birthday: 7/11/1767
Birthplace: Braintree, Massachusetts

Name: Abigail Smith Adams
Birthday: 0/0/1744
Birthplace: Weymouth, Massachusetts

Name:
Birthday: 0/0/0
Birthplace:

Select a family array index (-1 to quit): 0
Enter name (first<Enter> middle<Enter> last<Enter>):
John

Adams
Enter birth place (city<Enter> state<Enter> zip<Enter>):
Braintree
Massachusetts

Enter birth date (mm<Enter> dd<Enter> yyyy<Enter>):
10
30
1735

Select a family array index (-1 to quit): -1

Name: John  Adams
Birthday: 10/30/1735
Birthplace: Braintree, Massachusetts

Name: John Quincy Adams
Birthday: 7/11/1767
Birthplace: Braintree, Massachusetts

Name: Abigail Smith Adams
Birthday: 0/0/1744
Birthplace: Weymouth, Massachusetts

Name:
Birthday: 0/0/0
Birthplace:
```

✳ **DISCUSSION:** Function *readRelatives()* is almost identical to *writeRelatives()* except it opens the file in read mode and calls function *fread()* instead of *fwrite()*. If it cannot open the file, the function *returns* to allow the program to continue running rather than ending the program with a call to *exit()*.

Exercise 7:   Create links between structures.

✳ **DO:** In order to make this program really useful for family trees, you need to form links between the relatives. Solution file EX13-7.C shows how to use the structure member *spouseIndex* as a link to the husband or wife. You don't need to develop any new code yourself, but run the program and examine the source file to see how it produces the result below. (Copy EX13-7.C to FAMILY.C in order to use the project file FAMILY.PRJ.)

✳ **SOLUTION FILE:** EX13-7.C

✳ **RESULT:**

```
Name: John   Adams
Birthday: 10/30/1735
Birthplace: Braintree, Massachusetts

Name: John Quincy Adams
Birthday: 7/11/1767
Birthplace: Braintree, Massachusetts

Name: Abigail Smith Adams
Birthday: 0/0/1744
Birthplace: Weymouth, Massachusetts

Name:
Birthday: 0/0/0
Birthplace:

Select a family array index (-1 to quit): 0
Enter name (first<Enter> middle<Enter> last<Enter>):
John

Adams
Enter birth place (city<Enter> state<Enter> zip<Enter>):
Braintree
Massachusetts

Enter birth date (mm<Enter> dd<Enter> yyyy<Enter>):
10
30
1735
```

```
Enter the spouse index: 2
Select a family array index (-1 to quit): -1
Enter a name to search for(first<Enter> middle<Enter> last<Enter>):
John

Adams

Name: John    Adams
Birthday: 10/30/1735
Birthplace: Braintree, Massachusetts
--Spouse--
Name: Abigail Smith Adams
Birthday: 0/0/1744
Birthplace: Weymouth, Massachusetts
```

✳ **DISCUSSION:** You can search for any family member based on a name and display the full information about that person. Then, because the spouse index is present, a simple call to *showRelative()* displays the spouse information. You can extend this indexing technique to connect parents, children, and other relatives in order to display or print information in an organized layout.

Exercise 8:   Create a union.

✳ **DO:** Write a program that declares a union of three variables, *types char, int,* and *float.* Display the size of the union. Assign a value to each member of the union and display all members after each assignment. (Close the project file, FAMILY.PRJ, before running this program.)

✳ **SOLUTION FILE:** EX13-8.C

✳ **RESULT:**

```
The union size is 4 bytes.

(assign value 'A')
Character value = A
Integer value = 9793
Floating-point value = -0.000000

(assign value 123)
Character value = {
Integer value = 123
Floating-point value = -0.000000

(assign value 4.5e6)
Character value = @
```

```
Integer value = 21568
Floating-point value = 4500000.000000
```

✳ **DISCUSSION:** Only one member at a time has a valid value; it is the member last assigned a value.

Exercise 9: Declare bit-fields.

✳ **DO:** Write a program that shows which end of an integer a compiler starts assigning bit-field values. Hint: Combine a bit-field structure with an integer in a union.

✳ **SOLUTION FILE:** EX13-9.C

✳ **RESULT:**

```
The value of the whole integer is 1
```

✳ **DISCUSSION:** The above result shows that Turbo C++ begins assigning fields with the least significant bit of an integer. If it began with the most significant bit, the solution program would display a hex value of 100.

SUMMARY

Structures organize diverse data types under a single identifier. We recommend a two-step approach to structures: Declare a template having a tag identifier (possibly in a header file), then reuse the tag to define structure variables. Under ANSI C, you can assign entire structures between variables and you can pass a complete structure argument to a function, as well as return a structure from a function. You can define arrays of structures and you can use pointers with structures, and file I/O can be particularly easy with structures. You access individual members of a structure with the structure member operator (.) or the structure pointer operator (->). You can perform any operation with a structure member that you can with a separate variable, just remember to include the structure name. Much of the data processed by a computer program is interrelated. We urge you to think in terms of organizing data into structures whenever possible.

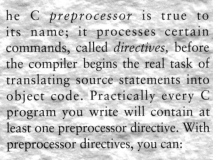

14

*Average time to
complete this chapter
(including lab and
quiz) is 6 hours.*

THE PREPROCESSOR

he C *preprocessor* is true to
its name; it processes certain
commands, called *directives*, before
the compiler begins the real task of
translating source statements into
object code. Practically every C
program you write will contain at
least one preprocessor directive. With
preprocessor directives, you can:

- ■ Copy the contents of
  header files into other
  source files.

- ■ Define symbolic constants.

- ■ Include or exclude
  sections of code based
  on defined constants.

- ■ Establish *macros* that act
  much like functions but
  actually become inline code.

In this chapter you will become
familiar with all these important
capabilities.

LECTURE

All preprocessor directives begin with the the pound sign (#) followed by a key word:

```
#keyword parameter(s)
```

One example is the familiar *include* directive:

```
#include <stdio.h>
```

Some of the older, non-ANSI compilers require that the pound sign be in column one of the source line. The ANSI standard allows spaces and tabs to precede a directive, but for the sake of portability we recommend you always place the pound sign in column one. Although it is legal to insert spaces between the pound sign and the directive key word, the usual form has no spaces until after the key word.

We'll discuss preprocessor directives in three categories:

1. Directives to define symbolic constants and macros (*#define* and *#undef*)

2. Directives to control conditional compilation (*#if, #ifdef, #ifndef, #else, #elif,* and *#endif*)

3. Directives to include files *(#include)*

Directives for Substitution

With the *#define* directive, you can substitute a character sequence of one or more lines for every occurrence of an identifier. The substitution can be either a constant (in the case of a symbolic constant), or it can be executable statements (in the case of a macro).

Symbolic Constants

The *#define* directive for a symbolic constant (also called *manifest constant*) has the form:

```
#define IDENTIFIER constant
```

This directive causes the preprocessor to locate every occurrence of *IDENTIFIER* in the source code and replace each instance with the defined constant. Any legal C identifier will do, but it is good programming practice to use uppercase letters so that substitutions are clearly visible in the source code. Here are several examples of defined symbolic constants:

```
#define PI 3.1416
#define TRUE 1
#define FALSE 0
#define ARRAY_SIZE 35
#define NEWLINE '\n'
#define ERRORFILE "ERRORS.LOG"
#define BYTE unsigned char
```

The *scope* (region where substitutions are made) of a *#define* starts at the directive and continues to the end of the file. Taking the first example, the preprocessor will replace every instance of PI in a file with 3.1416. The preprocessor performs a literal replacement—on the *#define* line it starts at the first non-space character after the identifier and uses everything to the last non-space character on the line for substitutions. So for the last example above, the preprocessor replaces *BYTE* with the two words *unsigned char* after removing leading and trailing spaces. Figure 14-1 shows a code fragment before and after the preprocessor runs.

You can use *#define* to substitute any item, but the result must ultimately be a syntax acceptable to the C compiler. For instance, you can change all occurrences of the word "oat" to uppercase letters with the following directive:

```
#define oat OAT
```

```
BEFORE PREPROCESSOR                          AFTER PREPROCESSOR

#define FALSE 0                              #define FALSE 0
#define TRUE  1                              #define TRUE  1
#define SPACE ' '                            #define SPACE ' '
#define ARRAY_SIZE 35                        #define ARRAY_SIZE 35

main()                                       main()
{                                            {
    int  i;                                      int  i;
    int  initialize = FALSE;                     int  initialize = 0;
    char name[ARRAY_SIZE];                       char name[35];

    if ( initialize == TRUE )                    if ( initialize == 1 )
    {                                            {
        for ( i=0; i<ARRAY_SIZE; ++i )               for ( i=0; i<35; ++i )
        {                                            {
            name[i] = SPACE;                             name[i] = ' ';
        }                                            }
    }                                            }
}                                            }
```

FIGURE 14-1 Effect of preprocessor substitution

But you better not do this if the file contains any floating-point type declarations because it will modify the key word *float* to *flOAT*. Because *#define* directives cause literal replacements, you can even redefine key words, such as:

```
#define for Do
```

This directive will cause all occurrences of *for* to become *Do* thereby making all *for* statements syntactically incorrect. You should steer clear of key words in *#define* directives—place them there only if you are certain of the effect.

The main advantage of a symbolic constant is that the preprocessor propagates a single constant to many places in a source file before compilation begins. This makes modification of constants easy and errorfree. By placing *#define* directives in a header file, you can make one symbolic constant serve any number of source files.

Macros

A more complex form of preprocessor substitution, called *macro* substitution, provides for arguments—the syntax is:

```
#define IDENTIFIER(argument list) substitution expression
```

For this directive the preprocessor first replaces arguments in the substitution expression with values from the argument list, then it replaces the *IDENTIFIER* with the whole substitution. For example, here is a macro definition that changes an uppercase letter to lowercase:

```
#define TOLOWER(letter) letter + 32
```

A reference to this macro in a program might look like this:

```
char lowercase;
lowercase = TOLOWER('A');
```

The preprocessor converts this statement in two steps. It first replaces argument *letter* with the value 'A', then it replaces the identifier *TOLOWER('A')* with the macro expression. The result is:

```
lowercase = 'A' + 32;
```

The preprocessor will make literal substitutions without regard to the effect, so you must take care how you set up and use macro expressions. For instance, you could write:

```
lowercase = TOLOWER(the bridge);
```

and the preprocessor would produce the following statement, resulting in a compiler error:

```
lowercase = the bridge + 32;
```

Even if you had defined variables named *the* and *bridge*, the juxtaposition of the two variables is illegal.

A COMMON MACRO ERROR

You will experience a natural urge to end a macro with a semicolon (;) as if it were any other C statement. You should avoid this practice because it often results in undesirable semicolons and compiler errors. Here is an example of this kind of error:

```
#define TOLOWER(letter) letter + 32;  /* Ends with semicolon */
printf( "Lower-case letter is %c", TOLOWER('A') );
```

After substitution, the statement has an extra semicolon after the 32 that will cause a compiler error:

```
printf( "Lower-case letter is %c", 'A' + 32; );
```

Any time a semicolon is needed, it belongs in the program statement that refers to a macro rather than in the macro definition.

You can define longer macros that span more than one line by appending a backslash character (\) to each continued line. Let's expand the *TOLOWER* macro to be more like the standard library function *tolower()*, which modifies only characters 'A' through 'Z', leaving a through z alone:

```
#define TOLOWER(letter) \
( letter >= 'A' ) && ( letter <= 'Z' ) ? letter + 32 : letter
```

This macro uses a conditional statement to return the unmodified letter if it is not in the range of uppercase 'A' through 'Z'. The entire statement is too long to fit on one line, so the first line has a continuation character (\) that connects the two lines. The conditional statement works well within a macro because it can return a value based on an expression test.

VERY LARGE MACROS

Some compilers limit the number of continuation lines; this is not normally a problem because the number of lines allowed is usually ample. However, you can overcome the limit for a very large macro by splitting it into two or more pieces. Here's the macro *TOLOWER* defined in two parts even though it's not big enough to require separation:

```
#define TOLOWER_TEST(letter) (letter >= 'A') && (letter <= 'Z') ?
#define TOLOWER_DO(letter) letter + 32 : letter
```

You then use both macro identifiers, each with the same argument, to refer to this two-part macro, the preprocessor will concatenate it as if it were one macro:

```
/* Original source line */
lowercase = TOLOWER_TEST('A') TOLOWER_DO('A');
/* Preprocessor output */
lowercase = ('A' >= 'A') && ('A' <= 'Z') ? 'A' + 32 : 'A';
```

You should not write large macros unless it is absolutely necessary.

The argument list for a macro can contain any number of values. The preprocessor substitutes all of the values in an argument list into the corresponding arguments of a macro expression. Here is a macro that finds the maximum of two values:

```
#define MAX(x, y) x > y ? x : y
```

The following statements will assign the values of 11 and 9.9 respectively to *maxInt* and *maxFloat*:

```
maxInt = MAX( 10, 11 );
maxFloat = MAX( 9.0, 9.9 );
```

Notice that this operation is type independent—it works regardless of the data type of the arguments! You can refer to one symbolic constant or macro within the definition of another. For instance, you can define a macro that uses a symbolic constant PI to calculate the circumference of a circle by multiplying the radius by 2 * PI:

```
#define PI 3.1416
#define CIRCUMFERENCE(r) 2 * PI * r
```

Some compilers don't care about the order, but it is best if the directive for PI precedes the definition for *CIRCUMFERENCE* so the preprocessor will know what value to substitute for PI in the macro.

Macro Errors

You need to be alert to particular subtle errors that can occur with macros. If you ask for the circumference of a circle with a radius of 2, the macro above correctly returns a value of 12.5664:

```
distance = CIRCUMFERENCE( 2 );  /* Original source code */
distance = 2 * 3.1416 * 2;      /* Preprocessor output */
```

However if you express the circumference as one plus one, the program will calculate the wrong answer of 7.2832:

```
distance = CIRCUMFERENCE( 1 + 1 );  /* Original source code */
distance = 2 * 3.1416 * 1 + 1;      /* Preprocessor output */
```

This error is representative of a whole class of similar errors due to incorrect order of operator application. To correct this problem, all you need to do is insert an extra pair of parentheses around each argument in the macro definition—the preprocessor will substitute the parentheses along with the argument value. Here's how you fix the above example:

```
#define CIRCUMFERENCE(r) 2 * PI * (r)
```

Now the preprocessor output is correct, with parentheses to force the addition to occur first:

```
distance = 2 * 3.1416 * (1 + 1);
```

These kinds of errors are completely avoidable if you always remember to insert parentheses around arguments in the macro expression.

Another serious error can occur if you use increment (++) or decrement (--) operators with macro arguments. Here's a simple example that calculates the square of an argument:

```
#define SQUARE(x) (x) * (x)
```

This works fine for just about any expression you give it as an argument, because we have enclosed each occurrence of the argument with extra parentheses. But look what happens when we use an increment operator:

```
int y = 2;
z = SQUARE( y++ );    /* Original source statement */
z = (y++) * (y++);    /* Preprocessor output */
```

The preprocessor copies the increment operator into the macro expression twice, so the resulting expression is incorrect. You might expect the answer to be four because the operator is a postfix increment, but the first instance increments the argument before the multiplication occurs, yielding an answer of six. You can avoid this type of error by never applying increment or decrement operators to macro arguments.

Comparison of Macros and Functions

Macros and functions have much in common: They both accept arguments, return a value, and have a similar "call" syntax. However the differences are more significant: A function accepts a copy of argument values, but a macro literally substitutes the arguments. A macro doesn't really "return" a value because the program doesn't declare a return data type or transfer control to a new location. As Figure 14-2 illustrates, a macro executes as *inline* code because the preprocessor actually copies the statement(s) into the program wherever the macro identifier exists.

Macro statements are repeated and recompiled for each occurrence of a macro reference, so a program that uses macros is larger than one that uses functions. However, macros are faster than functions because there is no time wasted in passing parameters, returning a value, and transferring control to a new location and back.

To summarize, you should use macros when speed is important or when type independence is an advantage; otherwise use them with restraint because they tend to hide part of the code and they can introduce subtle errors.

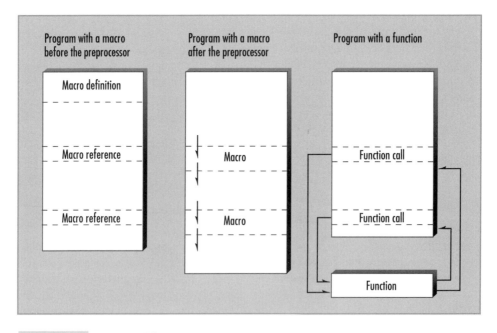

FIGURE 14-2 Macros and functions

Directives for Conditional Compilation

A group of preprocessor directives *(#if, #ifdef, #ifndef, #elif, #else, #endif)* allows you to include or exclude sections of code in a program selectively. The basic form of these directives in a program is:

```
#if ( constant expression )
    /* TRUE statements */
#else
    /* FALSE statements */
#endif
```

If the constant expression is TRUE, the preprocessor keeps the TRUE statements in the program and eliminates the FALSE statements; otherwise it discards the TRUE statements and keeps the FALSE statements. This is a way of inserting or deleting statements depending on some condition. The parentheses are optional (they just enhance readability). Symbolic constants are normally a part of the constant expression.

These directives allow you to modify data types, alter function calls, change header files, and otherwise alter statements in a program. You can use conditional compilation directives to customize a program for a particular computing environment. Here's an example of directives used as a tool to accomplish portability: For DOS compilers a 16-bit integer is type *int* and for DEC VMS compilers it is type *short*. With *typedef* you can declare a new data type *INT16* and adjust it with conditional compilation according to the operating system environment:

```
#define OS DOS  /* For a DEC environment change DOS to VMS */

#if ( OS == DOS )
    typedef INT16 int;
#elif ( OS == VMS )
    typedef INT16 short;
#endif
INT16 variable;  /* Define a 16-bit integer variable */
```

Directive *#elif* (meaning *else if*) in the previous example begins the second conditional branch. The best place to put the *typedef* statements is in a header file that can serve all of your source files.

You can also use conditional directives to control diagnostic statements in a program and turn them on or off at will. For example, you can insert *printf()* statements like this one into strategic places in a program:

```
#ifdef DEBUG
    printf( "Value = %d\n", value );
#endif
```

The *printf()* statements will only be active when the program is compiled with symbolic constant *DEBUG* defined. This way you can leave diagnostic statements in a program and only compile them during testing or during a period of program modification. If you insert the following directive at the beginning of your program, all of the debugging statements will be turned on:

```
#define DEBUG
```

Notice that you don't have to define a value for *DEBUG*—this form of *#define* merely declares that the symbolic constant exists. The *#ifdef* directive returns TRUE when the symbolic constant exists; it doesn't care what the value might be. Directive *#ifndef* (if NOT defined) reverses the test for existence of a symbolic constant. You might use it to exclude certain program sections when debugging is on:

```
#ifndef DEBUG
/* Statements not important to the debugging operation */
#endif
```

You could selectively turn off some of the diagnostic *printf()* statements by undefining and redefining *DEBUG*. Intervening conditional directives that depend on symbolic constant *DEBUG* will be disabled:

```
#undef DEBUG
.
.
.
#ifdef DEBUG
    printf( "String value = %s\n", string );
#endif
.
.
.
#define DEBUG
```

The above construction is a temporary convenience that eliminates selected lines of code as long as the *#undef* directive is in place. Figure 14-3 shows another way to define constants for a Turbo C++ compiler: Select *Define constants...* from the *Options* menu and type a symbolic name in the dialog box.

Directives for Including Header Files

You are already familiar with the *#include* directive for inserting header files into a program. We saved the discussion of *#include* for last to present additional techniques with headers that require some of the other preprocessor directives.

Location of Header Files

The *#include* directive has two forms:

```
#include <header.h>
#include "header.h"
```

Both cause the preprocessor to insert the header file into the program at the location of the directive. The difference is the manner in which the compiler searches directories for the header file. The form with angle brackets causes the compiler to search the directories designated by the IDE. With Turbo C++, you can set include directories by selecting *Directories...* from the *Options* menu and typing one or more directory paths in the *Include directories* dialog box. Either your AUTOEXEC.BAT file or your Turbo C++ *Include directories* item should be set to C:\TCLITE\INCLUDE, where the standard library headers reside.

Most other compilers will search for headers designated by angle brackets in directories specified by the operating system. DOS controls this via the INCLUDE statement in your AUTOEXEC.BAT file. The following line from an AUTOEXEC.BAT file tells the DOS environment to expect header files in directory C:\TCLITE\INCLUDE:

```
SET INCLUDE = C:\TCLITE\INCLUDE
```

Other operating systems have different methods for controlling include directories. Compilers usually have an option to establish search directories, and compilers will also have different rules governing the order of directory search.

The form of *#include* that uses double quotes causes the compiler to search the current directory for the header file, or another path that you designate within the

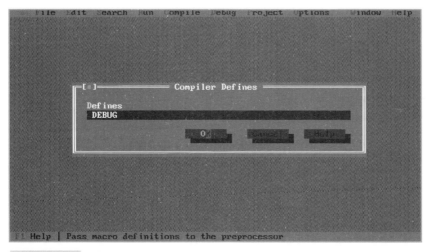

FIGURE 14-3 Defining constants for the Turbo C++ compiler

quotes. The Turbo C++ compiler first searches the source file directory (your current directory); if that fails, it will search the same include directory(s) as for the angle brackets. Here are two examples:

```
#include "myheader.h"
/* MYHEADER.H should be in the current directory */
#include "c:\private\myheader.h"
/* MYHEADER.H should be in directory PRIVATE */
```

As a rule, you should use the angle brackets to include standard library header files, and you should use double quotes to #*include* your own headers. So a typical file might begin with the following #*include* directives:

```
#include <stdio.h>
#include "myhead.h"
```

Headers Within Headers

It is often advantageous to segregate header items into different files. In this scheme the header files are smaller in size, and you can tailor headers to match particular groups of source files. Under this arrangement you may also want to include some header files within others. For example, you can reduce the number of directives in a file by inserting #*include* directives for several standard library headers within your own header. So the file MYHEADER.H could begin with:

```
#include <stdio.h>
#include <stdlib.h>
#include <string.h>
```

With one directive in a source file, you could include all four headers:

```
#include "myheader.h"
```

This is perfectly OK, but it can lead to a repeat *include* of the same file, or the dilemma of circular *includes* whereby header A *includes* header B, which *includes* header A, etc. Duplicate headers are not necessarily a problem, even though the compiler has to spend time on each occurrence, but circular *includes* cause the compiler to fail. The solution to this problem involves using preprocessor *include* guards. If you place an include guard in each of your header files, you will ensure that it will be included only one time for any source file. An *include guard* looks like this:

```
#ifndef _MYHEAD   /* First line in file MYHEAD.H */
#define _MYHEAD
 .
 .
 .
/* Other items in MYHEAD.H */
 .
 .
 .
```

```
#endif          /* Last line in file MYHEAD.H */
```

The first and last lines prevent any items in the header file from inclusion if the symbolic constant _MYHEAD is defined (exists). The second line defines _MYHEAD the first time the header is included, so subsequent #*include* directives with this file name will not have any effect. Notice the underline preceding the symbolic constant—this is the conventional naming scheme for include guards.

Contents of Header Files

If a program has more than a handful of preprocessor directives, or if the directives affect more than one source file, it is wise to put them in a header file. As a general rule, you should not place executable statements in a header file; nor should you put statements that define variables (allocate memory) in a header file. The main advantage of a header file is that you can include it in more than one source file, and you don't want to limit that capability by having executable statements in the header. Table 14-1 lists the items that are desirable in header files (roughly in best order of appearance).

Item	Example
Include guard	#ifndef _MYHEADER
	#define _MYHEADER
Other header files	#include "OTHER.H"
Symbolic constants	#define NEWLINE '\n'
Macros	#define ROUND(x) (int)((x) + .5)
Typedef statements	typedef BYTE unsigned char;
Structure templates	struct TAG
	{
	/* structure members */
	};
Function prototypes	void displayPrompt(char *message);
End of include guard	#endif

Table 14-1   Items for header files

The order of items is not a strict requirement, but certain items must precede others. Other header files should appear first because they could affect subsequent items. Symbolic constants and *typedef* declarations can be used in structure templates and function prototypes, so these items should appear last.

LAB

Exercise 1A: Define symbolic constants.

✳ **STARTER FILE: EX14-1A.C**

```
#include <stdio.h>
#define TRUE 1

void main()
{
    int x;

    while ( TRUE )
    {
        printf( "Enter an integer value: " );
        scanf( "%d", &x );

        if ( ( ( ( x > 100 ) && ( x < 120 ) ) &&
            ( ( x/2 >= 57 ) || ( x/2 <= 57 ) ) &&
            ( !( x == 'q' ) && !( x != 'r' ) ) ) )
        {
            printf( "Congratulations!"
                    " You've solved the stupid puzzle!\n" );
            break;
        }
    }
}
```

✳ **DO:** The starter program asks you to guess the value of a certain integer, and it uses a lot of logical and relational operators to test the answer. The FORTRAN language has different symbols for these operators, and many programmers find them easier to read than the C symbols. These operators are listed below:

Operator	C Symbol	FORTRAN Symbol
Equal	==	EQ
Not equal	!=	NE
Greater than	>	GT
Less than	<	LT
Greater than or equal	>=	GE
Less than	<=	LE

or equal

And	&&	AND
Or	||	OR
Not	!	NOT

Your task (besides guessing the integer) is to define symbolic constants corresponding to the FORTRAN symbols and insert them into the program.

✳ **SOLUTION FILE:** EX14-1B.C

✳ **RESULT:**
```
Enter an integer value: 112
Enter an integer value: 113
Enter an integer value: 114
Congratulations! You've solved the stupid puzzle!
```

✳ **DISCUSSION:** If you correctly substitute the FORTRAN symbols, the program will work exactly as the original. Some programmers like to use the FORTRAN symbols, while others see no advantage. Looking at the new source code, what is your opinion?

Exercise 1B: Use an #include directive.

✳ **DO:** If you haven't already done so, move the preprocessor statements for symbolic constants to a header file. Hint: Use double quotes (" ") in the #include directive. Run the program.

✳ **SOLUTION FILE:** EX14-1C.C and EX14-1.H

✳ **RESULT:** Same as Exercise 1A.

✳ **DISCUSSION:** You should place your header files in the same directory as source files and include them with double quotes.

Exercise 1C: Modify the #include directive.

✳ **DO:** Change the #include directive to enclose the header file name in angle brackets (< >)instead of double quotes (" "). Compile the program.

✳ **SOLUTION FILE:** EX14-1D.C

✳ **RESULT:**
```
Error: Unable to open include file 'EX14-1.H'
```

✳ **DISCUSSION:** Angle brackets cause the preprocessor to search for the header file in the directory specified by the IDE options; if your header is not in this directory, the compile error will occur.

Exercise 1D: Specify header location.

✳ **DO:** Use Turbo C++ to specify the directory where the header is located. Select *Options*, then *Directories...*, and type the directory name in the *Include directories* dialog box. Use a semicolon to separate the new directory from others that might already be in the *Include...* box. Run the program.

✳ **SOLUTION FILE:** EX14-1D.C

✳ **RESULT:** Same as Exercise 1A.

✳ **DISCUSSION:** This Turbo C++ option instructs the compiler where to search for header files enclosed by angle brackets.

Exercise 2:   Use an *#include* directive.

✳ **STARTER FILE:** EX14-2A.C

```
#include <stdio.h>

void displayMessage();

void main()
{
    displayMessage( "This is exercise 2" );
}

void displayMessage( message )
char *message;
{
    printf( "%s\n", message );
}
```

✳ **DO:** The starter program calls a function to display a message. The function is written with the "old style" C syntax—notice the absence of parameter declaration in the prototype and the extra line to define parameter *message* in the function definition. Use preprocessor directives to make this program portable to either a Common C or an ANSI C compiler. Hint: Define a symbolic constant *COMPILER* with value COMMON_C or ANSI_C that controls which type of function prototype and definition exists. Specify the ANSI compiler and run the program.

✳ SOLUTION FILE: EX14-2B.C

✳ RESULT:

```
This is exercise 2
```

✳ DISCUSSION: The Common C style of function definition is obsolete. Using the above method, you can make existing programs compatible with ANSI C while retaining compatibility with older compilers.

Exercise 3:   Write a macro.

✳ DO: Write a macro that rounds off a real number to the nearest integer value. Fractional values of .5 or greater round upward. Hint: You can round a number by adding .5 and truncating. Write a program that takes a number from the keyboard, uses the macro to round the number, and displays the result. Run the program and enter several values, including 1.4 and 1.5.

✳ SOLUTION FILE: EX14-3.C

✳ RESULT:

```
Enter a real number: 1.4
1.400000 rounded off is 1
Enter a real number: 1.5
1.500000 rounded off is 2
```

✳ DISCUSSION: The extra parentheses around the argument assures that the macro can accept an argument expression as well as a single value.

Exercise 4A: Compare macros with functions.

✳ STARTER FILE: EX14-4A.C

```c
#include <stdio.h>

void dayToDate( int, char * );

void main()
{
    int day = 200;
    char date[8];

    dayToDate( day, date );
    printf( "Day %d is %s\n", day, date );
}
```

```
void dayToDate( int day, char *date )
{
    if ( day > 334 )
        sprintf( date, "December %02d", day-334 );
    else if ( day > 304 )
        sprintf( date, "November %02d", day-304 );
    else if ( day > 273 )
        sprintf( date, "October %02d", day-273 );
    else if ( day > 243 )
        sprintf( date, "September %02d", day-243 );
    else if ( day > 212 )
        sprintf( date, "August %02d", day-212 );
    else if ( day > 181 )
        sprintf( date, "July %02d", day-181 );
    else if ( day > 151 )
        sprintf( date, "June %02d", day-151 );
    else if ( day > 120 )
        sprintf( date, "May %02d", day-120 );
    else if ( day > 90 )
        sprintf( date, "April %02d", day-90 );
    else if ( day > 59 )
        sprintf( date, "March %02d", day-59 );
    else if ( day > 31 )
        sprintf( date, "February %02d", day-31 );
    else
        sprintf( date, "January %02d", day );
}
```

✳ **DO:** The starter program calls a function to convert an integer (in the range 1 to 365) to month and day. Rewrite the function as a macro and run the program. With a DOS directory command, compare the sizes of the two executable files.

✳ **SOLUTION FILE:** EX14-4B.C

✳ **RESULT:**

```
Day 200 is July 19

(compare executable sizes)
C:\> dir EX14-4*.EXE

EX14-4A  EXE      9930 08-27-94   5:39a
EX14-4B  EXE      9728 08-27-94   5:37a
```

✳ **DISCUSSION:** This is a fairly long macro that requires the continuation character (\\) for multiple lines. The function version of this program is larger than the macro version because of processing associated with the function call. In the original program, we dispensed with the usual braces for each *if* clause because of the length of the statement.

Exercise 4B: Compare macros with functions.

✳ **DO:** Duplicate the call to convert and display a date in each of the two programs from Exercise 4A. In other words, have two identical function calls in one program and two identical macro references in the other. Run the two programs and compare the sizes of the executable files.

✳ **SOLUTION FILES:** EX14-4C.C and EX14-4D.C

✳ **RESULT:**

```
Day 200 is July 19

(compare executable sizes)
C:\> dir EX14-4*.EXE
EX14-4A  EXE      9930 08-27-94    5:39a
EX14-4B  EXE      9728 08-27-94    5:37a
EX14-4C  EXE      9934 08-27-94    5:44a
EX14-4D  EXE     10196 08-27-94    5:43a
```

✳ **DISCUSSION:** The function version of the program increased only slightly in size (from 9930 to 9934), but the macro version increased greatly (from 9728 to 10196) and is now larger than the function version. This illustrates how the size of a program expands as the preprocessor makes macro substitutions.

Exercise 4C: Compare macros with functions.

✳ **DO:** Compare the speed of the function call against that of the macro. Remove the *printf()* output statements from the two programs in Exercise 4B and insert a loop to repeat the date conversion 1 million times. Display the time just before entering the loop and again after it ends. Hint: A call to standard library function *time()* retrieves the time in seconds since January 1, 1970.

✳ **SOLUTION FILES:** EX14-4E.C and EX14-4F.C

✳ **RESULT:**

```
(EX14-4D.EXE, function version)
Start: 777993757
Stop: 777993863

(EX14-4E.EXE, macro version)
Start: 777993627
Stop: 777993730
```

✳ **DISCUSSION:** The function version took 106 seconds (the difference between the first Start and Stop times) to complete 1 million calls and the macro version took 103 seconds. The macro is only about 3 percent faster than the function in this case. Other macros can be significantly faster than functions, but often the difference is not important. Your results may be different than these timings (made on a 16 MHz 386 PC) because your computer may be faster or slower.

Exercise 5:   Use typeless macros.

✳ **DO:** Write a macro to exchange the values of two variables regardless of the data type of the variables. Write a program to use this macro to exchange two integers (values 1 and 2) and two floating-point numbers (1.1 and 2.2). Hint: Use a third macro argument that is a variable of the same type as the other two.

✳ **SOLUTION FILE:** EX14-5.C

✳ **RESULT:**

```
Original: i1 = 1, i2 = 2
Swapped: i1 = 2, i2 = 1
Original: f1 = 1.100000, f2 = 2.200000
Swapped: f1 = 2.200000, f2 = 1.100000
```

✳ **DISCUSSION:** Macros can perform a limited number of typeless operations, such as swapping or finding the maximum or minimum of two numbers.

Exercise 6:   Use macros containing functions.

✳ **DO:** Write a program that uses a macro to get an integer value from the keyboard. This macro requires two arguments: a pointer to a prompt message and a pointer to an integer variable. Run the program and enter the value 123.

✳ **SOLUTION FILE:** EX14-6.C

✳ **RESULT:**

```
Enter an integer: 123
Entered value is 123
```

✳ **DISCUSSION:** A macro such as *GETINT* in this exercise is likely to be used repeatedly. Macros, like functions, can replace blocks of repeated code.

SUMMARY

The preprocessor modifies source files before the compiler begins the main work of conversion to object code. Preprocessor directives allow you to include header files, define symbolic constants and macros, and control conditional compilations. You can avoid repetition by placing declarations and other nonexecutable statements in header files. Symbolic constants, usually identified with uppercase letters, make your programs more readable. Macros are like fast, inline functions. Conditional directives allow you to insert or delete lines of code selectively to achieve portability or add debugging statements.

15

PUTTING IT ALL TOGETHER

ongratulations on completing the 14 instructional chapters of *Certified Course in* C. You now have all the skills required to write a major program in C, and this final chapter will give you a chance to do just that! By designing and coding a large program, you will learn aspects of programming that you can't realize just by studying the separate elements of C. In particular, you will learn how to determine the functional specifications for a program, sketch its broad outlines, and code the functions in a top-down fashion. You also will gain experience in dealing with issues of data representation (What data structure do I use for this piece of information?), modularity (Which program operations should I place in separate functions?), and encapsulation (What information should I hide and how should my functions communicate with the main program?)

The program we've chosen for this exercise in "putting it all together" is the exam program that you've been using to take the chapter quizzes. It utilizes a broad range of features from the C language: different data types, arrays and strings, keyboard and screen I/O, file I/O, branching, looping, structures, preprocessor directives, and operators of many kinds. We'll first outline the design requirements for the exam program, then go step by step through developing the functions, allowing you to develop your own version of each function before revealing the source code for the supplied version.

Design of the Exam Program

The design is in three parts: (1) performance specifications, (2) data definition (structures and file layout), and (3) a flow diagram.

Performance Specifications

This is to be an on-line exam program that allows a user to take quizzes and a final exam interactively. Below is a short list of requirements that summarize how the program should work. The program should operate in the following sequence:

1. Display a list of available exams and accept the user's choice
2. Fetch the selected exam from a file
3. Display questions one at a time and accept the user's choice of answers
4. Grade the exam and display the results

The program and data must support the following capabilities and characteristics:

1. Color graphics display presentation with predominantly text output (also compatible with a monochrome screen)
2. One shared function to handle all display requirements (all screens will present similar generic layouts and a common display function simplifies the code)
3. Exam questions composed with a text editor and stored in files as ASCII data—one exam per file (this means the program can be used to present any multiple-choice exam)
4. User interacts with the program through a minimum number of keystrokes
5. User can quit at any time without completing an exam
6. User can freely move back and forth among questions and change selected answers
7. Results of an exam are not reported until all questions are answered

8. Results consist of a percentage grade and a list of questions with incorrect answers

9. User can request that a graded exam be printed

Data Definition

Specifying the data for a program goes a long way toward determining exactly what the program will do and how it will go about its operations. There are two important data items for the exam program: the files of exam questions and structure variables to hold the questions in RAM along with other data to support interactive testing.

File Layout

There are a total of 13 exams (12 chapter quizzes and a final) in 13 separate files. The quiz files are named QUIZ.XX, where XX is the chapter number (QUIZ.03 holds the quiz for Chapter 3). The final exam is named FINAL.EXM.

Each file contains numbered questions and lettered answers in the form of ASCII text. The first line of each question begins with a number followed by a period (for instance, 1. or 15.) The question continues on successive lines until an answer line occurs. Each multiple choice answer begins with a letter followed by a period (for instance, a. or d.) and is complete on one line. Answers for a question appear on successive lines until another question occurs. Here is an example of two questions with answers:

```
1. Why is the sky blue?
a. Because it's painted
b. Because of dust particles
c. Because of light refraction

2. Do I deserve to win the lottery?
a. Yes
b. No
c. None of the above
```

Data Structures

We'll declare data structures and place them in a header file for inclusion in all the files. The structures hold question and answer strings read from files, and they declare variables necessary to support the interactive exam process.

Questions and answers are strings of different sizes, so we plan to allocate memory for strings dynamically as the program reads an exam from a file. Figure 15-1 illustrates the basic concept for allocating memory and storing the questions and answers.

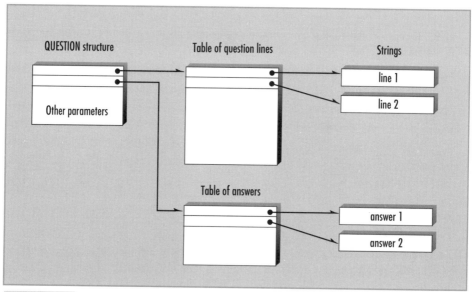

FIGURE 15-1 Memory management for questions and answers

The figure illustrates the layout of storage for one question. We'll allocate storage for the question strings (several lines) and for the answer strings (one line per), then store pointers to the strings in tables. We also plan to allocate storage for the tables (which are lists of pointers) as the questions and answers build up. A *QUESTION* structure (shown at the left in Figure 15-1 and detailed below) will tie the string information together for each question.

```
struct QUESTION
{
    int numLines;             /* Number of question lines */
    char **lineTable;         /* Pointer to table of question lines */
    int correctAnswer;        /* Table index of correct answer */
    int selectedAnswer;       /* Table index of selected answer */
    int numAnswers;           /* Number of answers in the table */
    char **answerTable;       /* Pointer to table of answers */
};
```

The *QUESTION* structure must have a pointer to a table of question lines and a pointer to a table of answers. Both of these tables are lists of pointers to character strings, so the variables (*lineTable* and *answerTable*) in structure *QUESTION* are pointers to pointers. The *QUESTION* structure must also have integer members to keep track of how many question lines and answer lines exist,

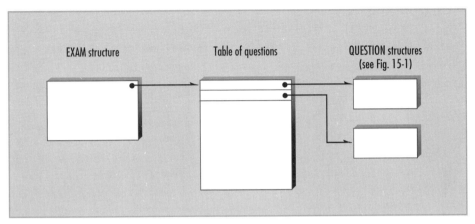

FIGURE 15-2 Organization of memory for an exam

and it must hold an indicator for the correct answer and the user's selected answer.

At a higher level, an exam is a group of questions. So each question will be listed in another table of dynamically allocated pointers. Figure 15-2 illustrates the higher-level memory scheme.

A structure for the basic variables that make up an exam includes a pointer to a title, a pointer to the above table of questions, and the number of questions in the table:

```
struct EXAM
{
    char *pTopic;                   /* Title for the examination */
    int numQuestions;               /* Number of questions in the table */
    struct QUESTION **questionTable; /* Pointer to table of questions */
};
```

The question table is a list of pointers to question structures, so the *questionTable* member is a pointer to a pointer.

This design accommodates a variable number of questions per exam, a variable number of lines per question, a variable number of answers per question, and variable lengths for question and answer lines. If the specifications allowed all these parameters to be fixed instead of variable, you could define arrays to hold all the data and simplify the program somewhat, but the storage requirements would be greater.

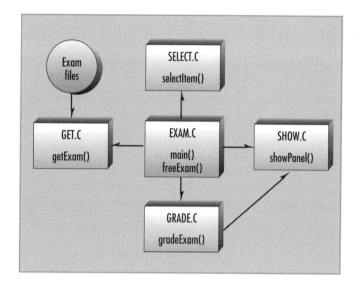

FIGURE 15-3 Exam program

Flow Diagram

Figure 15-3 is a diagram of the major components of the exam program; each module in the diagram represents a file containing the listed function(s). The arrows show the direction of data flow and function calls.

The main function is in the EXAM.C module; it implements the four steps listed in the performance specifications by calling other functions.

Step 1: Display a list of available exams and accept the user's choice. The main function calls *showPanel()* and *selectItem()* for this purpose.

Step 2: Fetch the selected exam from a file. Function *getExam()* reads the selected exam file and dynamically allocates memory for the data as needed. When it is done with the exam, the *main()* program calls another function, *freeExam()*, to release the allocated memory.

Step 3: Display questions one at a time and accept the user's choice of answers. The *main()* program uses a loop to process each question; once again it calls functions *showPanel()* and *selectItem()*, but with different parameters than in Step 1.

Step 4: Grade the exam and display the results. Function *gradeExam()* serves this purpose and it calls *showPanel()* to display the results. Function *gradeExam()* also prints the graded exam on request from the user.

Notice that *showPanel()* does triple duty; in Step 1 it displays available exams, in Step 3 it displays exam questions, and in Step 4 it displays the results. Also, *selectItem()* is used to choose an item from different lists in Steps 1 and 3. This reuse of modules is a characteristic of efficient program design.

Develop the Exam Program

We'll develop the program in five phases according to the schedule in Table 15-1.

Phase	Operation	Functions Developed
1	Display list of exams	*main()* and *showPanel()*
2	Select an exam	*main()* and *selectItem()*
3	Get the exam	*main()* and *getExam()*
4	Take the exam	*main()*
5	Grade the exam	*main()* and *gradeExam()*

Table 15-1   Schedule for development

Figure 15-4 is a flow diagram of the *main()* function.

The program initializes the graphics display, then enters an indefinite loop. In this loop the program calls functions *showPanel()* and *selectItem()* to allow you to select an exam or quit. After you select an exam it calls *getExam()* to read questions from the appropriate file and then enters an inner loop to display the questions. Function *selectItem()* reads answers from the keyboard and *showPanel()* displays another question until you indicate that you are finished, then *main()* calls *gradeExam()* to display the results. After grading you can select another exam or retake the current one.

Source for the supplied functions is approximately 700 lines of code. Given the above design information, an average development pace of ten fully debugged lines per hour might be reasonable, for a total time of 70 hours estimated to complete a new version of the program. We strongly encourage you to develop your own version of the program based on the design given. You will gain valuable experience by making this effort, even if you need to look at the supplied files for assistance. If you need to shorten the time commitment, a worthwhile exercise might be to develop just one or more of the functions, using the supplied *main()* function as a base. Details about calling parameters and return values are available in comments at the beginning of the supplied source files (EXAM.C, GET.C, GRADE.C, SELECT.C, SHOW.C).

Phase 1— Display a List of Exams

For Phase 1 you need to have the *main()* program initialize the graphics display and call function *showPanel()* with appropriate arguments to display the list of 13 exams. Your task in developing your own version of this program is twofold: To use the Turbo C++ help system to look up examples of how to use the graphics

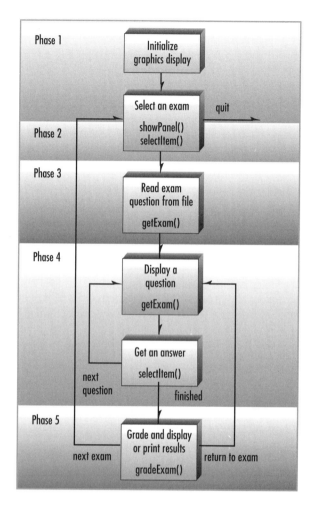

FIGURE 15-4 Exam program

system, and to generalize function *showPanel()* so that it can display the list of exams, or (later on) an exam question with answers, or (still later) the graded results. Hint: The function can display general purpose fields on the screen. A generic panel consists of a title field at the top of the screen, followed by information text fields (questions on the question screen, or results on the grade screen), and item selection fields below that (available exams on the first screen, or answers on the question screen), then a prompt field at the bottom (listing the active keys). You should develop your own version of these capabilities before proceeding to the rest of this section for an explanation of how the supplied program works.

Turbo C++ Graphics

The first few executable lines in *main()* initialize the graphics screen:

```
initgraph( &gdriver, &gmode, "" );
if ( graphresult() != grOk )
{
    printf( "Unable to open graphics driver.\n" );
    exit( 1 );
}
setbkcolor( DARKGRAY );
```

This code is copied from the examples that are available by looking up the header file GRAPHICS.H under the IDE help menu. Other important graphics functions are:

- *closegraph()*, called at the end of *main()*
- *clearviewport()*, called by *showPanel()* to clear the screen
- *setcolor()*, called by *showPanel()* to change colors
- *settextstyle()*, called by *showPanel()* to set the text font
- *moveto()* and *lineto()*, called by *showPanel()* to draw lines
- *outtextxy()*, called by *showPanel()* to display text strings

In the graphics display mode, you have the capability of changing text appearance by selecting fonts, colors, sizes, and character coordinates. Turbo C++ requires file EGAVGA.BGI and appropriate font files (*.CHR) to be in the executable directory path in order to process graphics functions.

Function *showPanel()*

If you look at a listing of file SHOW.C, you will see that *showPanel()* is a rather simple function that displays a screen of information in sections. It displays a title, some text, some selection items, and a prompt line, each with similar code statements. Below is the code fragment that displays selection items:

```
setcolor( LIGHTGRAY );
settextstyle( SMALL_FONT, HORIZ_DIR, 6 );
for ( i=0; i<pSelect->numItems; ++i )
{
    outtextxy( INDENT, y, pSelect->itemTable[i] );
    y += 1.5 * textheight( "H" );
}
```

The first two lines set the color and font, then a loop calls *outtextxy()* to display text strings from a table (*pSelect->itemTable[i]*). After displaying each line, the code moves the vertical position, *y*, a distance equal to 1.5 character heights ("H" is just a convenient argument for graphics function *textheight()*). Pointer *pSelect* is the key to how shareable function *showPanel()* operates. See the comments at the top of SHOW.C for information about *showPanel()*. There are four parameters to this function (one for each displayed field), each a pointer to a *GROUP* structure declared in header EXAM.H:

```
struct GROUP
{
    int numItems;        /* Number of items in the table */
    char **itemTable;    /* Pointer to table of display items */
};
```

GROUP contains a pointer to a table of string pointers (*itemTable*), so that *showPanel()* can receive a table of strings (a ragged array) from the calling function. Thus, *showPanel()* is generic and can display any information passed as parameters; it merely positions the four fields of string data, sets the colors, and accomplishes the final display. Notice the macro *CENTERTEXT()* in the sections of *showPanel()* that display the title and prompt lines. *CENTERTEXT()* is defined in EXAM.H; it calculates a horizontal coordinate that will center the text string on the screen, then calls *outtextxy()* to display the text.

To display the available exams, *main()* defines and initializes a ragged array of exam strings (*examTable*), assigns it to the *selectGroup* structure, and passes a pointer to *showPanel()* in the fourth argument. The main program also initializes strings for the title and a prompt, then similarly assigns them to *GROUP* structures and passes pointers to *showPanel()*. In file EXAM.C, this occurs in the seven lines of code under the comment:

```
/*--- Display available exams ---*/
```

Phase 2 — Select an Exam

In this phase your task is to write the *selectItem()* function and add a call to it in *main()* in order to choose one of the available exams. Remember, a little later in the program we also want *selectItem()* to get answers to displayed questions interactively. This function should accept the same *GROUP* pointer argument that was given to *showPanel()* to display the available exams. You want to use certain keys to highlight and select an item on the list, then return the index of the selected item in the *GROUP* table. You can review detailed specifications for *selectItem()* in the comments at the beginning of SELECT.C. The following paragraph explains the code supplied for *selectItem()*.

We have chosen the following seven keys for item selections: (CURSORUP) or (CURSORDOWN) highlights selection items, (PAGEUP) or (PAGEDOWN) requests a new exam question (not active for Phase 2), (ESCAPE) quits, (END) signals that you are finished answering exam questions, and (ENTER) selects the currently highlighted item. *main()* calls *selectItem()* in a *do while* loop that ignores return codes for (PAGEUP) and (PAGEDOWN) keystrokes. Function *selectItem()* assumes that selection items have already been displayed by *showPanel()*. The bulk of *selectItem()* is a *do while* loop that reads a character from the keyboard, ends when you press (ENTER), and uses a six-branch *if else* statement to handle other responses. If the keypress corresponds to (CURSORUP) or (CURSORDOWN), the function updates a vertical *y* coordinate accordingly, highlights the new item, and "lowlights" the previous item. Any of the other four keys cause the function to return with a code that signifies which key was pressed. When you press (ENTER), the function returns the index of the currently highlighted item in the *GROUP* table. The fact that it uses a *GROUP* structure pointer passed from the calling function makes *selectItem()* independent of the data items being displayed and selected; thus you can place exam answers in a *GROUP* structure and use it for processing questions too.

Phase 3 — Get the Exam

After selecting an exam in Phase 2, you have an index to the desired exam. Your task now is to call *getExam()* with the name of the exam file as an argument and read questions from that file. You need to read question and answer lines from the file and allocate memory for the data strings and table pointers as the data is read. Figure 15-5 is a flow diagram for completed function *getExam()*.

The main function (in EXAM.C) uses the exam index from Phase 2 to retrieve the file name from an array of initialized name strings and passes the name to function *getExam()*. (Refer to the source code in GET.C while reading the following explanation.) *getExam()* opens the file and allocates storage for an EXAM structure. A *while* loop reads lines from the file until no more data exists. For each line, the function looks for a period (.) in the first three characters that signifies a new question or answer. A flag, *mode*, assists the process—it begins with a value of SEARCH then cycles between NEWQUESTION, MOREQUESTION, and NEWANSWER as the different kinds of line occur. Any line that follows a NEWQUESTION line that is not a NEWANSWER is a continuation of the question (MOREQUESTION). Three blocks of code independently process each of these three kinds of line—look for the three *if* statements preceded by the following comments in the source code:

```
/*--- Insert a new question ---*/
if ( mode == NEWQUESTION )
{
/* This block of code expands the question table with a call to realloc(),
allocates memory for the new question with a call to calloc(), adds the new
memory pointer to the expanded question table, then sets the mode to
MOREQUESTION to let the next block of code insert the actual data line. */
}

/*--- Accumulate question lines ---*/
if ( mode == MOREQUESTION )
{
```

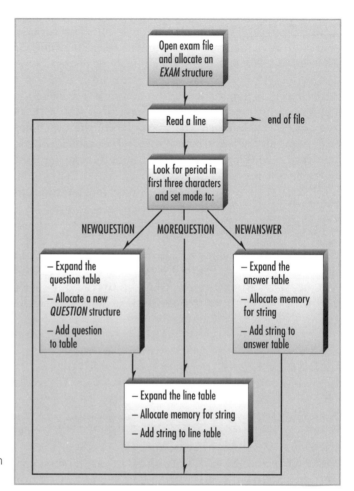

FIGURE 15-5 Read exam
data from a file

```
/* This block of code increments the question line count, expands the
question line table (with a call to realloc()), allocates memory for the
line data (with a call to malloc()), then copies the data string to the new
memory. */
}

/*--- Insert a new answer ---*/
if ( ( mode == NEWANSWER ) && ( pDot != NULL ) )
{
/* This block of code expands the answer table (with a call to realloc()),
allocates memory for the line data (with a call to malloc()), then copies
the data string to the new memory. */
}
```

When it reaches the end of file, *getExam()* returns a pointer to the *EXAM* structure that, in turn, contains pointers to the question table and answer table.

Phase 4 — Take the Exam

In this phase of the development you need to display one question at a time with *showPanel()* and call *selectItem()* to accept the user's answer. This section must also respond to (PAGEUP) and (PAGEDOWN) keystrokes by moving to a new exam question. If the (END) key is pressed, the program must proceed to the next phase and grade the exam.

All the code for this phase is in the main function in EXAM.C below the comment:

```
/*----- Take the Exam -----*/
```

A *while* loop encompasses a call to *showPanel()* that displays the current exam question. An inner *while* loop calls *selectItem()* to get an answer, ending when *selectItem()* returns a negative value in response to a (PAGEUP), (PAGEDOWN), (END), or (ESCAPE) key. (PAGEUP) and (PAGEDOWN) cause variable *questionIndex* to decrement or increment, thereby selecting another exam question. An (END) key return code takes the program to the final phase to grade the exam.

Phase 5 — Grade the Exam

The last task that you need to complete is to write function *gradeExam()* to report the results of the test. This function must scan the answers given to the exam to see if all questions were answered and to record the wrong answers. If there are any unanswered questions, the function returns to allow the user to complete all questions; otherwise it displays the percentage correct and lists questions with incorrect answers. After displaying the result, at the user's request you should print the exam, complete with grade and incorrect answers.

If you look at the supplied file GRADE.C, you will see function *gradeExam()*, which has one parameter: a pointer to the *EXAM* structure. Near the beginning, a loop checks the exam, counting the total number of answers and the number correct, and forming a string of wrong answers. If the user needs to complete some unanswered questions, the function formats a message to that effect and displays it in red at the bottom of the screen. Next, function *gradeExam()* formats some text strings to report the result and calls *showPanel()* to display them. This occurs in the section of code under the comment:

```
/*----- Report the Grade -----*/
```

The rest of the function is devoted to printing the exam if the user requests it by pressing (ENTER).

Final Comments

Obviously, this program needs some way to signify the correct answer to each exam question. We won't tell you how we did this, but maybe you can figure it out from the supplied source code—or perhaps you can think of some good methods of your own. We purposely hid the answer marks so you wouldn't be too tempted to cheat, and if you can figure out how we did it, you probably don't need to cheat anyway.

We congratulate you on completing *Certified Course in C!* Good luck with your future programming endeavors, and don't forget to mail in the final exam to receive your certificate.

ASCII TABLE

IBM Character Codes					IBM Character Codes			
DEC	**HEX**	**Symbol**	**Key**		**DEC**	**HEX**	**Symbol**	**Key**
0	00	(NULL)	`CTRL` `2`		27	1B	←	`ESC`
1	01	☺	`CTRL` `A`		28	1C	⮂	`CTRL` `\`
2	02	☻	`CTRL` `B`		29	1D	↔	`CTRL` `]`
3	03	♥	`CTRL` `C`		30	1E	▲	`CTRL` `6`
4	04	♦	`CTRL` `D`		31	1F	▼	`CTRL` `-`
5	05	♣	`CTRL` `E`		32	20		`SPACEBAR`
6	06	♠	`CTRL` `F`		33	21	!	`!`
7	07	•	Beep		34	22	"	`"`
8	08	◘	`BACKSPACE`		35	23	#	`#`
9	09		`TAB`		36	24	$	`$`
10	0A	■	Newline		37	25	%	`%`
			(linefeed)		38	26	&	`&`
11	0B	♂	`CTRL` `K`		39	27	'	`'`
12	0C	♀	`CTRL` `L`		40	28	(	`(`
13	0D	♪	`ENTER`		41	29	)	`)`
			(carriage return)		42	2A	*	`*`
14	0E	♫	`CTRL` `N`		43	2B	+	`+`
15	0F	¤	`CTRL` `O`		44	2C	,	`,`
16	10	►	`CTRL` `P`		45	2D	-	`-`
17	11	◄	`CTRL` `Q`		46	2E	.	`.`
18	12	↕	`CTRL` `R`		47	2F	/	`/`
19	13	‼	`CTRL` `S`		48	30	0	`0`
20	14	¶	`CTRL` `T`		49	31	1	`1`
21	15	§	`CTRL` `U`		50	32	2	`2`
22	16	▬	`CTRL` `V`		51	33	3	`3`
23	17	↨	`CTRL` `W`		52	34	4	`4`
24	18	↑	`CTRL` `X`		53	35	5	`5`
25	19	↓	`CTRL` `Y`		54	36	6	`6`
26	1A	→	`CTRL` `Z`		55	37	7	`7`

DEC	HEX	Symbol	Key	DEC	HEX	Symbol	Key
\multicolumn{4}{}{IBM Character Codes}				\multicolumn{4}{}{IBM Character Codes}			
56	38	8	⑧	95	5F	_	⌴
57	39	9	⑨	96	60	`	'
58	3A	:	⦂	97	61	a	ⓐ
59	3B	;	⦂	98	62	b	ⓑ
60	3C	<	⦉	99	63	c	ⓒ
61	3D	=	⊜	100	64	d	ⓓ
62	3E	>	⦊	101	65	e	ⓔ
63	3F	?	⑦	102	66	f	ⓕ
64	40	@	ⓐ	103	67	g	ⓖ
65	41	A	Ⓐ	104	68	h	ⓗ
66	42	B	Ⓑ	105	69	i	ⓘ
67	43	C	Ⓒ	106	6A	j	ⓙ
68	44	D	Ⓓ	107	6B	k	ⓚ
69	45	E	Ⓔ	108	6C	l	ⓛ
70	46	F	Ⓕ	109	6D	m	ⓜ
71	47	G	Ⓖ	110	6E	n	ⓝ
72	48	H	Ⓗ	111	6F	o	ⓞ
73	49	I	Ⓘ	112	70	p	ⓟ
74	4A	J	Ⓙ	113	71	q	ⓠ
75	4B	K	Ⓚ	114	72	r	ⓡ
76	4C	L	Ⓛ	115	73	s	ⓢ
77	4D	M	Ⓜ	116	74	t	ⓣ
78	4E	N	Ⓝ	117	75	u	ⓤ
79	4F	0	Ⓞ	118	76	v	ⓥ
80	50	P	Ⓟ	119	77	w	ⓦ
81	51	Q	Ⓠ	120	78	x	ⓧ
82	52	R	Ⓡ	121	79	y	ⓨ
83	53	S	Ⓢ	122	7A	z	ⓩ
84	54	T	Ⓣ	123	7B	{	⓵
85	55	U	Ⓤ	124	7C	¦	⓵
86	56	V	Ⓥ	125	7D	}	⓵
87	57	W	Ⓦ	126	7E	~	⌃
88	58	X	Ⓧ	127	7F	Δ	CTRL ←
89	59	Y	Ⓨ	128	80	Ç	ALT 128
90	5A	Z	Ⓩ	129	81	ü	ALT 129
91	5B	[	⓵	130	82	é	ALT 130
92	5C	\	⓵	131	83	â	ALT 131
93	5D	]	⓵	132	84	ä	ALT 132
94	5E	^	⌃	133	85	à	ALT 133

IBM Character Codes

DEC	HEX	Symbol	Key		DEC	HEX	Symbol	Key
134	86	å	(ALT) 134		173	AD	¡	(ALT) 173
135	87	ç	(ALT) 135		174	AE	«	(ALT) 174
136	88	ê	(ALT) 136		175	AF	»	(ALT) 175
137	89	ë	(ALT) 137		176	B0	3	(ALT) 176
138	8A	è	(ALT) 138		177	B1	6	(ALT) 177
139	8B	ï	(ALT) 139		178	B2	9	(ALT) 178
140	8C	î	(ALT) 140		179	B3	3	(ALT) 179
141	8D	ì	(ALT) 141		180	B4	4	(ALT) 180
142	8E	Ä	(ALT) 142		181	B5	5	(ALT) 181
143	8F	Å	(ALT) 143		182	B6	6	(ALT) 182
144	90	É	(ALT) 144		183	B7	7	(ALT) 183
145	91	æ	(ALT) 145		184	B8	8	(ALT) 184
146	92	Æ	(ALT) 146		185	B9	9	(ALT) 185
147	93	ô	(ALT) 147		186	BA	:	(ALT) 186
148	94	ö	(ALT) 148		187	BB	;	(ALT) 187
149	95	ò	(ALT) 149		188	BC	<	(ALT) 188
150	96	û	(ALT) 150		189	BD	=	(ALT) 189
151	97	ù	(ALT) 151		190	BE	>	(ALT) 190
152	98	ÿ	(ALT) 152		191	BF	?	(ALT) 191
153	99	Ö	(ALT) 153		192	C0	@	(ALT) 192
154	9A	Ü	(ALT) 154		193	C1	A	(ALT) 193
155	9B	¢	(ALT) 155		194	C2	B	(ALT) 194
156	9C	£	(ALT) 156		195	C3	C	(ALT) 195
157	9D	¥	(ALT) 157		196	C4	D	(ALT) 196
158	9E	Pₜ	(ALT) 158		197	C5	E	(ALT) 197
159	9F	ƒ	(ALT) 159		198	C6	F	(ALT) 198
160	A0	á	(ALT) 160		199	C7	G	(ALT) 199
161	A1	í	(ALT) 161		200	C8	H	(ALT) 200
162	A2	ó	(ALT) 162		201	C9	I	(ALT) 201
163	A3	ú	(ALT) 163		202	CA	J	(ALT) 202
164	A4	ñ	(ALT) 164		203	CB	K	(ALT) 203
165	A5	Ñ	(ALT) 165		204	CC	L	(ALT) 204
166	A6	ª	(ALT) 166		205	CD	M	(ALT) 205
167	A7	º	(ALT) 167		206	CE	N	(ALT) 206
168	A8	¿	(ALT) 168		207	CF	O	(ALT) 207
169	A9	Z	(ALT) 169		208	D0	P	(ALT) 208
170	AA	?	(ALT) 170		209	D1	Q	(ALT) 209
171	AB	½	(ALT) 171		210	D2	R	(ALT) 210
172	AC	¼	(ALT) 172		211	D3	S	(ALT) 211

IBM Character Codes					IBM Character Codes			
DEC	HEX	Symbol	Key		DEC	HEX	Symbol	Key
212	D4	T	(ALT) 212		234	EA	Ω	(ALT) 234
213	D5	U	(ALT) 213		235	EB	δ	(ALT) 235
214	D6	V	(ALT) 214		236	EC	∞	(ALT) 236
215	D7	W	(ALT) 215		237	ED	φ	(ALT) 237
216	D8	X	(ALT) 216		238	EE	ε	(ALT) 238
217	D9	♣	(ALT) 217		239	EF	∩	(ALT) 239
218	DA	♫	(ALT) 218		240	F0	≡	(ALT) 240
219	DB	▪	(ALT) 219		241	F1	±	(ALT) 241
220	DC	▪	(ALT) 220		242	F2	≥	(ALT) 242
221	DD	▬	(ALT) 221		243	F3	≤	(ALT) 243
222	DE		(ALT) 222		244	F4	⌠	(ALT) 244
223	DF		(ALT) 223		245	F5	⌡	(ALT) 245
224	E0	α	(ALT) 224		246	F6	÷	(ALT) 246
225	E1	β	(ALT) 225		247	F7	≈	(ALT) 247
226	E2	Γ	(ALT) 226		248	F8	°	(ALT) 248
227	E3	π	(ALT) 227		249	F9	•	(ALT) 249
228	E4	Σ	(ALT) 228		250	FA	·	(ALT) 250
229	E5	σ	(ALT) 229		251	FB	√	(ALT) 251
230	E6	μ	(ALT) 230		252	FC	η	(ALT) 252
231	E7	τ	(ALT) 231		253	FD	²	(ALT) 253
232	E8	Φ	(ALT) 232		254	FE	▪	(ALT) 254
233	E9	Θ	(ALT) 233		255	FF	(blank)	(ALT) 255

Note that IBM Extended ASCII characters can be displayed by pressing the (ALT) key and then typing the decimal code of the character on the keypad.

GOOD PROGRAMMING STYLE

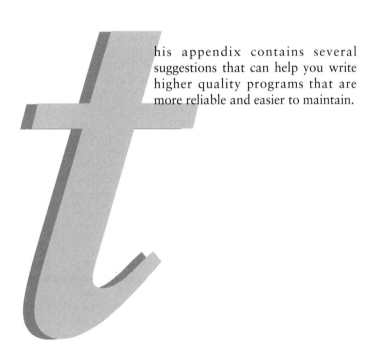

his appendix contains several suggestions that can help you write higher quality programs that are more reliable and easier to maintain.

Refrain from Programming Tricks

C sometimes tempts you to show off and take a short cut or do something unusual with a program. For example you could (but shouldn't) use the left-shift operator (<<) to accomplish multiplication by a power of two.

Do this:

```
x = 4 * y;
```

not this:

```
x = y << 2;
```

You should resist abuse of the language in favor of producing clearly understandable code. It is rare that an obscure construct actually results in any measurable increase in efficiency, but it usually *does* result in confusion later on (for others and possibly for you) about what the code is doing.

Use Symbolic Constants

Programs invariably use many numeric constants to set the size of arrays and to control the limits of loops, among other things. It is wise not to use explicit numbers for constants; symbols are more descriptive and readable. You can use the *#define* directive or *const* qualifier for this purpose. For example, rather than insert the number 17 everywhere that a program requires the number of districts in a county, you would use a symbolic constant called NUM_DISTRICTS defined either with a preprocessor directive:

```
#define NUM_DISTRICTS 17
```

or with the *const* qualifier:

```
const int NUM_DISTRICTS = 17;
```

Then when you set up an array or initiate a loop you would do it this way:

```
districts[NUM_DISTRICTS];

for (i=1; i<=NUM_DISTRICTS; ++i)
```

Later on you could change the number of districts for the whole program by modifying just one statement (either the *#define* or the *const* statement).

Organize Reusable Functions into Libraries

In moderate- and large-sized programs you will find functions that are called repeatedly. It is a good idea to group similar functions into categories and place each group in an object library (for example, put all file functions in one library and all math functions in another). Libraries simplify the process of compiling and linking larger programs.

Design Error Handling into Your Programs

Explicit error handling is important because a perfectly good program can experience trouble when it encounters bad data or a changing environment (like running out of memory). If you haven't anticipated such events with error handling, your program could quit awkwardly or, worse, crash the system or corrupt some important data files. You can avoid disaster by writing a specialized function for processing error conditions and by placing calls to this function wherever errors might occur. Figure B-1 is an example of this approach to error handling.

```
/******************************************************************************
Example program that uses error handling
*******************************************************************************
#include <stdio.h>

#define FILE_ERROR    0
#define ALLOC_ERROR   1
#define ZERO_DIVIDE   2
#define INVALID_DATA  3

int main ()
{
    static int dividend;
    static int divisor;
    static int answer;

        if (divisor== 0)
        error (ZERO_DIVIDE) ;
answer = dividend / divisor;
printf ("The answer is %d", answer) ;
}
/******************************************************************************
Example handling function
*******************************************************************************
void error (int error_id)
{
    static char *message [] = {"File open failure",
                               "Memory alocation error",
                               "Attempt to divide by zero",
                               "Invalid data"};
    printf("\nUnrecoverable error: %s", message [error_id]);
    printf("\nExiting the program...");
    exit (1);
}
```

FIGURE B-1   Error handling function

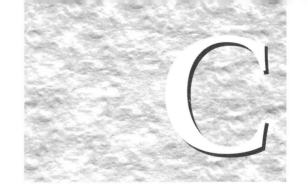

BORLAND C/C++ PRODUCTS

ince the introduction of Turbo C in 1987, Borland has offered a wide range of compilers and development tools for C and C++. Table C-1 lists key events in the history of Borland C products, ending with the introduction of C++ development support for the 32-bit Windows environment.

May 1987	Borland announces Turbo C, a full-featured C development environment lauded for its fast and compact code generation.
August 1988	Borland moves into professional programmer market with Turbo Pascal Professional, Turbo C Professional, and a new Turbo Assembler and Debugger.
May 1990	Turbo C++ Professional ships. New tool incorporates object-oriented programming and is aimed at the world's more than two million developers who use the "C" programming language.
February 1991	Borland C++, the only complete C and C++ programming environment for building DOS and Windows applications, ships.
May 1991	Borland enters into agreement with IBM to develop specific object-oriented programming languages and development tools for OS/2 2.0. Company announces that first product will be Borland C+ for OS/2 2.0.
July 1991	Borland introduces "The World of C++", a video training course that introduces software developers to the world of object-oriented programming.
	Borland ships Turbo C++ & Turbo Vision, a programming language product comprised of Borland's award-winning Turbo C++ compiler and Turbo Visions for C++, an application framework to streamline software development.
September 1991	Borland ships Borland C++ & Applications Frameworks, its C++ programming languages with application frameworks to accelerate the development of software programs for Microsoft Windows and DOS operating systems.
November 1991	Borland ships more than one-half million units of its C++, Turbo C++ & Turbo Vision, and Borland C++ & Application Frameworks.
	Borland ships three object-oriented software tools: Turbo C++ for Windows 3.0, Borland C++ 3.0, and Borland C++ & Application Frameworks 3.0.
February 1992	Borland ships Turbo C++ 3.0 for DOS, a product built on Borland's third-generation compiler. The product allows entry-level programmers to learn and use C and C++ for $99.95.
June 1992	Borland ships five language products—Borland C++ and Applications Frameworks 3.1, Borland C++ 3.1, Turbo C++ for Windows 3.1, Turbo Pascal for Windows 1.5, and ObjectVision 2.0 for OS/2 2.0.

May 1993	Borland announces Borland C++ for Win32 Early Experience Program at the Borland International Conference and Exposition. Borland C++ for Win32 runs under both Windows and Windows NT.
January 1994	Borland announces Borland C++ 4.0, making Borland the first to offer both 16- and 32-bit development capabilities in a single box.
December 1994	Borland ships Borland C++ 4.5 and Database Tools with easy OLE 2.0 automation, VBX32 support, and a faster compiler for development.
January 1995	Borland ships Borland C++ 2.0 for OS/2, providing ObjectWindows Library support and OS/2 Warp compatability.

Table C-1   **Borland International, Inc., corporate milestones**

Figure C-1 shows which Borland language products can be used to develop applications for the DOS or Windows operating environments, and it places the products on a price scale (current prices could be different from the approximate values shown).

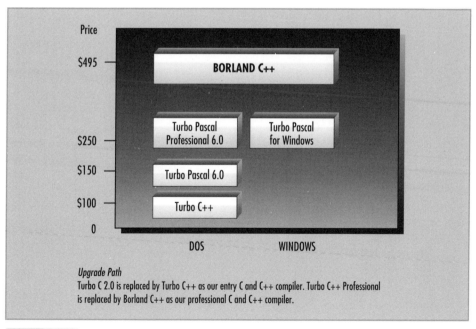

FIGURE C-1   Borland languages

Turbo C++ is the low-cost, entry-level compiler for ANSI C and C++ in the DOS environment. The compiler supplied with this book, Turbo C++ Lite, is a version of this product intended for teaching of C and C++.

Borland C++ is a full-featured compiler for professional developers in both the DOS and Windows environments. The current version of this product is Borland C++ 4.0; Borland C++ 4.5, containing Windows Object Linking and Embedding (OLE 2.0) component support, which was released in late 1994.

CERTIFICATION AND COURSE CREDIT

aite Group Press and the University of Phoenix (UoP) are pleased to offer you the opportunity to obtain a two-level certification for the C programming language knowledge you've gained from completing *Certified Course in C*. After you complete the first level, UoP will recognize your achievement by awarding a certificate. Completion of the first level allows you to move on to the second level, where you can earn three undergraduate course credits by passing a more thorough final exam, which involves writing C program code.

To become eligible for the first-level certification, you must take the final exam with the testing program included on the enclosed disk. When you have completed the exam, the program will prompt you to save it to disk as file FINAL.XAM. You then need to copy it to a separate 3.5 inch floppy disk, and label the disk with your name, phone number, and the title "Certified Course in C: Final

Exam." Submit this disk, the completed original (not a photocopy) of the University of Phoenix Certification Application found in the back of this book, and a $10 ($15 for orders outside of North America) processing fee (make check payable to University of Phoenix) to:

University of Phoenix
Technology Programs Department
7800 East Dorado Place
Englewood, CO 80111

Attn: Certified Course in C Exam

Within two weeks of receipt, the University of Phoenix will grade your answers to the exam and return the results. To pass this exam, you must achieve a score of 75 percent or better.

If you do not achieve a 75 percent score, you will receive your score, a list of chapters you should emphasize when you review the material in the book, and a new card that entitles you to retake and resubmit the exam. Each time you submit your final exam for evaluation, you must pay the $10 ($15) processing fee. You may attempt to pass the final exam from the book a maximum of three times.

If you do achieve a 75 percent score, you will be awarded your certificate (similar to the one shown in Figure 1-4 in the book). In addition, you will receive an application to attempt the second-level exam. The second-level exam requires you to write one or more C programs. Upon achieving a 75 percent or better score, you will be awarded three undergraduate college credits. The processing fee for the second-level exam is $35 ($45 for orders outside of North America), and you may attempt it only once. Both passing and failing candidates will receive brief comments from a University of Phoenix grader. The second-level exam application will explain the application, testing, and fee details more thoroughly.

INDEX

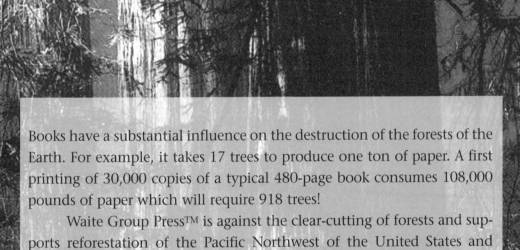

Books have a substantial influence on the destruction of the forests of the Earth. For example, it takes 17 trees to produce one ton of paper. A first printing of 30,000 copies of a typical 480-page book consumes 108,000 pounds of paper which will require 918 trees!

Waite Group Press™ is against the clear-cutting of forests and supports reforestation of the Pacific Northwest of the United States and Canada, where most of this paper comes from. As a publisher with several hundred thousand books sold each year, we feel an obligation to give back to the planet. We will therefore support organizations which seek to preserve the forests of planet Earth.

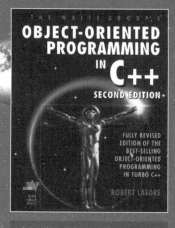

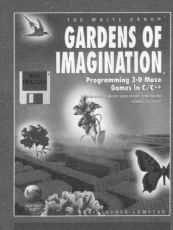

This is a legal agreement between you, the end user and purchaser, and The Waite Group®, Inc., and the authors of the programs contained in the disk. By opening the sealed disk package, you are agreeing to be bound by the terms of this Agreement. If you do not agree with the terms of this Agreement, promptly return the unopened disk package and the accompanying items (including the related book and other written material) to the place you obtained them for a refund.

SOFTWARE LICENSE

1. The Waite Group, Inc. grants you the right to use one copy of the enclosed software programs (the programs) on a single computer system (whether a single CPU, part of a licensed network, or a terminal connected to a single CPU). Each concurrent user of the program must have exclusive use of the related Waite Group, Inc. written materials.

2. The program, including the copyrights in each program, is owned by the respective author and the copyright in the entire work is owned by The Waite Group, Inc. and they are therefore protected under the copyright laws of the United States and other nations, under international treaties. You may make only one copy of the disk containing the programs exclusively for backup or archival purposes, or you may transfer the programs to one hard disk drive, using the original for backup or archival purposes. You may make no other copies of the programs, and you may make no copies of all or any part of the related Waite Group, Inc. written materials.

3. You may not rent or lease the programs, but you may transfer ownership of the programs and related written materials (including any and all updates and earlier versions) if you keep no copies of either, and if you make sure the transferee agrees to the terms of this license.

4. You may not decompile, reverse engineer, disassemble, copy, create a derivative work, or otherwise use the programs except as stated in this Agreement.

GOVERNING LAW

This Agreement is governed by the laws of the State of California.

LIMITED WARRANTY

The following warranties shall be effective for 90 days from the date of purchase: (i) The Waite Group, Inc. warrants the enclosed disk to be free of defects in materials and workmanship under normal use; and (ii) The Waite Group, Inc. warrants that the programs, unless modified by the purchaser, will substantially perform the functions described in the documentation provided by The Waite Group, Inc. when operated on the designated hardware and operating system. The Waite Group, Inc. does not warrant that the programs will meet purchaser's requirements or that operation of a program will be uninterrupted or error-free. The program warranty does not cover any program that has been altered or changed in any way by anyone other than The Waite Group, Inc. The Waite Group, Inc. is not responsible for problems caused by changes in the operating characteristics of computer hardware or computer operating systems that are made after the release of the programs, nor for problems in the interaction of the programs with each other or other software.

THESE WARRANTIES ARE EXCLUSIVE AND IN LIEU OF ALL OTHER WARRANTIES OF MERCHANTABILITY OR FITNESS FOR A PARTICULAR PURPOSE OR OF ANY OTHER WARRANTY, WHETHER EXPRESS OR IMPLIED.

EXCLUSIVE REMEDY

The Waite Group, Inc. will replace any defective disk without charge if the defective disk is returned to The Waite Group, Inc. within 90 days from date of purchase.

This is Purchaser's sole and exclusive remedy for any breach of warranty or claim for contract, tort, or damages.

LIMITATION OF LIABILITY

THE WAITE GROUP, INC. AND THE AUTHORS OF THE PROGRAMS SHALL NOT IN ANY CASE BE LIABLE FOR SPECIAL, INCIDENTAL, CONSEQUENTIAL, INDIRECT, OR OTHER SIMILAR DAMAGES ARISING FROM ANY BREACH OF THESE WARRANTIES EVEN IF THE WAITE GROUP, INC. OR ITS AGENT HAS BEEN ADVISED OF THE POSSIBILITY OF SUCH DAMAGES.

THE LIABILITY FOR DAMAGES OF THE WAITE GROUP, INC. AND THE AUTHORS OF THE PROGRAMS UNDER THIS AGREEMENT SHALL IN NO EVENT EXCEED THE PURCHASE PRICE PAID.

COMPLETE AGREEMENT

This Agreement constitutes the complete agreement between The Waite Group, Inc. and the authors of the programs, and you, the purchaser.

Some states do not allow the exclusion or limitation of implied warranties or liability for incidental or consequential damages, so the above exclusions or limitations may not apply to you. This limited warranty gives you specific legal rights; you may have others, which vary from state to state.

BORLAND

NO-NONSENSE™ LICENSE STATEMENT AND LIMITED WARRANTY

If you have any questions, please contact our Customer Service Department at (408) 461-9000. Customers outside the U.S. should contact their local Borland office.

This software is protected by copyright law and international copyright treaty. Therefore, you must treat this software just like a book, except that you may copy it onto a computer to be used and you may make archive copies of the software for the sole purpose of backing up our software and protecting your investment from loss.

By saying "just like a book," Borland means, for example, that this software may be used by any number of people, and may be freely moved from one computer or location to another, so long as there is no possibility of it being used by more than one person at a time. Just as a book can't be read by two different people in two different places at the same time, neither can the software be available for use by two different people in two different places at the same time without Borland's permission (unless, of course, Borland's copyright has been violated).

TRANSFERRING THE SOFTWARE

You may transfer all of your rights to use the software to another person, provided that you transfer to that person all of the software, diskettes, and documentation provided in this package (including this statement), and transfer or destroy all copies in any form. Remember, once you transfer the software you no longer have any right to use it, and the person to whom it is transferred may use it only in accordance with the copyright law, international treaty, and this statement.

If you have purchased an upgrade version of the software, it constitutes a single product with the Borland software that you upgraded. For example, the upgrade and the software that you upgraded cannot both be available for use by two different people at the same time, and cannot be transferred separately, without written permission from Borland.

This software is subject to U.S. Commerce Department export restrictions, and is intended for use in the country into which Borland sold it (or in the EEC, in the case of software Borland first sold into the EEC). Except as provided in this statement, you may not transfer, rent, lease, lend, copy, modify, translate, sublicense, time-share, or electronically transmit or receive the software, media, or documentation.

ADDITIONAL LICENSE TERMS FOR DEVELOPMENT PRODUCTS

If you have any questions, please contact our Customer Service Department at (408) 461-9000. Customers outside the U.S. should contact their local Borland office.

Borland products, including the one in this package, may include one or more libraries intended to help you develop your own application programs. For example, Borland products may also include some source code, either with the libraries or as sample programs. In addition to the rights you have under copyright law and Borland's No-Nonsense™ License Statement to use this software like a book, Borland, under its copyright, also grants you a license to use such libraries and source code included in this package in the manner described below, so long as you comply with all of the conditions in this statement.

COMPILED PROGRAMS

You may write and compile your own application programs using the Borland software contained in this package, including any libraries and source code included for such purpose with the product. If you are the licensed, registered user of this product, you may use, reproduce, give away, or sell any program you write using this product, in executable form only, without additional license or fees, subject to all of the conditions in this statement.

REDISTRIBUTABLE COMPONENTS

Borland products, including the one in this package, may include certain files intended for distribution by you to the users of programs you create ("Redistributables"). Redistributables in this package may include various run-time files or drivers intended to permit stand-alone operation of your programs. Redistributables may also include utilities intended to enhance operation of your programs, such as utilities that facilitate installation of your programs.

The Redistributables for this product are only those files specifically designated as such by Borland in the documentation included in this package. From time to time, Borland may designate other files as Redistributables. You should refer to the documentation and the "readme" file included in this package for additional information.

Under Borland's copyright, and subject to all of the conditions in this statement, Borland authorizes the licensed, registered user of this product to reproduce and distribute exact copies of the files designated as "Redistributables" for this product, provided that such copies are made from the original disks in this package (or a set of backup copies made directly from them).

Copies of Redistributables may only by distributed with and for the sole purpose of executing application programs permitted under this statement that you have written using this Borland product. Under no circumstances may any copies of Redistributables be distributed separately. You may not reproduce or distribute any Borland documentation without Borland's permission.

GENERAL TERMS THAT APPLY TO COMPILED PROGRAMS AND REDISTRIBUTABLES

The license granted in this statement for you to create your own compiled programs and distribute your programs and the Redistributables is subject to all of the following conditions:

- All copies of the programs you create must bear a valid copyright notice, either your own or the Borland copyright notice that appears on the original diskette label in this package.

- You may not remove or alter any Borland copyright, trademark, or other proprietary rights notice contained in any portion of Borland's libraries, source code, Redistributables, or other files that bear such a notice. You may not remove or alter any identifying screen that is produced by a Borland Redistributable.

- Borland provides no warranty at all to any person, other than the Limited Warranty provided to the original purchaser of this package.

- You will remain solely responsible to anyone receiving you programs for support, service, upgrades, or technical or other assistance, and such recipients will have no right to contact Borland for such services or assistance.

- You will indemnify and hold Borland, its related companies, and its suppliers harmless from and against any claims or liabilities arising out of the use, reproduction, or distribution of your programs.

- Your programs must be written using a licensed, registered copy of this Borland product.

- Your programs may not be merely a set or subset of any of the libraries, code, Redistributables, or other files included in this package.

- You may not use Borland's or any of its suppliers' names, logos, or trademarks to market your programs, except to state that your program was written using this Borland product.

- All Borland libraries, source code, Redistributables, and other files remain Borland's exclusive property

- Regardless of any modifications that you make, you may not distribute any files (particularly Borland source code and other non-executable files) except those that Borland has expressly designated as Redistributables. Nothing in this license statement permits you to derive the source code of files that Borland has provided to you in executable form only, or to reproduce, modify, use, or distribute the source code of such files. You are not, of course, restricted from distributing source code that is entirely your own. Code that you generate with a Borland code generator, such as AppExpert, is considered by Borland to be your code.

- All other requirements of the copyright law, international treaty, and Borland's No-Nonsense License Statement and Limited Warranty continue to apply except as provided otherwise above.

If you wish to distribute copies of your compiled programs or Redistributables on other terms, please call our OEM licensing department.

LIMITED WARRANTY

Waite Group Press warrants the physical media and physical documentation provided by Waite Group Press to be free of defects in materials and workmanship for a period of ninety (90) days from the original purchase date. If Waite Group Press receives notification within the warranty period of defects in materials or workmanship, and determines that such notification is correct, Waite Group Press will replace the defective media or documentation.

The entire and exclusive liability and remedy for breach of this limited warranty shall be limited to replacement of defective media or documentation and shall not include or extend to any claim for or right to recover any other damages, including but not limited to, loss of profit, data, or use of the software or special, incidental or consequential damages or other similar claims, even if Borland has been specifically advised of the possibility of such damages. In no event will Borland's liability for any damages to you or any other person ever exceed the lower of the list price or the actual price paid for the package or the license to use the software, regardless of the form of the claim.

BORLAND SPECIFICALLY DISCLAIMS ALL OTHER WARRANTIES, REPRESENTATIONS, OR CONDITIONS, EXPRESS OR IMPLIED, INCLUDING BUT NOT LIMITED TO, ANY IMPLIED WARRANTY OR CONDITION OF MERCHANTABILITY OR FITNESS FOR A PARTICULAR PURPOSE. ALL OTHER IMPLIED TERMS ARE EXCLUDED.

Specifically, Borland makes no representation or warranty that the software or documentation are "error-free," or meet any user's particular standards, requirements, or needs. In all events, any implied warranty, representation, condition, or other term is limited to the physical media and documentation and is limited to the 90-day duration of the limited warranty.

Borland is not responsible for, and does not make any representation, warranty, or condition concerning product, media, software, or documentation not manufactured or supplied by Borland, such as third-parties' programs that are designed using Borland software or which include Borland programs or files.

GENERAL PROVISIONS

This statement may be modified only in writing signed by you and an authorized officer of Borland. If any provision of this statement is found void or unenforceable, the remainder will remain valid and enforceable according to its terms. If any remedy provided is determined to have failed of its essential purpose, all limitations of liability and exclusions of damages set forth in the limited warranty shall remain in effect. Use, duplication, or disclosure of the software and documentation in this package by the U.S. Government is subject to the restricted rights applicable to commercial computer software (under FAR 52.227-19 and DFARS 252.227-7013).

This statement shall be construed, interpreted, and governed by the laws of the State of California, U.S.A. This statement gives you specific legal rights; you may have others which vary from state to state and from country to country. Borland reserves all rights not specifically granted in this statement.

About the University of Phoenix

Technological Leadership Begins with Educational Leadership

The University of Phoenix (UoP) was founded in 1976 by Dr. John Sperling. Concerned that American business was losing its competitive edge in the global marketplace, Dr. Sperling built a university dedicated to making a difference. Sperling's vision was to recapture our entrepreneurial and technological leadership and forge new paths in creative and innovative management through continual education of the American workforce.

More than 150,000 students have attended the University of Phoenix. Its programs are acclaimed by employers for their role in providing students with timely and relevant education that combines theoretical knowledge and practical applications to the real world.

Every Program Is Geared for Working Adults

More than 60 percent of UoP students have 11 years or more of full-time work experience. This profile is different from that of traditional college programs—and it is a profile the University understands. Each of its degree programs is constantly evaluated and updated in light of this profile. Concrete objectives are set for each course, so students and faculty have a clear road map of what they need to accomplish. As the nation's leader in adult education, the University of Phoenix continues to set educational standards that are emulated by both traditional and nontraditional institutions alike.

Courses are designed and taught by working professionals who are recognized leaders in their field. Classes usually meet for four hours, one night per week, allowing students to complete their degree programs without delay. UoP provides students with a variety of options for meeting course objectives outside of the classroom.

Master of Science in Computer Information Systems (MSCIS)

The MSCIS program provides students with a thorough grounding in key technologies so that they can effectively deal with system integration issues. Even if a student's primary interest is object-oriented programming and design, he or she will understand the concepts of telecommunications, operating systems, and databases—the key elements of most systems with which the student will be involved. The bridges between each of these key technologies consist of effective management principles and techniques.

All students must complete a common set of foundation courses consisting of project management, CIS management, effective oral and written communications, data communications and local area networks, file and database concepts, software engineering, and Open Systems computing (UNIX and C programming). Upon completion of the foundation courses, students must complete their degrees by taking a series of elective courses from the management (such as strategic planning, risk management of CIS assets, and CIS economics) and/or technology (such as object-oriented design, reengineering the software development process, and enterprise-wide networking) areas. A practical, work-related project completes the degree program.

Bachelor of Science in Business/Information Systems (BSB/IS)

Keeping in step with today's evolving business climate requires keeping up with information systems technology. The University of Phoenix BSB/IS degree is designed to bridge the gap between a traditional business education and a working knowledge of computer information systems. The degree supports students by providing the necessary skills to design, develop, and implement a successful integrated business information system.

When a student enrolls in the BSB/IS program, the Core Curriculum consists of business courses including: Organizational Behavior, Business Communications, Computers and Information Processing, Marketing, Business Statistics, and Finance and Accounting for Managers. A series of information systems classes is then required to complete the major course of study. These courses include Introduction to Software Engineering, Project Planning and Implementation, Computer Architecture, Data Design and Information Retrieval, Database Management Systems, Telecommunications, Programming Concepts, Structured Programming Techniques Using the C Language, and Information Resource Management.

It is not necessary to be an experienced information systems professional to enroll in the University of Phoenix MSCIS and BSB/IS programs. Students with diverse backgrounds and skill levels are able to benefit from these programs.

Accreditation

The University of Phoenix is accredited by the Commission on Institutions of Higher Education of the North Central Association of Colleges and Schools (NCA). Institutional accreditation ensures that UoP and its programs meet the stringent standards set by the NCA.

To Obtain More Information

You may request more information about the University of Phoenix by writing, calling, or sending email.

University of Phoenix Technology Programs
7800 E. Dorado Place
Englewood, CO 80111
(303) 755-9090, ext. 116
Internet: moreinfo@hawaii.uopcol.uophx.edu

CERTIFIED COURSE IN

Certification Application

I have read and completed *Certified Course in* C by Waite Group Press, have taken the final exam on the enclosed disk, and wish to apply for the first-level certification (described in Appendix D of this book). I understand that only the original form from the book (not a photocopy) can be accepted as an official application by the University of Phoenix.

I understand that the University of Phoenix will grade my exam and notify me of my score within two weeks (allow longer for orders outside of North America). Additional information about the second level of certification will also be sent at that time.

Name

Address

City   State   Zip

Daytime phone

Signature

❏ I have enclosed one 3.5" floppy disk containing my completed FINAL.XAM. I have labeled the disk with my name, phone number, and the title "Certified Course in C: Final Exam." (Disk will not be returned.)

❏ I have enclosed a check (made payable to University of Phoenix) for $10 ($15 for orders outside of North America) the exam processing fee.

Send to:

University of Phoenix
Technology Programs Department
7800 East Dorado Place
Englewood, CO 80111
Attn: Certified Course in C Exam

SATISFACTION REPORT CARD

Please fill out this card if you wish to know of future updates to
Certified Course in C, or to receive our catalog.

Company Name:

Division/Department: Mail Stop:

Last Name: First Name: Middle Initial:

Street Address:

City: State: Zip:

Daytime telephone: (   )

Date product was acquired: Month   Day   Year   Your Occupation:

Overall, how would you rate *Certified Course in C?*

☐ Excellent   ☐ Very Good   ☐ Good
☐ Fair   ☐ Below Average   ☐ Poor

What did you like MOST about this book?

What did you like LEAST about this book?

Please describe any problems you may have encountered with installing or using the disk:

How did you use this book (problem-solver, tutorial, reference...)?

What is your level of computer expertise?

☐ New   ☐ Dabbler   ☐ Hacker
☐ Power User   ☐ Programmer   ☐ Experienced Professional

What computer languages are you familiar with?

Please describe your computer hardware:

Computer _____ Hard disk _____
5.25" disk drives _____ 3.5" disk drives _____
Video card _____ Monitor _____
Printer _____ Peripherals _____
Sound Board _____ CD-ROM _____

Where did you buy this book?

☐ Bookstore (name):
☐ Discount store (name):
☐ Computer store (name):
☐ Catalog (name):
☐ Direct from WGP   ☐ Other

What price did you pay for this book?

What influenced your purchase of this book?

☐ Recommendation   ☐ Advertisement
☐ Magazine review   ☐ Store display
☐ Mailing   ☐ Book's format
☐ Reputation of Waite Group Press   ☐ Other

How many computer books do you buy each year?

How many other Waite Group books do you own?

What is your favorite Waite Group book?

Is there any program or subject you would like to see Waite Group Press cover in a similar approach?

Additional comments?

Please send to: **Waite Group Press**
Attn: *Certified Course in C*
200 Tamal Plaza
Corte Madera, CA 94925

☐ **Check here for a free Waite Group catalog**

- **NEW!** 16-bit optimizing linker and profiler help speed up your 16-bit Windows applications.
- **NEW!** Faster 32-bit compilation is 50% faster and code runs up to 25% faster!

Borland Turbo C++ 3.0 for DOS

Turbo C++ is a full-featured compiler that makes programming in C and C++ easy. With context-sensitive help, color syntax highlighting, and the Programmer's Platform IDE, you can create great applications quickly. A complete tutorial helps you quickly navigate the development environment and gain insight into C and C++ languages. Novices and professionals alike will appreciate the intuitive help system that answers your questions instantly. There's even sample code that you can paste into your own applications.

Borland Turbo C++ 3.0 for DOS features:

- Easy-to-use Programmer's Platform IDE with color syntax highlighting
- Macro-based editor that supports full undo and redo, and editing of large files
- Integrated debugger with data and Object Inspectors,® and conditional breakpoints
- 100% ANSI C–compatible runtime libraries
- Turbo Librarian™ for creating and managing .LIB files
- On-line, context-sensitive help system
- Hands-on tutorials on C and C++ programming

This offer good in the U.S. only. International customers please contact your local Borland office for the offer in your country. Corporate Headquarters: 100 Borland Way, Scotts Valley, California 95066-3249, 408-431-1000. Internet: http://www.borland.com/ CompuServe: GO BORLAND. Offices in: Australia (61-02-911-1000), Canada (416-229-6000), France (33-1-41-23-11-00), Germany (49-6103-9790), Hong Kong (852-2572-3238), Japan (81-3-5350-9380), Latin American Headquarters in U.S.A. (408-431-1074), Mexico (52-5-687-7582), Netherlands (31-020-540-5400), Taiwan (886-2-718-6627), and United Kingdom (44-1734-321-150)

Name _____

Address _____

City _____

State/Province _____ Zip/Postal code _____

Phone (_____) _____ Fax (_____) _____

To redeem this coupon, mail the original coupon (no photocopies, please) along with payment and shipping information to: Borland, P.O. Box 660005, Scotts Valley, CA 95067-0005.

Select one:

❏ Borland® C++ 4.5 for DOS, Windows, and Win32 (regularly $499)	CD-ROM	**$199.95**
❏ Borland Turbo C++ 3.0 for DOS (regularly $99.95)	3.5″ disks	**$69.95**

Method of payment: ❏ Check enclosed†
❏ VISA   ❏ MasterCard   ❏ American Express

__ __ __ __ - __ __ __ __ - __ __ __ __ - __ __ __ __
card number

Expiration date: __ __ / __ __

Z1136

Subtotal	$ _____
State sales tax*	$ _____
Freight ($10.00 per item)	$ _____
Total order	$ _____

Limited to one per customer. Offer expires April 30, 1996.
*Residents of AZ, CA, CT, DC, FL, GA, IL, MA, MD, MN, MO, NC, NJ, OH, TN, UT, and VA, please add appropriate sales tax. CO, MI, NY, PA, TX, and WA residents, please calculate tax based on product **and** freight charges. †Make checks payable to Borland International, Inc. Offer good in U.S. only. Purchase orders accepted upon approval—$500 minimum. Terms: Net 30 days. Borland reserves the right to modify or cancel this offer at any time. Copyright © 1995 Borland • BOR 6929.3

STOP!

BEFORE YOU OPEN THE DISK OR CD-ROM PACKAGE ON THE FACING PAGE, CAREFULLY READ THE LICENSE AGREEMENT.

Opening this package indicates that you agree to abide by the license agreement found in the back of this book. If you do not agree with it, promptly return the unopened disk package (including the related book) to the place you obtained them for a refund.